PENGUIN HANDBOOKS
THE MEDIA ROOM

Howard J. Blumenthal is a television producer and writer who has produced a wide variety of shows for both cable television and videodisc and videocasette use. He was one of the founders of the innovative Qube Cable TV project, for which he designed hundreds of games utilizing its interactive capabilities. He is also the author of *The Complete Guide to Electronic Games* and *Everyone's Guide to Personal Computers*. Mr. Blumenthal lives in New York City.

THE MEDIA ROOM

CREATING YOUR OWN HOME ENTERTAINMENT AND INFORMATION CENTER

by Howard J. Blumenthal

PENGUIN BOOKS

Penguin Books Ltd, Harmondsworth,
Middlesex, England
Penguin Books, 40 West 23rd Street,
New York, New York 10010, U.S.A.
Penguin Books Australia Ltd, Ringwood,
Victoria, Australia
Penguin Books Canada Limited, 2801 John Street,
Markham, Ontario, Canada L3R 1B4
Penguin Books (N.Z.) Ltd, 182–190 Wairau Road,
Auckland 10, New Zealand

First published 1983

LIBRARY OF CONGRESS CATALOGING IN PUBLICATION DATA
Blumenthal, Howard J.
  The media room.
  (Penguin handbooks)
  Filmography: p.
  Includes index.
  1. Home video systems.   2. Microcomputers.
I. Title.   II. Title: Creating your own home
entertainment and information center.
TK9961.B59 1983   384   82-19003
ISBN 0 14 046.538 3

Printed in the United States of America by
Halliday Lithograph Corporation,
West Hanover, Massachusetts
Set in Videocomp Times Roman
Designed by Beth Tondreau

THIS BOOK IS FOR SHARI

CONTENTS

ACKNOWLEDGMENTS

This was a complicated book to write, because the information in it spans so many different fields.

Brian Smith of RCA was particularly helpful in describing some of the more elusive technical details, spending many patient hours on the phone with me and offering some fine ideas for additions to the manuscript. Panasonic's Mike Abrams was also helpful on the technical side, especially in the area of VCRs.

My longtime cohort Andy Hejnas was helpful in the computer area, as was Atari's Jerry Jessup.

In more general areas, Ron Tomczyk of Panasonic, Frank McCann and his staff at RCA, Steve Cody at Geltzer and Company, and Bruce Apar of *Video* magazine provided indispensable assistance, as did Richard Meidenbauer of Toshiba, Tom Lauterback of Quasar, Ken Kai and his staff at Pioneer, and all the good people on the JVC account at Burson-Marsteller. My good friends Ginny Junkhe, Sandy Archer, Margaret Lasecke, and Peter Nelson at Atari were wonderfully supportive as always, as were Joan Gasperini, Claudia Bloom, and Janice Bender at Edelman Public Relations.

The good people at New York Giant Screen TV Center, especially Louise and Giovanni Cozzi, were kind enough to let me photograph almost everything in their store.

Wendie Owen, Anita Mazzerelli, Fritz Friedman, Bob Shortel, Jim Murphy, Hollace Brown, Sandy Smith, Judie Sefcovic, and other software people were very helpful (and patient with me as well). Thanks also to Linda Stern Rubin, Al Filipeli, Marcia Klein, Bruce Blackwell, Frida Schubert, Theodore Van Sickle, Richard Ziff, Ed Leonardo, Pam Speigel, Jon Tisch, Howard Holtzman, and to Michael Marcovsky, Dr. Vivian Horner, Michael Dann, Harlan Kleiman, and, most recently, Al Markim for getting me so excited about the whole area of new television media in the first place.

Two very special people, who had faith in this project from the beginning, were essential in making this book a reality: Jeanne Glass, my agent, who helped me mold the concept into a book, and Gerry Howard, my editor, who believed so strongly in the idea from the beginning.

Thank you also to my father, who encouraged a lifelong interest in television, and to my mother. A special thanks to my wife, Shari, who always seems to become involved in all of my crazy projects.

To all of you, my most sincere thanks.

PREFACE: WHAT IS A MEDIA ROOM?

When I was about ten years old, in 1962, I remember leaving my father's office in Rockefeller Center in New York City, crossing Forty-ninth Street, and wandering into an incredible world of the future called the RCA Exhibition Hall. As a child, I was mesmerized by the idea of videotape machines as toys for the home, and by color TV sets that could be worn on the wrist like a watch. At the time, color television itself was a relatively new idea (the program my father produced, *Concentration*, was not broadcast in color until 1968), and home video recorders, picture phones, and TV sets that could be carried in a shirt pocket seemed very far away.

Twenty years later, seated in my very own home media room, I can watch not only videotapes but video*discs* as well. I can also play a wide variety of videogames, a craze that RCA could never have foreseen in the days when Jayne Mansfield, The Jetsons, and Ben Casey were hot stuff. (I'm still waiting for my wristwatch color TV—black-and-white wristwatch TVs are about as close as we've come so far.)

It is no accident that the 1980s are the era of personalized entertainment and information.

We're all growing more technologically sophisticated, we're better educated as a people than any other group in history, and, probably most important, we have more leisure time—time to think and time to play—than our ancestors. These changes in life-style have been accompanied by a constant rise in the sheer amount of information available on this planet and, to a lesser extent, in the amount of entertainment programming available as well. The technology to deliver almost any kind of message to any place on earth currently exists—the real questions for the 1980s have to do with refinements, and, most important, with marketing.

All these converging trends, combined with our all-American fascination with fancy gadgets, will make the home media room (and the office media room) a ubiquitous reality in the 1980s. Every home that currently owns a TV set (98 percent of U.S. households) will probably have some form of media room by 1990, and will certainly have one by the year 2000, less than twenty years from today.

What, then, is a media room? In its simplest form, it is a room whose center of attention is a color TV set that is used to watch not only off-the-air signals but other kinds of programming as well. On one side of the TV set there is likely to be some kind of video player, probably with recording capability. On the other side you're more than likely to find a videogame system.

It is that game system, in reality a game-playing computer, that dictates just how the room functions. It is with videogames that a family room begins to become a media room. If you've lived with a videogame console on the *side* of your TV set for a while, you will realize that the system should really sit a few feet *in front* of the set instead—that way you won't have to get up to change cartridges. The best place for a videogame console is usually a table that can be reached by someone sitting on the couch normally reserved for TV viewing.

Once you've added that special coffee table (usually one with a drawer or shelf for the storage of the game cartridges and the controllers), you've begun a process that has altered the room's function. You have started to create a media room. The room has gained a function. The former reading room is now, in effect, an arcade, or, with the addition of a videocassette recorder (VCR), a movie theater. Once you've bought the VCR, you will buy some blank and preprogrammed tapes, and you'll probably eliminate some books in the bookshelves to accommodate them. Welcome to the world of the future.

Once you have a mini movie theater in your home, you will probably start thinking about accouterments. A giant projection TV screen dramatically enhances the theatrical ambience (if you watch a lot of TV, why not see images as large as life?). The old coffee table may be transferred to another room, to make way for a TV projector—built into a new coffee table.

If you're very serious about your TV viewing, you could take the concept of a media room to heart, gut the family room entirely, and create a full-scale futuristic environment. If this is your bent, this book will guide you in all aspects of assembling a media room to satisfy even the most ambitious fantasies.

A word of caution, though. The consumer electronics industry is racing ahead with fantastic speed, and today's wonder may be tomorrow's antique. You'll be on reasonably solid ground with a home VCR, a color TV, a video camera, and a videogame—all these products will be improved, but not dramatically reshaped, within the next five years or so. Cable is the safest bet of all, because you rent the service; you can never be stuck with out-of-date purchases. Videodiscs, projection TVs, and, to a lesser extent, personal computers are a little more risky, because they're still finding their place in the market.

There is no guarantee that the products described in this book will be available for years and years. Some will be obsolete due to competition from other manufacturers; others will be made less desirable because of a manufacturer's own improvements. Atari, for example, now sells three incompatible videogame units—the VCS, the Home Entertainment System 2500, and their personal computers. Will all three retain popularity until 1985? 1990? Will cartridges continue to be made for all three systems? It's impossible to predict.

At the time this book was written, two videodisc systems were vying for leadership, and neither was succeeding in even reaching the manufacturers' own sales projections. The release of a third system was delayed due to poor market conditions. Again, it is impossible to predict public taste, particularly when consumers are routinely barraged with so many new electronic marvels. Industry experts and analysts cannot project beyond a year or so, even when armed with all available product reports and marketing studies.

Since the home electronics industry will not slow down for at least ten years (probably fifteen to twenty, in fact), you might as well dive in as soon as you have an idea of what you want and you have the money to pay for it. Try to design your media room for flexibility and even replacement (permanent installations are a bad idea if products are custom-fitted, for example). Consider what you really *need* first, and then buy with as much information at hand as you can muster. This book will supply most of the necessary information—and will tell you where to find updates.

You should start building and buying as soon as you've decided you want to have your own media room. You could wait forever for prices to fall (they may or may not), for items to be redesigned (they *are*, every year, and will continue to be), for someone to tell you what to buy (read this book and you'll have a good idea of what to buy and how to make your equipment work in an overall room design). No more excuses—if you don't take the plunge and buy a VCR or a videogame or a small computer, you'll never really understand what all the excitement is about.

New York City, 1982   H.B.

THE
MEDIA ROOM

JUST WATCHING TV

As I write this, I am seated in front of a conventional typewriter keyboard. The "typewriter," however, holds no paper. Instead, characters appear on a television screen, and as my thoughts become cohesive, I can improve upon what I've written, using a few simple commands to move words, sentences, and even full paragraphs around in the text. Three years ago, the idea of this sort of word processing at home (I do my best writing on the kitchen table) was a wild idea right out of a science fiction movie. Three weeks ago I packed up my Smith-Corona and its assorted ribbon cartridges and buried the box in a closet.

I now do all my writing (and most of my accounting) on the computer, taking breaks for a quick game of Pac-Man between chapters. Compared with the combination of my Atari personal computer system (the hardware), the Letter Perfect word processor (the software), and a Panasonic 7-inch color television set, the Smith-Corona is an antique. It cannot do the job anymore. As anyone who has ever written a book will tell you, the hardest part of book writing is the conceptualizing, but the most time-consuming task is the need to submit hundreds of pages of cleanly typed manuscript to an editor. On the typewriter, my hands do all the work. On the word processor, the software does the work of setting margins, numbering pages, making those pages look uniform, even making instantaneous corrections of typing errors (word processors will someday put Liquid Paper out of business). Some word-processing programs can even be used with software that will correct spelling errors. Once you've used a word processor, it is nearly impossible to understand why (cost aside) people use typewriters. To put it bluntly, word processors are now making typewriters obsolete, and it seems likely that the typewriter will soon join the icebox, the steam engine, and the telegraph as a pivotal invention replaced by superior technology. Typing on TV—one of many futuristic notions now routine in my daily life.

A UTILITY CALLED TELEVISION

Teenagers who play videogames are acutely aware of the multiple uses of the TV screen. Children who learn computing in their *Sesame*

Street years adapt to education via TV, regardless of the programming. Video reality is more than TV shows—it's computer graphics, space battlescapes, word-processing readouts, a place to see home movies. Videogames are merely the first wave of pop culture to alter our perceptions. Computers will be the second wave.

All this technology comes as a direct result of the invention of the microcomputer chip, a tiny slice of silicon that inexpensively houses a vast number of electronic circuits. Chips are the reason why calculators, digital watches, electronic games, and even microwave ovens are so small, and so reasonably priced. They are at the heart of all miniaturized electronic devices, from personal computers to Sony's Walkman personal stereos and Watchman pocket TV sets. These very same chips are the key to interactive television, to videodisc technology, and, increasingly, to the workings of television sets themselves.

I've always thought of television as a utility, like electricity or running water. Watching television, regardless of *what* is being watched, is an activity in and of itself. TV's kin are not really newspapers, theater, or the movies; watching television is more closely linked with eating, sleeping, and turning on a light—our routine daily activities. Marshall McLuhan said that TV's message was its glow, its noise, its presence, and that *what* was being shown hardly mattered. A. C. Nielsen says the average American basks in that glow for 4¼ hours every day, making the activity third in the human hierarchy, directly after work (8–9 hours) and sleep (6–8 hours).

For most of its history, the television set has been a passive instrument in the home. You turned it on and watched what came in over the airwaves. The average viewer touched only two controls on the TV set—an on/off/volume control and a knob to switch channels.

That there are four networks seems as normal as the fact that there is hot water and cold water. Each time you turn on the television set, there are the same three commercial networks, plus PBS, plus the same number of local stations in your area. That this seems "normal" is merely a result of years of limited options; until the mid-1970s there were no alternatives except some independent stations (featuring off-network programming) and PBS.

That has now changed swiftly and dramatically. Television in the 1980s is being transformed into an *active* instrument—active in two respects. First, the viewer has an increasingly active role in choosing what to watch—selecting a program from dozens of cable channels or, in the case of videocassettes, videodiscs, and videogames, from a rack in a retail store. Second (and to an admittedly limited extent), the viewer can control the video images themselves, by using videogames and computers and interactive cable TV consoles, which allow select Qube viewers to express opinions and make suggestions on live television programs (see page 99). We can also now speed up, slow down, or freeze the recorded images from a videotape or a videodisc.

The effect of these two changes (and their variations) will cause Americans to consider their TV sets to be far more than "idiot boxes." The most sophisticated among us will see TV as a tool, a new kind of window on the world, the display component of a sophisticated communications system. The rest of us will enjoy television's alternatives as a natural facet of life—causing a domino effect among TV network ratings, advertisers, and, ultimately, the business and creative community that supplies the grist for the electronic mill that is American television.

TELEVISION OF ABUNDANCE

The new video technology is here to stay. The products themselves, however, are in varying stages of consumer acceptance. Cable television is currently millions of households ahead of all other new technologies combined. Cable TV advocates have promised a new "television of abundance," a world where people watch *what* they want to watch, *when* they want to watch it, via cable TV. Educators and community leaders, who will finally have the means to reach into the community, are readying for this revolution.

But that phrase "television of abundance" is not new. In fact, it is over thirty years old. It was originated when radio started losing ground to the then-new TV, in the early 1950s. At that time educators and culturemongers and local, ethnic, religious, and political leaders all foresaw themselves as broadcasters. Unlike radio, whose stations were used mainly for news and entertainment for the masses, television would serve loftier concerns. There would be opera and ballet, legitimate theater, and uplifting programs from the colleges. This *was*, in fact, the case, albeit on an extremely limited basis. Early TV schedules included some highbrow programming, but most slots were filled with cheap-to-produce boxing and wrestling coverage, and a continuation of radio's staples: variety shows, sitcoms, and soap operas.

Television, as those well-intentioned individuals soon discovered, is an expensive way to communicate. Americans are unaccustomed to paying for broadcast entertainment and information directly (a tradition established in early radio, despite loud protests about the disastrous potential of advertising on the public airwaves). Advertisers are only too happy to pay to communicate—but only to the largest audiences. (This is now changing with the advent of specialized cable-TV audiences, but only to a limited degree.) Entertainment programs almost always deliver higher audience shares than cultural or educational programs, and so TV, in order to support the enormous costs of production, has always been programmed to reach the largest audiences.

Just listening to radio, late 1920s.
(Photo courtesy RCA)

Studios in the late 1940s cost hundreds of thousands of dollars to build and equip (today's medium-size studio costs about a million dollars). The cost of a transmitter, a technical staff (requiring highly specialized training on finicky equipment), and the overall operation (sets, costumes, writers, producers, directors, etc.) was prohibitive, except for the largest organizations—the networks and their allies, the advertisers.

It is true that TV began as something of a cultural cornucopia, with programs like *You Are an Artist*, *Author Meets the Critics*, *Meet the Press*, and *Science Circus* in prime-time slots. The reasons had very little to do with crafty programming—before 1950, nobody really understood what would "work" on the new medium.

Within ten years, programmers had a very good idea of what the public would accept on the new medium, and even the finest of the dramatic anthology series had been replaced by the likes of *77 Sunset Strip*, *Perry Como's Kraft Music Hall*, *Bonanza*, *The Ed Sullivan Show*, and *Perry Mason*.

Television had become a business.

Programmers learned not to take chances, to develop their wares according to the "least objectionable program" principle. Schedules were

STEP-BY-STEP GUIDE: NETWORK TV BROADCASTING

1. Whether in the studio or in the field, a camera (or several cameras) records the action. In the case of most network programs, the action is recorded and edited for playback at a scheduled time.

2. The edited tape is stored until needed, then played on a videotape machine in a network playback center. The signal travels via telephone lines to local television stations across the country.* (Some programs are "fed" once for the East Coast and a second time for the West Coast because of time differences.)

(Photos courtesy RCA)

3. The local TV station, broadcasting on a prescribed channel, can transmit the program in either of two ways. Most often, it simply passes

* Networks currently use satellites only for specialized distribution. As more and more local TV stations buy satellite receivers, the networks will use satellite transmission with greater regularity.

the network signal directly to its local transmitter (common for most regularly scheduled network shows), roughly in synchronization with the other local stations of the network. The local station may, however, record the network feed for later broadcast. For instance, if a football game is scheduled for 8 p.m. on a Friday night, the local station might rebroadcast the network program fed at that time later in the evening or on another night.

4. Local television transmitters serve a specific area of coverage, generally a city and its suburbs. Home television antennas are designed to receive all local television transmissions on VHF and UHF channels.

5. There are three ways to receive local television channels. You may connect your television set to an outdoor antenna (recommended if you're on the outskirts of a coverage area), you may use an indoor "rabbit ear" antenna, or you may connect to cable TV (see page 134).

filled almost entirely with formula action/ adventure series and situation comedies. By the mid-1960s, the biggest hits were *The Beverly Hillbillies* and *Peyton Place*.

The educational and cultural contingent, feeling left out by the early 1960s, started talking up the need for a fourth network, guided not by ratings but by nobility of purpose. The result was a ragtag syndicate of educational television stations called National Educational Television. Plagued by an overabundance of unpopular UHF stations in key cities, a severe lack of funds, and continual political intervention from the Johnson Administration, NET nevertheless persevered. Now called the Public Broadcasting System, this network is still chronically short of funds, but now represents a substantial force in American broadcasting.

False starts in programming were accompanied by dubious technological decisions. Early in television's development, before the medium became a money machine, it was a blank slate, just a box that received and played pictures and sound. Engineers weren't sure what, exactly, they had invented. With radio as popular as it was (just about every home had one in the 1930s), why would anybody buy a "radio with pictures"? TV was seen as superfluous, possibly an invention without any useful purpose at all. There were experiments to explore all possible uses of television. One group of inventors was certain that television would not be successful unless each set included a printer that could reproduce the screen image for permanent storage (this process is now called a "screen dump" and is frequently employed by personal computer users). Another group was reluctant to introduce the device without a well-developed system of reproducing color pictures, as was becoming popular in the movies. Nobody really knew what television was *for*. And almost nobody knew how to sell it to Americans. Nobody, that is, except RCA.

Television was a novelty item when it was ex-

hibited at the 1939–40 World's Fair, a new product that RCA hoped to mass-produce by early in the 1940s. World War II delayed that start, since the electronics industry went to work for the war effort. RCA was back with an improved system almost immediately after the war. By that time, NBC, CBS, ABC, and the now-defunct DuMont network were testing programs on the air. RCA encouraged its radio stars to try television on NBC. By 1950, Arthur Godfrey, Frank Sinatra, *The Goldbergs*, Ed Wynn, Kate Smith, and Burns and Allen had made the transition from radio to TV. The prime-time schedules were filled with programs, and TV had become a popular novelty in American households. Ten years later, it was a necessity. Twenty years later, it was an addiction.

A typical family scene, watching TV in the days of *Howdy Doody*, *Playhouse 90*, and *This Is Your Life*. At this time, there were four networks: ABC, NBC, CBS, and the now-forgotten DuMont network. (Photo courtesy RCA)

PERSONAL TELEVISION

Since the transition to color in the mid-1960s, television has not changed dramatically. It has regularly served a very useful purpose, both as an entertainer (some say baby-sitter) and as an information source, for thirty years.

Now change is afoot. Technology is changing the world, and television is at the forefront of the new communications system. The revolution has seen uneven success, and no one knows how it will end up. In the late 1970s most people did not want cable television (fewer than one in four subscribed in areas where cable was available) because it offered little more than improved reception and some movies. Cartrivision, the first home videotape system, was almost universally ignored by the general public, again because there was precious little software available for its cartridges. Magnavox introduced Odyssey, the first home videogame, in 1972, but it never caught on, probably because of its limited graphic capability. Despite the current hype, fewer than one in one hundred homes owns a personal computer, and 95 percent of American households did *not* own videocassette machines as of early 1983.

Despite slow starts, though, substantial changes are now taking place. Videogames are a national obsession, both in the arcades and at home. Most schools have computers, and an increasing number own the equipment needed to produce TV shows. Watching videotaped movies at home is no longer an exotic experience, just a little out of reach for some because of high prices. Videodiscs will presumably make viewing off-the-shelf movies and special programs possible at more reasonable prices. Slowly but surely the passive concept of "just watching TV" is fading away. Television viewing is becoming an individualized affair now, with personal-size screens and stereos and one's own library of cassettes and discs. Perhaps this is all part of the "me" sensibility so often cited in magazines.

There are several reasons why the 1980s will almost certainly be the decade of the media room. Baby-boom couples, the group that filled the colleges in the late 1960s and the 1970s, are settling down. Many are not starting families immediately, so there is more time and more money for leisure. Work weeks are a bit shorter, and people are spending more time at home. Investments in a living environment are making sense to many people; it's expensive to go out. We buy microwave ovens and Cuisinarts and stereo systems and video equipment, but think twice about the second car, because the car itself is outrageously expensive and gas is still going up in price. Home entertainment seems to be the better investment.

Shifts in programming tastes are also contributing to change. I find myself turning on the VCR more and more often, because I am bewildered by the networks' choice of *That's Incredible!* and *Diff'rent Strokes* as prime-time fare. It seems that the networks are programming for somebody else. The days when I could watch network TV for an entire night are clearly over. Having grown up in the 1960s, I still expect a full night of entertainment along the lines of *The Ed Sullivan Show—The Smothers Brothers Comedy Hour—Mission: Impossible* (8:00 p.m.–11:00 p.m. Sundays, CBS, 1967), or *Mr. Novak—The Man from U.N.C.L.E.—That Was the Week That Was—The Bell Telephone Hour* (7:30 p.m.–11:00 p.m., NBC, 1964), or such amiable junk as *The Flying Nun—Bewitched—That Girl* or *Dragnet—The Dean Martin Show* (8:00 p.m.–9:30 p.m., ABC; 9:30 p.m.–11:00 p.m., NBC, 1968). When the best of a weekday night (Tuesday, 1982) is *Hart to Hart, Flamingo Road, Three's Company, The Dukes of Hazzard*, and *Happy Days*, I either head for PBS (on this night, an excellent BBC series called *Life on Earth*) or Home Box Office (*The Black Hole*—oh well!). On a bad night, the networks can be beaten in ratings by HBO or other cable television channels. Clearly there is room for alternatives (at least in my house).

The growth of alternatives has been further augmented by time-shift viewing, the recording of programs for later replay. Current technology makes this videotaping possible automatically. Many people record the day's soap operas for viewing in the evening. Others record old movies broadcast late at night for subsequent viewing at a more reasonable hour, or on a "bad" TV night.

Cable TV has also grown quickly in the past five years, because of the complementary growth of new cable channels and the easing of government regulations that previously limited its growth in many areas, particularly the big cities. Some words of caution are in order, however. The magical potential of cable may ultimately become another "television of abundance"—lost in a money-grubbing shuffle. The technologies seem to race forward: while you're weighing the virtues of a videotape machine versus an RCA SelectaVision disc player, an entirely new disc system may be introduced. The smart video consumer is the one who continually updates his or her information.

THE DANGER ZONE

Incompatibility—the inability to use one system's hardware to play another's software—is the biggest problem most people face in making video decisions. Intellivision videogame cartridges don't fit the Atari videogame (in fact, Atari makes three totally incompatible cartridges for their three game systems); RCA's videodiscs won't work on any other videodisc system; Beta cassettes are too small for the VHS (Video Home System) cassette format. It's all very confusing, and more than a little scary, when as much as $1000 can be paid for a device that could be obsolete within a year of purchase.

The story of quadraphonic stereo, introduced less than ten years ago and now all but forgotten, is a poignant example of a "great idea" that became obsolete less than two years after its introduction. Several "quad" systems were intro-duced in the mid-1970s that could play four different channels from four different speakers, thus doubling the stereo effect. Quadraphonic amplifiers, turntables, and tape decks were manufactured and purchased by a limited number of listeners. There were several—incompatible—systems, some requiring special records and tapes, which could not be played on any non-quad system. The end of the story is bitter for those who bought quadraphonic equipment—quadraphonic records are no longer sold.

The consumer electronics industry offers several examples of much-publicized products that have drifted into obsolescence. Polaroid introduced a home movie camera that processed its own pictures under the name "Polavision," in 1977, only to withdraw it months later (much to the chagrin of consumers who could no longer buy film for the system). Eight-track audio cartridges, once quite popular in the early days of car stereos, have now been almost entirely edged out by more efficient audiocassettes.

With three different videodisc players currently on the market, all incompatible, and a vast number of incompatible computer products, it is wise to research very carefully before you make any investment—it's the only way to protect yourself against costly mistakes. This book will help you make informed decisions with buying checklists and background information, but nobody can guarantee against obsolescence. Ultimately, all the products mentioned in this book *will* be obsolete—it is simply a matter of time.

Matters of taste provide another reason for caution. In a home lovingly decorated in an early-American motif, a giant projection TV will be almost certainly out of place. Videocassette machines and videogames can be hidden away in smoked-glass cabinetry, but screens, even if they fold up into themselves, are usually too large to disguise. Questions of practicality also figure. A television writer I know in Los Angeles has both the space and the money to accommodate a giant screen, but his wife keeps asking a very practical question: "What do you *need* it for?" She wins every time.

This media room business is *not* for people who are concerned about every penny. It's an expensive pursuit, one guaranteed to cost you more than you had originally anticipated. Whether you plan a specialized and modest information center dominated by a computer linked to the Dow Jones News/Retrieval service and some videotapes of old movies, or a full-scale, high-tech redesign of your den or family room, with all the latest equipment, creating a media room is a complicated and costly affair. It's an individual art, one that should conform to needs and resources rather than dreams. You may find that a media-room-in-a-briefcase, containing a hand-held computer and related accessories, plus a Watchman, or pocket-size television set, may be everything you need. You may also find that passive home entertainment is all you really want, just a place to comfortably watch TV shows and prerecorded movies with life-size images. Whatever your goals, look at your needs carefully, and then buy *slowly*. Start simply, with a videogame or a videodisc machine, and then build up to the more complicated (and expensive) devices. (Chapter 10, "Putting It All Together," provides specifics on building a media room just right for you.)

If your home is anything like the typical American household, the room where your media environment begins to roost is likely to be the busiest one in the house. Just as soon as the first videogame arrives, the arguments will begin. One family member will want to watch *60 Minutes*, while another will want to play Defender or Missile Command. Add more equipment and you'll add more options and, if you have more than two family members, even more occasions

for argument. One television set will simply not suffice. You may need almost as many television sets as there are people in the house. You will also need some way to switch different signals into different sets, so that you're not spending half the night moving and rewiring VCRs and videogames.

To put this another way, once you've bought your first videodisc player or videogame, you have begun a *process*. You've agreed to change your viewing habits, probably forever.

New buyers tend to make light of this "process" notion. The author hereby warns every reader of this book that a videogame will almost certainly lead to habit-forming activities (both in playing the game itself and in checking with your local store to see if any new games have arrived). A VCR will lead to similar habits, particularly if you like movies and have a videocassette rental store in the neighborhood. This process extends beyond software. If you own a VCR, you'll probably keep your eye out for new kinds of videotape, for other related devices, for anything that will reduce the clutter of wires. Then there is the matter of storage—once you've surpassed the capacity of your bookshelf, you'll be thinking a lot about redesigning the space to accommodate not only today's tapes but the new disc player that you're planning to buy for Christmas. A media room is the embodiment of electronic addiction. It's a room that could change several times a year, each time the consumer electronics industry unleashes a new gadget, or an improvement on an old one.

In order to best use all your new equipment, you will certainly need more screens. Sometimes the bigger the better. Sometimes the smaller the better. In any case, the process begins with a television set.

■ 2 ■

THE BEST PICTURES

American consumers buy, on the average, *fifteen million* television sets each and every year. We buy about twice as many color sets as we do black-and-white sets, but the total amount of sales is remarkably consistent—with a slow but steady rise as many families replace their first (ailing) color sets.

When television began just before World War II, with fuzzy little black-and-white screens and thirteen channels (Channel 1 was later retired to municipal communications, leaving a total of twelve: 2–13), the very idea of a television in every home was hopeful at best. The first problem: There was almost nothing to *watch* on television, almost no programming at all. The second problem: Radio was an intimate part of American life, a situation some thirty years in the making. The solution to both problems began with RCA, a company that not only manufactured most of America's radios (and televisions) but also owned the nation's largest radio (and television) programmer, NBC. The mother company encouraged NBC's favorite stars to try television, and soon the best stars and the best shows were no longer on radio. They were on television instead. *You Bet Your Life* (hosted by Groucho

Marx), *Your Hit Parade*, *Dragnet*, and the *Original Amateur Hour* eventually eliminated their radio runs. By the early 1950s, RCA's coaxing, combined with the magic of the first major TV star, a heretofore undistinguished radio comic named Milton Berle, piqued America's interest in TV. The stories about people lining up outside stores that sold TV sets to watch Uncle Miltie's Tuesday night show through the window, and about neighbors "just dropping by" in the middle of each Tuesday's prime time, are exaggerated but for the most part true. By the mid-1950s, most families either owned a television set or were thinking seriously about buying one.

Color television took longer to win consumer acceptance. Although first introduced in 1954, and incessantly promoted by such gimmicks as NBC's "Color Weeks" (when all programming was presented in color—big news for the early sixties), the redoubtable NBC Peacock, and their signature as "NBC: The Full Color Network," color television was not an institution until as recently as the early 1970s. In the first ten years of color TV, only one home in thirty owned a color set. It was an expensive luxury, a good investment only as a replacement for an old black-and-

Color television sets have been sold since 1954, but they did not gain widespread acceptance until more than ten years later. Note the rounded picture tube, a relic. (Photo courtesy RCA)

white set. By 1970 or so, most American homes had witnessed the death of their first black-and-white set—and replaced the old Raytheon or Philco with a new color TV.

Manufacturers have spent millions of man-hours perfecting the basic color television set, improving picture tubes, tuners, circuitry, and mechanical and electronic parts, justifying claims that a new TV set should last a decade or more. The picture tube, despite the best manufacturing skills, is almost always the first part to go. (Mechanical tuners, described below, are also subject to early replacement.) Other components (all considerably less expensive than the picture tube) usually last longer. Most standard warranties will protect your picture tube for two years, the other parts for one year, and allow only 90 days of labor at no charge. Certain manufacturers don't reach this standard, others offer better warranties, but most are close to industry average. There are dozens of warranties available—

you should ask your retailer about the term of warranty on the picture tube, on other parts (the tuner, the electrical system), the question of repair or replacement of faulty parts, and service contracts (extended warranties for a price).

Electronics industry data forecast a very good to excellent chance that you will buy a new television set before this decade is over. If you are shopping for a "bedroom set," a second set that you can use to watch *The Tonight Show* or a late movie, you'll probably buy a black-and-white 12-inch model for just under $100 (there are dozens available, all very much alike). If you're shopping for an AC/DC portable that will work on house current or batteries, you must consider size, weight, viewing situations, color vs. black-and-white, and your need for built-in accessories like a cassette player, or AM/FM or clock radio. If you need a new color set for your new media room or the living room, the options are surprisingly varied. Nearly all the top manufacturers and dozens of small importers sell color sets. It would be fair to say that there are up to 500 different models of color television sets available in America. How to make a decision among them? Try the checklist on pages 28–29, and consider the points below before you even start to shop.

Screen sizes currently vary from $1\frac{1}{2}$ inches to 10 feet. (They won't get much smaller, but they may get larger.) Sizes are always expressed by "height," but the measurements are always taken *diagonally*, from the upper left to the lower right, or vice versa. Technically speaking, the screens capable of the absolute best pictures, those capable of the most accurate color rendition and the finest reproduction of the lines and tones on test patterns are either 19 inches, 21 inches, or 25 inches high (Sony has created a "limited-edition" 30-inch screen that is excellent, but expensive.) Smaller screens do not offer as fine detail as these sizes; larger screens are available only in projection formats, whose overall picture quality is always inferior to glass-enclosed screens.

TOP B/W TELEVISION BRANDS (Rated by sales)*

(Courtesy of *Television Digest*)

1. RCA
2. Zenith
3. GE
4. Sears
5. Panasonic
6. Sony
7. Sanyo
8. Quasar
9. J. C. Penney
10. Montgomery Ward
11. Sylvania
12. Philco

(All of the above have at least a 2 percent share of the market.)
*1981

TOP COLOR TELEVISION BRANDS (Rated by sales)*

(Courtesy of *Television Digest*)

1. Zenith
2. RCA
3. GE
4. Sears
5. Sony
6. Magnavox
7. Quasar
8. Sylvania
9. Montgomery Ward
10. Panasonic
11. Sanyo
12. Hitachi

(All of the above have at least a 2 percent share of the market.)
*1981

There is no single manufacturer who consistently produces the best color television sets. As a matter of fact, there is no best maker of television sets, period. Certain makers have maintained reputations for extraordinary quality, sometimes because their sets are legitimately better than most, but more often because their higher prices represent higher quality in the eyes of the consumer public. Most of the name-brand manufacturers sell good sets, with basically the same warranties. Only a few have functional service networks among local dealers and repair shops nationwide. (RCA in particular has a fine, dependable service network for many of their products.) RCA and Zenith color TV sales regularly account for one third of the U.S. market.

The latest color television sets offer not only remote control but stereo sound, 105-channel cable tuning, and remarkably lifelike colors. This is one of the more advanced sets, General Electric's 25EM2870P. (Photo courtesy General Electric Television Division)

CHECKLIST: HOW TO BUY A COLOR TV SET

PART 1: AT HOME

With hundreds of color TV sets available, it's wise to determine your needs before you start to shop. Use this checklist to analyze your needs, then compare three sets to make a final decision.

1. SCREEN SIZE   RANGE: _____

Pictures can be as small as 3.7 inches (measured diagonally) and as large as 30 inches (projection systems aside). Most people buy in the 13-inch area for small rooms; in the 19-inch area for larger rooms.

The chart below is based on maximum feasible viewing distance from the screen.

DISTANCE FROM SCREEN	SCREEN SIZE
1–3 feet	5 inches or less
3–5 feet	5–7 inches
5–8 feet	5–10 inches
8–10 feet	8–13 inches
10–12 feet	13–19 inches
12–15 feet	15–21 inches
15–18 feet	21–25 inches
18 feet or more	25 inches (and you should consider projection television)

2. TUNER   CHOICE: _____

See pages 31–33 before making selection. Select your preference for tuning control.
a. Rotary (least expensive)
b. Push-button
c. Seesaw switch
d. Digital keypad (most expensive)

3. REMOTE CONTROL   CHOICE: _____

What's it worth to you?
a. Additional $100 or more
b. Additional $50
c. Additional $25
d. No additional money

4. CABINET STYLE   CHOICE: _____

This is totally dependent on your personal taste. The salesmen will tell you that plastic isn't particularly durable, and that wood or metal is best. Pay heed if you plan to move within the next few years. If the set will be in one place through most of its life, don't worry about a plastic cabinet.

a. Plastic table model
b. Metal table model
c. Simulated wood table model
d. Small floor console
e. Large floor console
(Make your decision and *stick to it*!)

5. NEW FEATURES

Check the appropriate column for each of these new features.

	Essential	Desirable	Unnecessary
a. Cable-ready tuning			
b. AC/DC operation			
c. Use as monitor or TV			
d. Built-in clock			
e. Built-in telephone			

6. HOW MUCH WILL YOU SPEND?   PRICE: _____

a. $200–$250
b. $250–$300
c. $300–$350
d. $350–$400
e. $400–$450
f. $450–$500
g. $500–$600
h. $600–$700
i. $700–$800
j. Over $800

7. SERVICE   CHOICE: _____

Where will the set be serviced?
a. Store/repair shop
b. Store/repair shop or home
c. Home

8. SERVICE CONTRACT   VALUE: _____

What is the value of an annual service contract to you and your family?
a. $0–$50
b. $50–$100
c. Over $100

PART 2: IN THE STORE

Using the checklist, visit the store in your area with the largest stock and the most knowledgeable salespeople.

Rate each of the sets that interest you with a number on the chart below. The set with the *highest* number will suit your needs most completely.

Reception in some stores will be less than perfect, so it is best to test all sets by using the same videodisc or videocassette machine as programming.

	SET 1	SET 2	SET 3
a. Confidence in manufacturer (rate 0–10)			
b. Picture quality (rate 0–100)			
c. Number of front-of-set controls (times 2)			
d. Number of side-of-set controls			
e. How many days long is the warranty for parts?			
f. For labor?			
g. Home service? (0 if no, 25 if yes)			
TOTALS			

Two more steps before you actually buy the set:

First, shop around and compare prices for precisely the same set in at least three different stores.

Second, make your decision based not only on price but on the store's reputation as well. Discounters are fine, but be sure you can return the set *for cash* if there's anything wrong during the first seven days (and keep all paperwork, just in case).

Enjoy your new color television set.

This is now something of an industry rule. The reason has everything to do with quality—and distribution. A chart of the sales leaders in color and B/W appears on page 27.

The decision as to which set to buy, whether it's a cassette/clock/TV/radio combo or a wall-size projection unit, usually comes down to features—which ones you need and which ones you're willing to pay for. The checklist on pages 28–29 will help you recognize your needs, while the step-by-step guide on pages 32–33 offers specifics on how television sets work. This will be surprisingly helpful when you shop. If the salesperson senses you've taken a serious interest in your purchase, he or she will probably be more helpful. Get to know the various features by their names, understanding, of course, that some manufacturers call the same feature by different names.

BLACK-AND-WHITE SETS

There isn't much difference between the quality of black-and-white sets, except with respect to their size, weight, and price. The most popular black-and-white TVs are 12-inch, AC-only, which offer VHF/UHF dial tuners and a passable level of picture quality. The main reason for buying a 12-inch B/W portable is convenience. These are basic television sets—don't expect much and you won't be disappointed. Priced under $100, the 12-inch sets are quite a bargain.

Black-and-white sets are also designed as portables, perfect for the back yard. Look for sets that can be powered by batteries and by the cigarette-lighter socket in your car. Remember to consider the weight of the batteries when comparing portables. This tip goes for all portable gear: Whenever you consider any portable equipment, be sure to check the weight, *including batteries.*

Buying a B/W set is principally a matter of taste, and of price comparisons. Stick to the major manufacturers for best results.

Quasar's 12-inch black-and-white portable is typical of the "second sets" used in America's kitchens and bedrooms. (Photo courtesy Quasar)

COLOR SETS

Unlike black-and-white TVs, all color TV sets are different, even within the product line of a single manufacturer. As you can see from the Step-by-Step Guide: How Color TV Works (pages 32–33), all color sets show the full-color spectrum by combining red, blue, and green stripes, broken into tiny segments by a black mask (or, in older sets, red, green, and blue *dot patterns,* also masked in black). There are no alternatives to this system—this is the way all color television sets work. (For the nuances of other countries' systems, though, see pages 154–55, "About Foreign TV Systems.") Although the mask patterns may vary slightly, you should know that there is very little difference between the masking systems available (although salespeople may try to tell you otherwise).

Most sets have four basic picture controls: BRIGHTNESS, CONTRAST, COLOR, and HUE. BRIGHTNESS is used mainly to adjust the picture for the room's light level; treat BRIGHTNESS as if it were a dimmer control for an electric lamp and adjust for your comfort in each room lighting situation. An Automatic Brightness feature contains a sensor that reads the amount of room light and adjusts for "normal" brightness. You should be able to override the sensor at any time if you disagree with the sensor's perception of brightness needed.

The control for HUE, which adjusts for a little more green or violet, and the one for COLOR; which adds or subtracts the overall intensity of all colors, are for personal preference, having little to do with technical color accuracy. The real technical color controls are usually behind the set's back cover. They allow a knowledgeable technician to increase the intensity of the red stripes, the green stripes, and/or the blue stripes. If you don't know exactly what you're doing, *do not* adjust the set yourself. Messing with those color controls can knock the whole picture hopelessly out of whack—and only a technician will be able to reset the proper color relationships.

CONTRAST controls are very important for your overall picture quality. Adjust the darkest area on the screen to show just a small amount of detail in order to get the whole picture right.

You might find two other controls on the front (or side) of a TV set: SHARPNESS and PICTURE. The degree to which a picture is "sharp," with all the fine details crisply defined, is difficult to determine during regular viewing of an average TV show. Technicians use test patterns to adjust sharpness; they generally involve a series of thin, almost fragile lines, grouped very close to one another. Sharpness is usually expressed as "resolution" by the pros; about 150 discrete lines of resolution can be identified on a properly adjusted 19-inch screen. (The new home monitors, described on page 34, reach over 200 lines of resolution, so the pictures are very

clearly detailed.) Sharpness can be improved only slightly with front-of-set controls. Most of the real adjustment can be done only by a technician, using back-of-set controls. A PICTURE control is similar to sharpness on some sets, but it is more of a contrast controller on others. Ask for a demonstration to be sure of what you're buying.

When advertisers speak of television broadcast engineers adjusting color immediately prior to transmission, they speak the truth. Encoded data relating to numerical values of colors (every color has a numerical equivalent in the spectrum) is indeed transmitted along with the picture, and a system, in some sets called VIR (short for "Vertical Integral Reference"), locks to that color information so that your set reproduces precisely the colors preset by the broadcast engineer. Not all programs are transmitted with VIR color information, and so, ColorTrak was created. ColorTrak, an RCA feature, locks to the VIR signal (when available), and adjusts all incoming signals to reproduce the most pleasing "normal" colors possible. System 3 (Zenith), Automatic Color Lock (Mitsubishi), Signal Tracker (Hitachi), Automatic Balanced Color (Toshiba), and Trimatic (Sanyo) are all similar, and sometimes encompass automatic brightness and fine tuning as well.

TUNING

Most sets have an AFT, or Automatic Fine Tuning, push button. Although AFT may improve color and overall picture quality, it is strictly a tuning aid, used to find the exact spot in the spectrum of channels, the exact frequency where the broadcast signal is strongest. AFT controls are sometimes sensitive to heat, and will occasionally drift with time.

Individual tuning systems vary among sets,

STEP-BY-STEP GUIDE: HOW COLOR TV WORKS

1. The television signal can reach the receiver via antenna or cable or a direct video feed like the signal from a VCR. The tuner selects the channel you wish to see. Every channel travels at a different frequency. The television tuner locks on to a particular frequency, or channel.

2. The television signal, or, more accurately, the RF (radio frequency) signal (see page 39), contains three elements: the picture, the sound, and the synchronization code. In actual fact, the RF signal "carries" the picture and sound over short and long distances.

3. The audio signal is directed into an amplifier and later into a speaker. The sequence works much like radio.

4. At the same time, the picture or video signal, whether it comes from an over-the-air channel or a videogame or any other source, is directed toward the picture tube. The signal is changed in the tube from a stream of electronic

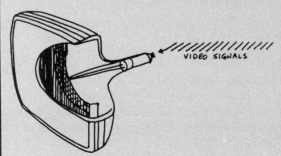

signals to a stream of *electrons*. These electrons are projected onto the reactive surface of the television screen and cause the screen to glow.

5. A closer look reveals not one but *three* video signals, one red, one green, and one blue, which operate in perfect synchronization. Each of these signals actually interacts only with specific portions of the screen. A black mask behind the screen, popularly called a "blackstripe" or

"black matrix," ensures that the red, blue, and green screen lines are kept separate. Our version is, of course, in black-and-white. Take a very close look at your color TV and you'll see three different colored stripes in a similar pattern.

6. The synchronization signal works three ways. First, it keeps the audio and the video simultaneous, so that sound matches picture. Second, it causes the electron stream to scan the reactive screen elements at a steady interval (actually 30 times per second). Third, it channels the electrons so that they create pictures "line by line." If you look closely at any television picture, you will see that hundreds of horizontal lines compose the image; similarly, if you look closely at any newspaper photo, you'll see thousands of tiny dots composing the printed image. These lines are actually the path followed by the electron stream.

7. All the action described above happens very quickly, on a microscopic scale. Normal viewing occurs at a distance of several feet from the screen, so the illusion of moving colored pictures is created every time we turn on the television set.

and some are better than others. "Frequency synthesis" is the single best tuning system available. It is usually operated by a 0–9 digital keypad, or a seesaw switch rocked in one direction for higher channel numbers, in the opposite direction for the lower numbers. A frequency synthesis tuner will lock onto one frequency (channel) and then electronically check to make sure the tuner has reached the proper frequency. It's drift-free, but every channel's push button must be pretuned (sometimes with tiny dials—note size before you buy). Ask for a demonstration of the frequency synthesis tuner when you buy—and be sure all of your preprogramming will remain intact ("non-volatile") even after the set is turned off.

"Electronic varactor" tuning is usually operated by push buttons. Each button sends a specified amount of electrical voltage to an electronic tuning circuit. There's no double checking as in frequency synthesis, but varactor tuning is a superior system.

"Rotary-dial" tuners, where each channel is tuned by twisting a dial, are the most familiar of all, but in today's electronic age, they're old-fashioned. The rotary is a 13-position switch whose contact points get dirty and wear out after a few years.

Two other advances in tuning make your choice even more complicated. Many sets are now being built with their own cable tuners. The actual number of cable channels, and which cable channels can be received, may vary with manufacturers, and even within manufacturing lines. There is no standard, so it is best to compare sets and the technical channel layout of your cable system at your local retailer before you buy. Be sure to check both present and future plans for cable TV in your area (see Chapter 7) before spending money on a cable-ready set that may be outmoded only a year after the purchase. The second tuning variation is a bit more exotic; some television sets are built without tuners.

MONITORS

Up until now television sets have always been manufactured as one-piece units containing screen, tuner, audio amplifier, and support electronics. But some of the more aggressive manufacturers have found a way to serve the more demanding buyer by separating the tuner and the audio section from the screen unit and creating discrete components, as you would find in a stereo system. They have invented "component video." There are several discrete TV tuners and screens already available (this has been the case in the industrial and professional video fields for many years), allowing a buyer to select the best equipment for his or her needs. Let's say you've just bought a top-of-the-line videocassette recorder, complete with push-button electronic tuning. Why, then, buy a television set with a tuner as well? Why pay for the same component twice? You can now buy a screen, with or without the audio system, and use the tuner in your videocassette recorder. And you may not need a television audio system either, because you can use the same electronic tuner that is connected to your stereo system to hear the television signal—at much higher fidelity than you would through a small TV speaker.

The perfect media room will contain not a single television set but a monitor screen, an audio system, and the best component tuner money can buy. In theory, the degree of quality now standard in the audio field will become the standard in video as well. And that means the best possible pictures—sometimes at the highest possible prices. Monitors are now being made with outlets labeled VIDEO IN, VIDEO OUT, AUDIO IN, and AUDIO OUT, which allow easy connection to other video and audio components. The use of these outlets is a little more complicated than they at first appear, because there are two kinds of signals involved. See page 39 for more about the differences between RF and video/audio signals.

Note: The word "monitor" is now being used to describe high-quality TV sets with monitor-like features. Generally speaking, it's best to buy a separate screen, audio system, and tuner, but price and new products may dictate otherwise.

SOUND

The present state of TV sound, or "audio," is worthy of discussion. Most television sets are built with almost no care for quality sound reproduction, using small speakers for barely adequate sound rendition. With the advent of stereo videodiscs and stereo videocassettes, and stereo cable-TV channels like Warner-Amex's MTV, a rock-music cable channel, quality sound has finally become important. Some sets already feature an enhanced sound capability, itself quite primitive when compared with even an inexpensive stereo system. Enhanced-sound sets usually include larger-than-normal speakers and a better amplifier. If you are going to connect a television set to your stereo system (easily done—see the explanation on page 134), think twice about buying a set with enhanced sound. If you're going to watch your new set *without* a stereo connection, have a salesperson demonstrate a console TV with built-in stereo speakers—you're bound to be impressed. The newest sets can operate as monitors, permitting easy hookup to your stereo system.

REMOTE CONTROL

One last feature to consider before you buy a set has little to do with picture or sound—it's purely a convenience item, which has been available for

Remote control is the most-asked-for feature on new TV sets. On Sony's KV-1945RS TV, you can select from 105 channels (including most cable channels), and adjust picture and volume using the remote controller. (Photo courtesy Sony Corporation)

many years on specially equipped sets. Remote control, now the single most popular feature on new sets, is available with plenty of variations, at various prices. All remote controllers will turn your set on and off, provided their "electronic eye" has a direct line of sight to the target on the set itself (no wire is required). Some controllers will let you control the volume and change channels; some will even tune cable channels. In the not-so-distant future cable operators may provide their own remote-control tuners for use on all TV sets.

PORTABLES

There are three kinds of portable television sets: miniature black-and-white sets, small color sets, and combination sets, which include some combination of small screen, radio, audiocassette, videocassette, clock, extra speakers, and battery power.

Portables usually contain a screen measuring 12 inches or less, so they're small enough to be carried from room to room. Many can be operated on house current or with a battery pack. Black-and-white sets are generally available with 12-inch, 10-inch, 9-inch, 5-inch, and smaller screens—including the 1½-inch described below. Color sets are available at 12 inches and then at intervals down to just over 2 inches. In either case, you'll not find every size in every manufacturer's product line, because no one manufacturer sells sets at every interval. To make this even more complicated, one manufacturer's 9-inch screen may come in a larger or heavier portable cabinet than a competitor's 10-inch, so screen size and set size are not always matched. Picture and color quality vary among portables, so it is best to compare prices and features before you finally buy.

The smallest screens currently available are only 1.5 inches high (measured diagonally), or about 1.3 inches up and 1 inch across. The TR–1000 series of Travelvision sets is made by Panasonic and is available with an optional built-in AM/FM stereo radio. Small enough to be carried in your pocketbook or jacket pocket, the screen is best used with a detachable magnifier. This kind of portability is a pleasure when you're away from home. And the set is battery-operated, good for about an hour without a recharge from either AC outlet or car battery. You can use either the accessory battery pack (included) or four alkaline penlight batteries. The set seems like a magical toy of sorts; one does not normally expect such a small box to be a television set—with such good pictures to boot!

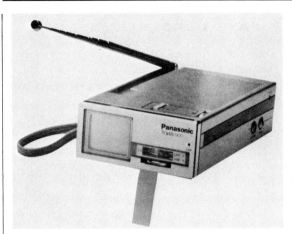

Panasonic's TR-1010P is about the size of a paper-back book. You can actually carry it around in a shoulder bag. (Photo courtesy Panasonic Company)

known as MGA). Nearly all these sets offer special features, like radios and audiocassette recorders, built-in. Sony's 5-inch B/W TV contains a timer mechanism, so it can be used as an alarm clock.

The portable category extends through the 7–8–9–10-inch sizes, with most manufacturers represented somewhere in this range.

Toshiba's CA-045 is a color portable, with a 4½-inch screen and an optional battery pack. (Photo courtesy Toshiba America, Inc.)

Sanyo makes a similar unit. Sony's vest-pocket B/W portable called Watchman, the logical successor to that company's Walkman, may well revolutionize portable entertainment.

A 5-inch screen is a practical size for most viewers on the go. Viewing at close quarters, you can comfortably enjoy even the longest movies while seated as close as a foot from the screen. Yet the very same 5-inch set can be used some six feet from the viewer, making it perfect for bedside viewing as well. In color, try Toshiba's 5-inch CA-045. It can be used either as a television set or as a monitor, to be connected to your portable videocassette camera when you're out shooting. It can be powered by either an AC outlet, an optional battery pack, or your car's cigarette lighter. It fits neatly on top of the computer console and doesn't take up much space, making it perfect for use as a display. Panasonic, Hitachi, and JVC are among those who manufacture similar units.

Your choices in 5-inch black-and-white sets are not nearly as limited. Quasar makes a good one. So do Panasonic, Sony, and Mitsubishi (also

A small portable color television set is perfect for use with a desk-top computer. Here the computer is an Atari 800, and the television is Panasonic's CT-5551. The author used this combination, with some additional equipment, to create the manuscript for this book. (Photo by H. Blumenthal)

Panasonic's CT-7711 is a fine example of a slightly larger portable designed to meet a variety of needs. Indoors, you can use the set at the foot of your bed, or even on the far side of a small room. Outdoors, it's small and light enough to be used beside the pool, at the stadium, on camping trips, or in the car. Those who see the 5-inch format as uncomfortably small may feel at home with a slightly larger portable, without sacrificing convenience. It can be powered by AC/DC battery pack or by car battery.

Nearly every manufacturer makes a 12-inch or 13-inch set, most often used as a bedroom or kitchen TV. The black-and-white version is just about the best TV value around—look through the newspaper for advertisements—some appliance dealer or department store is always selling a Zenith or a Sanyo or some other 12-inch set for under $100.

In color, the 12-inch or 13-inch size is usually the least expensive set you can buy. (For smaller sets, you'll pay a premium for miniaturization.) A 12-inch set is available from most manufacturers for under $300.

RCA, for example, has three 13-inch sets in their line. The most advanced of these has many of the features associated with larger sets, including automatic color control, frequency synthesis tuning via digital keypad, and cable-ready tuning for up to twenty-three CATV channels. Yet it's small enough to sit on a kitchen cabinet or nightstand. It also comes in an enhanced model with remote control, and in a second cabinet style.

Standard-size color sets, those in the 19-inch–25-inch class, remain the most popular group. It is here that the greatest number of features are available, and here that manufacturers find the greatest competition. Use the checklist on pages 28–29 to help make your decision, and then *shop around*! You'll find as much as a $100 spread between retailers, sometimes almost $200 during a price war or a sale in this range, so it really pays

The 13-inch size is perfect for color television viewing in smaller rooms. This is the EF338R by RCA. (Photo courtesy RCA Consumer Electronics)

to compare and to consider buying from a discounter. Be sure to get the manufacturer's warranty, and to check the condition of your set before you leave the store (or get a cash-back guarantee).

RCA and Zenith have made consistently good products in this size category, with Japanese makers like JVC, Hitachi, Panasonic, Quasar, Sanyo, and Toshiba providing healthy competition. Two makers, Sony and Mitsubishi, have maintained relatively high prices, while providing craftsmanlike quality through the years. (Some say that the long-maintained quality gap between Sony and the competition has been closed, and that the price difference is no longer justified; others disagree.) It's wise to be wary of color TV manufacturers you've never heard of before—low prices on the sets of unknown makers may be a false economy.

It's best to buy name brands from reputable stores, and to compare prices and model numbers while you shop for a real bargain. You should know that some manufacturers sell low-, medium-, and high-priced lines. There is a difference in picture quality, tuner, and cabinet.

Example: RCA sells its least expensive sets under the XL-100 banner, its better sets as Color-Trak TVs, and its best as ColorTrak 2000 sets.

GIMMICKS AND COMBO SETS

Although you really should select your set based on picture quality and price, there are gimmicks that will no doubt affect your purchase decision. Zenith advertises a device called "Space Phone," for example, which allows you to receive and place phone calls using a telephone built into your living room TV set. No additional equipment is needed—the touch-tone dialer is built into the remote control. Space Phone doesn't look any different from a standard set, except that the phone number appears on the screen, but the idea is fun.

Sampo, one of the smaller Oriental importers, has been selling a large color set with three screens for a few years. On this set, originally designed for security systems, two of the screens are preprogrammed to receive only a limited number of channels. While watching full-screen color programming on a big screen, you can preview a second channel on one black-and-white screen and keep an eye on the baby in the crib (with the help of a video camera) on the other black-and-white screen. Only the color picture has sound. This product is similar to a device once sold by Sharp, called "Dualvision" (now discontinued), wherein a second picture from a camera input or a second channel was inserted into the corner of an otherwise standard television picture.

Multiple-screen television sets have not been very successful because they're clumsy. If you buy one multiple-screen set, it won't be nearly as versatile as several individual sets, which can be

JVC's portable color TV combo, the CX-500US. (Photo courtesy U.S. JVC Corporation)

Sony's FX-414 combo, with 3.7-inch screen and stereo speakers. (Photo courtesy Sony Corporation)

used in different rooms of the house. Multiscreen sets look flashy, but they're not very practical.

Combo sets are usually full of gimmicks. JVC's CX-500US (see picture) looks like one of those large silver-gray speaker "boxes" frequently seen (and heard) blasting down city sidewalks. The key difference: JVC's "box" has a 3-inch color TV screen on the top and an AM/FM/Public Service Band radio. Sony's FX-414 (see picture) offers a black-and-white screen, but matches it with two very powerful speakers and

ABOUT TV SETS, MONITORS, AND RF

In order to service the new home video recording boom, traditional TV manufacturers have started selling "monitors" and "TV/monitors." There is a definite difference between a monitor and a television set; each one has its own specific function.

A television set generally consists of a picture tube, an audio system, an electronic chassis, and a tuner. More accurately called a television *receiver*, this is the standard "box" that sits in living rooms across the nation and around the world.

A monitor, in the classic sense of the word, literally *monitors* the video and the audio signal being put out by a secondary video device (like a VCR or a TV studio's control room switcher). In its purest form, a monitor shows video only, and a parallel audio system monitors the sound.

The principal difference between TV receivers and monitors lies not in the fact that only the TV has a tuner but in the kind of signals used by each device.

A monitor deals with an *audio* and a *video* signal. A television receiver does not deal with audio or video signals directly; instead, it works with *one* signal, called RF (short for "Radio Frequency").

An RF signal is a "carrier" frequency; that is, it carries or transports weaker signals from place to place. Audio and video signals are not strong enough to travel from the TV station antenna to your home on their own; they must be carried on another signal. The RF signal, then, is composed of audio, video, and the carrier frequency itself.

A monitor generally reproduces better pictures than a TV set because it is using pure video to show pictures. Whenever RF is introduced, there is a possibility of interference on the RF carrier's frequency.

All television signals use RF to get from place to place. Some home video gear, however, has been built to take advantage of pure audio and video signals.

The easiest way to determine whether your equipment can be used to pass audio and video directly is to look at the cables and connectors. Audio and video signals are almost always passed with RCA phono plugs (the kind used to attach your turntable to your stereo amplifier). RF signals are always passed through coaxial cables (the thick black or white wires used by the local cable system), with RF connectors at each end (an RF connector looks like a tiny cup with a single strand of wire sticking out of the middle, and is usually screwed onto a small post on the machine itself). You will almost always get better pictures by connecting via audio and video rather than RF. Try it and see for yourself (assuming, of course, that yours is one of the newer TV sets that offer a choice between RF and audio/video inputs).

This Technicolor portable does not contain an audiocassette, nor does it contain a radio. Instead, this is a one-piece media room, with 7½-inch color TV/monitor and ¼-inch format videocassette recorder. It can be used in the field with a camera, and will operate on either AC, self-contained battery, or car or boat battery.
(Photo courtesy Technicolor)

a stereo audiocassette player/recorder. Sharp makes a clock/TV/radio for the night table. Comparatively few combo units offer color screens as of this writing, but more color combos are on the way—that's a promise from the manufacturers.

PROJECTION SETS

The consumer electronics industry has high hopes for a relatively new kind of television set, the large-screen projection system. The smallest projection screens are about 40 inches (measured diagonally), or just under 4 feet high. Prices generally start over $2000 (although less expensive, clearly inferior systems are available). The largest projection screen will fill a wall that's ten feet high.

There is nothing exotic about the way in which projection television works. The principle is remarkably simple. All television sets emit light. The simplest projection sets are actually TV sets with a single lens mounted on the screen, rather like a nose cone attached to the front of an upside-down TV. By placing the nose-cone-with-TV unit a specified number of feet from a special screen, you'll see a large, impressive picture. It's like magic, particularly when you consider how long we've been living with 7-inch newsmen talking about 6-inch space shuttles, and so forth. The price: about $500–$600, *plus* the cost of a proper-size color TV, which may be detached from the lens for normal viewing, though not easily.

This rudimentary "one-gun" projection system (a picture tube "shoots" the light beam to the screen, so it is called a gun) soon gives way to the more sophisticated "three-gun" unit. Here, the red, green, and blue elements project their own pictures (go back to "How Color TV Works," pages 32–33). The proper registration of three individual color images was tricky in the

The heart of this one-lens projection TV is an ordinary picture tube. The left half of this unit is a TV set. (Photo by H. Blumenthal)

earliest projection sets, but nowadays the lenses are more dependably made and consistently show perfect pictures with minimal adjustment.

Once again, three separate television picture tubes (one red, one green, one blue) focus projected light to form an image on a custom-shaped reflective screen. If the screen is close to the projector, the image will be relatively small; if the screen is farther from the projector, the image will be larger. Smaller projected images will be slightly crisper, because distance from the lens tends to dissipate picture clarity. Manufacturers customize screens to minimize these kinds of problems, rounding the corners so that they are several inches closer to the lens than to the center of the screen, for instance. Distance from projector to screen is always prescribed by the size of the screen you buy; the screens come in fairly standard sizes, usually starting at just over 3 feet (measured diagonally) and ranging to 6 feet, with various increments along the way.

The first projectors were rather ugly, resembling sawed-off pyramids. Designed to sit about six feet from the screen (with an unobstructed view, of course), they were cumbersome for all but the largest of rooms. As design of projectors progressed, the pyramids became funny-looking coffee tables and, after some design improvements, not-so-funny-looking coffee tables. The need for an unobstructed view from lens to screen, however, remains in some models to this day (but now, there are options).

Manufacturers chose to solve the problem of obstructed view in two ways. The simplest solution was the longest in coming: hang the projector from the ceiling! Specially built ceiling-mount projectors are available from Sony, Kloss, and a few other manufacturers.

More practical for most families is the one-piece projection system, where the projector and the screen are built into a single piece of furniture. A mirror reflects the projected image, allowing the entire process to occur in a reasonably comfortable 3-to-4-foot area.

Sony's popular two-piece projection system, the KP-5020, uses a coffee-table projector, which contains all controls on one side and the projection "guns" on the other, and a 50-inch screen (measured diagonally). A similar system is available from Sony with a 72-inch screen. (Photo courtesy Sony Corporation)

Exotic counterbalancing systems have been designed so that the projectors and mirrors fold back into the base of the units, out of sight when not in use. Some units are built to look like hutches and other furniture when shut, hiding the screen behind doors or louvers. Although the resulting piece of furniture is still a little on the monstrous side, projection televisions are not nearly as hideous today as when they were first introduced.

Of more limited appeal is the rear-projection system, housed in a box that looks like an overgrown TV set. The projector inside also uses mirrors to reach the screen, but the image is emitted from behind and seen by viewers through a translucent screen. This system takes up less floor space (it's about 2 feet deep, com-

Sony's KP-5040 is a one-piece system whose three projectors bounce the image off a mirror and onto the screen. (Photo courtesy Sony Corporation)

The rear-projection TV, like this one with additional cabinetry, sold by GE (sold separately), is highly functional in appearance. Picture quality, however, is limited. (Photo courtesy General Electric)

pared to almost twice that amount for the smallest of the single front-projection systems). The width and height are about the same, about 4 to 5 feet high, and 3 to 4 feet wide. Most rear-projection pictures are slightly inferior to those produced on a front-projection screen. The picture's overall brightness, color, and contrast are not nearly as vibrant, but more bothersome is the fact that a rear-projection screen must be viewed almost head-on to be seen properly. Still, the contained "RP" has great potential in both home and business. With a wider angle of view, RP is likely to become the dominant large-screen format.

When you're ready to buy a projection system, it's best to look at the simple, inexpensive ones first, and work your way up. Try to shop in a store where you can see all kinds of units, and test every one with the same program (preferably the same prerecorded tape) *under identical lighting conditions*. Try to see the screen in room light similar to the light in your own home (incandescent lamps instead of the usual store fluorescents, for example) before you buy. Video specialty stores are the best places to buy, for selection and for knowledgeable salespeople.

Start with the single-lens "nose-cone" units. If you want a large picture for about $1000, and you're willing to sacrifice some quality to get it, you'll do well to shop around. Many stores have created their own single-lens products, while others work with small manufacturing concerns to service the "low-end" customers. As of this writing, none of the major manufacturers was offering a one-gun-projection television system.

The most popular projection systems are front-projection units, built into single pieces of furniture. These can be viewed fully 30 to 60 degrees off-center, give or take a few degrees. This angle of viewing, equivalent to an arc of up to 120 degrees, or one third of a circle, is quite sufficient for nearly all home-viewing situations. Mitsubishi's VS-5050 and VS-510UD (pictured on page 43) are essentially the same system

Mitsubishi's projection system, available in several cabinet styles, open . . .

. . . and closed! Some projection systems even include doors to cover the screen. The resulting unit looks more like a wooden hutch than a piece of expensive electronic hardware. (Photos courtesy Mitsubishi Electric Sales America, Inc.)

housed in different furniture. Both deliver clear pictures with a good amount of contrast. Electronic tuning is standard (as it is on most projection sets), as is a two-speaker audio system that can be used for stereo programs. Sony, Advent, Pioneer, RCA, and Zenith make similar sets, but the most demanding critics give Mitsubishi an extra point for picture quality. This is likely to be a short-lived advantage, however, because new projection sets are likely to appear annually for the next few years.

The front-projection systems are best represented by Sony, which makes two units. The projector is identical in both systems; only the screen size (and the screen-to-projector distance) varies. Electronics pioneer Henry Kloss manu-

This video screen measures 6½ feet diagonally. The projector unit doubles as a coffee table. It sells for just over $3000, and is made by Kloss Video. (Photo courtesy Kloss Video)

WHAT'S HAPPENING INSIDE YOUR MACHINE: PROJECTION TELEVISION

The workings of a projection set are similar to that of most color television sets, except in the way in which the image actually reaches the screen.

1. Immediately after the video signal is electronically changed to a stream of electrons, the red, the blue, and the green streams are sent to their own "projection tubes" (the three circles in the photo below). Each tube is a combination television screen and projector.

2. Follow the arrows on the diagram, and you'll see how projection television works.

3. Let's look at one of the three separate projection tubes, as designed for a Kloss projector; follow the arrows carefully. First, the stream of electrons enters the tube and is projected onto the target, which is physically quite similar to the reactive surface on all television screens. This

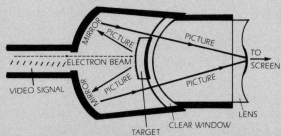

action creates a television image, albeit one in a single color (let's say blue). Second, this television image is deflected toward the back of the tube, where mirrors reflect the image back and through the lens. Third, the blue image, in continuous synchronization with the red and green images, is projected onto a screen.

4. If you look carefully at the projection set in operation, you will see the lens portion of all three projection tubes. Notice, however, that these projectors are not facing the screen. Instead, they are focused onto a mirror, which reflects the image onto a screen. Mirror construction has been vital to the development of popular-size projection systems. (You will find mirrors, incidentally, both in front projection systems [pictured] and in rear projection systems.)

Here's a closer look at the Kloss Model One projector. It's available with either a ceiling (pictured) or floor mount. (Photo courtesy Kloss Video)

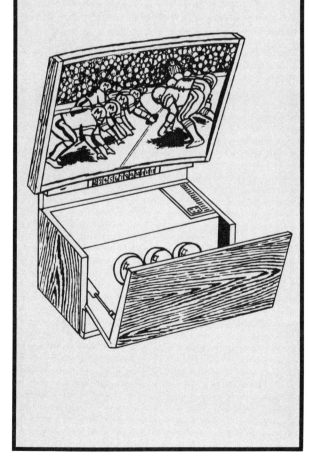

factures an impressive coffee-table projector*—impressive because it works equally well with a standard concave screen (about 5 feet high) or with a roll-down home-movie screen (about 10 feet high). The latter is a highly reflective surface, showing clear and colorful pictures even in normal room light. The size of the images is very exciting—I saw Rod Stewart, as large as life, in a full-scale video concert in my living room (in stereo, which added to the sensation of reality). After you watch a 10-foot picture, it is difficult to be moved by anything you see on a 19-inch screen. If Kloss's system is any indication, wall-size television will be a necessity for the future. There's nothing dwarfing about the sheer size. You feel as if you're looking at real life passing by. You experience the screen image not as "big" but as realistic and life-size. The images seem to join you in your living room.

*A portable projector-on-wheels is now available as well.

On this 10-foot screen, the sense of reality is simply fantastic. The people on the screen seem real. (Photo by H. Blumenthal)

And when you've finished watching, you just tug on the screen (as you would tug on a window shade), and it rolls up and out of sight!

You can also buy front-projection systems with smaller screens. Room size, layout, and light levels are considerations that *must* be worked out before you buy any projection set (the Kloss unit notwithstanding—that's a special case). For more about just how large you can go, and whether your room can accommodate a large screen at all, read Chapter 10.

A last reminder: Whether you are buying a large screen projection set or the smallest 3.7-inch color portable, you should consider where you will be watching it. Buy it knowing that you'll use the screen not only to watch NBC, CBS, ABC, and PBS but for a combination of cable, videodiscs, videocassettes, videogames, computer programs, and more. Keep your eyes open when shopping, and talk to salespeople— they're your best source of current information in this rapidly changing world of home video.

■ 3 ■

VIDEODISCS

I f you currently own a late-model color television set, you'll probably buy a second piece of video equipment in the near future. The videodisc player was designed to be a "video record player"—easy to operate but technically superb. You can buy a player for a few hundred dollars. Individual discs aren't very expensive either—you'll spend as little as $20 for an entire motion picture (versus $50–$70 for a prerecorded videocassette). The videodisc player, which *plays* programs but *does not record*, is the perfect start for your media room.

Choosing a videodisc machine is not a simple matter of comparing price and features. There are three completely different disc machines now available, and each machine requires its own type of disc. Videodiscs are not interchangeable between systems: they are "incompatible." All three are out to be the one that remains after the marketing battle, but the competition won't be over for a few years. Until two of the systems capitulate, or relegate themselves to the industrial, institutional, or educational market, anyone who buys a disc player will be playing Russian roulette, because there's a 2-to-1 chance that

your machine format will be obsolete within the next five years.

Briefly, here are the players: the CED (Capacitance Electronic Disc system), developed by RCA to be a simple video record player, is the cheapest—and the least versatile. It plays video records, with three features on each machine: visual scans forward or backward at several times normal speed, fast forward or reverse, and pause, along with the standard PLAY mode. Second in price is VHD (Video High Density system), developed by JVC and Japan's giant Matsushita organization (represented in the U.S. by Panasonic, Quasar, and Technics, an audio line). VHD players physically resemble CED players, but VHD has many more features and uses smaller discs. LaserVision players are the most expensive, and as versatile as the VHD players. Laserdisc players look like record players. Laserdiscs look and feel like futuristic silver records; the VHD and CED systems never allow you to see the discs, because a plastic sleeve always protects them from the dust and grease of the outside world.

Each of these systems is backed by major engineering, manufacturing, and marketing dollars,

The VHD system also uses a caddy to protect the videodisc inside. (Photo courtesy Quasar)

and each is being sold by several manufacturers with slightly different arrays of features. As of late 1982, here's who sells what:

CED	LASERVISION	VHD
RCA	Pioneer	Panasonic
Toshiba	Magnavox	Quasar
Zenith	Sylvania	JVC
Sanyo		General Electric
Radio Shack		Toshiba
Montgomery		Yamaha
Ward		J. C. Penney
Elmo		
Sears		

In an effort to expand hardware sales, some of these companies have entered the software, or programming, business. RCA's SelectaVision sells discs for its own machine, on an RCA disc label, a logical extension of RCA Records and other RCA entertainment activities. The Laser-Vision companies created Optical Program Associates (OPA) to produce programs that demonstrate the still frame and visual search fea-

tures of their disc system. OPA is responsible for the likes of *The First National Kidisc*, which you'll find explained in some detail on page 167. VHD Programs, Inc. was organized to acquire and produce original programs for VHD players.

Each of the movie companies (Columbia Pictures, Warner Brothers, Walt Disney, Paramount, Twentieth Century-Fox, MCA/Universal, and MGM/UA) releases programs for the three disc systems, but not every movie is available for every format (since the disc-pressing plants are still being built). Smaller disc labels are a new idea (one presses a disc in the same way one presses a record—it is essentially a process of stamping vinyl from a permanent master).

BUYING A DISC SYSTEM

The essential question in buying a disc system is very straightforward: Which format should you buy? Each has its own selling points, with Laser-Vision and VHD offering the greatest number of features for a slightly higher selling price. You must decide whether you want or need these features, or simply want a video record player. You must also consider software—whether the programs you want are available on one system and not on another. The competition is really one of marketing, where public relations and advertising will be used to sway you in favor of one kind of disc format over another. All three basic products are of good quality, so you'll have to make decisions based on (1) available programs and (2) available features. An inordinately large number of disc programs is being made available in a relatively short time, under a wide range of subject headings, to entice the consumer into buying a disc system.

There really isn't much difference among the three disc systems. Each is used primarily to play movies and prerecorded programs, each is as easy to operate as any household appliance. All three can scan the program material to repeat a scene or to skip a particularly boring or gory one; it is the degree to which you can control the playback that distinguishes the various systems. Your buying decision should be made on the fine points, determined by hands-on familiarity of each machine before purchase—and a knowledge of which programs are available and which programs will shortly become available for each system.

CED

The CED is the simplest system. You play a disc by inserting a plastic sleeve (called a "caddy"), with the disc inside, into the mouth of the player. When the disc is accepted, you pull out the sleeve. To remove the disc, the caddy is reinsert-

An RCA disc, with caddy exposed (you'll never see a disc—it will either be inside the caddy or inside the machine). (Photo by H. Blumenthal)

ed. You never touch the disc itself. (If you could see the disc, you'd find that it looks and works much like an audio record, except that there are many more grooves and the vinyl used carries a slight electrical charge.) A stylus (the "needle" in any record player is properly called a stylus) rides in the grooves, electronically reading the peaks and valleys and related tracking and sync signals, which become sound and pictures. The reason for the caddy is simply a matter of sanitation: greasy, scratchy discs will not play properly (they skip, causing jumpy pictures or missed frames), and may even damage the stylus. RCA engineers developed the caddy concept only a short time after the long-playing record was invented, but the practical consideration of replacing all of America's record players has delayed the concept's introduction until now. It's a very good idea, because the discs will remain in mint condition for about as long as you own them (under normal playing conditions, of course). The CED stylus, incidentally, is easily replaced at home.

The stylus can be advanced across the grooves (without damaging anything, of course—the stylus is not really a needle, but a blunt-tipped wedge), to scan the grooves visually at many times normal speed. This "visual search" can be operated in either forward or reverse direction. Rapid access is much faster, but you can't see the pictures scanning on the screen. You can use either of these methods to find specific minutes (e.g., three minutes on side 1), the approximate start position of a particular song, scene, or chapter. Minutes are indicated on a small readout on the front of the player.

Aside from a pause control (which blanks the screen—it is *not* a still-frame display), a three-position switch (OFF/PLAY/LOAD) and an automatic stylus cleaner (every time a disc is removed, a pad dusts off the stylus), that's the whole story behind RCA's CED player. Connection and operation are easier here than with any video device—you'll be watching your favorite

WHAT'S HAPPENING INSIDE YOUR MACHINE: CED VIDEODISC

1. CED videodiscs are manufactured like records. Each disc begins as molten plastic (in this case, plastic with a conductive carbon additive), which is stamped into the shape of a record with an accurate reproduction of the stamper disc's grooves. The disc is then inserted into its permanent caddy.

2. In this top view of an RCA CED machine, you can see the videodisc in place. Notice that there is no tone arm, as there would be in a normal record player. Instead, the stylus is located inside the tracking arm (the wide horizontal bar at the top of the picture). The tracking arm moves toward the front of the machine as the record plays.

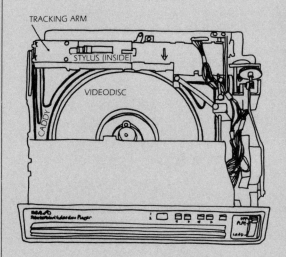

3. Once you remove the caddy and switch into the PLAY mode, the disc starts to spin at 450 rpm (thirteen times faster than an audio LP). The grooves are far more narrow on a videodisc than on an audiodisc.

38 VIDEO DISC GROOVES

ONE AUDIO DISC GROOVE

4. A microscopic diamond stylus glides through the *V*-shaped grooves, reading the peaks and valleys by electronic sensing. The stylus does not actually bump along in the grooves—it rides above instead.

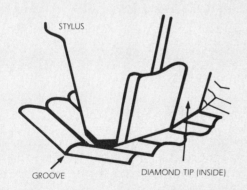

STYLUS

GROOVE

DIAMOND TIP (INSIDE)

5. The sensor's readings are translated into audio, video, and RF signals by the disc machine's circuitry. The composite signal is sent to your TV set.

prerecorded movie or sporting event within a minute of unpacking the carton. One "coaxial cable" (see page 137) connects the back of the player with the TV set's antenna (sometimes via an adapter). It's *very* easy.

The RCA machine was first introduced at the lowest possible price, and that meant monophonic (one-channel) sound. RCA now sells several stereo units, including one with remote control. All monophonic discs will play on the new stereo players, and vice versa (but they will play back in mono, of course).

VHD

The VHD system also uses discs in protective sleeves, albeit discs which are slightly smaller than those used in the CED players (CED sleeves are about 12 inches square, and VHD sleeves are just over 10 inches). There are no traditional grooves on VHD discs, but rather electrically charged particles that guide the stylus in a groove-like track. The stylus reads micropits in the disc surface, and receives encoded audio, video, and related information (frame numbers, for example) from these micropits. Since there is no pressure from the stylus, the discs should show almost no signs of wear. And the machine is very durable—I actually saw one operate *upside down*!

The VHD disc sleeve pops in and out of the player in precisely the fashion described for the CED. You touch only the sleeve, never the disc itself. Searching can be done in three ways—by individual frames, in a variable-speed slow or fast search mode, or in forward/reverse speed (with no picture). Every frame and every chapter (e.g., every song on a video music album) is numbered, and you have access to any spot on the disc in seconds. With these frame numbers and some fancy preprogramming, you can use these discs not only for out-of-the-ordinary view-

HOW SINGLE FRAMES CREATE THE ILLUSION OF MOTION

When you look at a strip of motion picture film, you actually see individual frames, photographs that are projected at a constant speed (24 frames per second) to simulate motion.

Television works in much the same way. Broadcasts transmit *30* individual pictures every second, but your mind can't assimilate images that quickly, so the single frames blur into a simulation of moving pictures.

On the Laserdisc, each of these frames fills one complete rotation of a videodisc, one circle. If the laser/stylus is moved to any point on the disc, therefore, it picks up exactly one frame, one still picture. Each of these frames can be numbered (the recorded disc contains this data as well as picture, sound, and tracking information), and each can be selected, by number, by using a keypad.

The VHD system is similar, except that it has a smaller disc, so each frame fills only half a rotation, half a circle.

Still frames can also be seen on specially designed VCRs (see Chapter 4), but they cannot be seen as clearly as disc pictures because of other technological considerations.

ing situations but for immediate feedback in educational programs (example: a multiple-choice question whose answers are found in specific frame numbers). Bear in mind that thirty individual TV frames pass your eyes every second and that a single still frame buried in those thirty is just barely perceptible. You could, therefore, be watching a continuously programmed segment, not realizing that some single frames within it are actually answers to questions posed elsewhere on the disc. It's a neat trick, one that allows producers of original programs for the VHD (and the Laserdisc, which offers the same feature) unique creative possibilities for response-type viewing.

All VHD machines are designed for high-quality stereo sound and will no doubt be used to play new pictureless audio records (called AHD, for Audio High Density) as well as videodiscs. The stereo feature is valuable for two reasons: first, true-to-life sound reproduction, and second, as a tool for bilingual programming (Spanish on Channel 1, English on Channel 2— you may listen to either or both). A similar system may be used for foreign films, and for all sorts of instruction. You'll find more about specialized disc programs on pages 165–72.

LASERVISION

Laserdiscs look different from other videodiscs in that they resemble the shiny platinum records awarded to top-selling recording artists. There is no protective caddy, only a clear acrylic coating on the disc itself. Laserdiscs are shiny silver, and they're exactly the same size as standard record albums. There are grooves beneath the plastic surface of the Laserdisc and tiny bumps and ridges in those grooves. A small laser beam, mounted ever so accurately in the base of the Laserdisc player, reads those bumps and ridges and translates them to electronic impulses,

The Laserdisc looks like a record album, except that it's silver. (Photo by H. Blumenthal)

which are in turn translated into television sound and pictures and into data (e.g., frame and chapter numbers).

LaserVision players feature a variable-speed slow scan, a visible-speed search in either forward or reverse, a pictureless fast forward, and a visible still frame which can be advanced in either direction. The Pioneer player allows access to individually numbered frames and chapters through a digital keypad; the less expensive

The LaserVision player looks like a futuristic record player. (Photo by H. Blumenthal)

Magnavox player will also allow access to chapters, but not by number.

CHOOSING A VIDEODISC PLAYER

As for specific machines, three units tell the story.

The CED, developed by RCA, is represented by the SGT 250, a full-function stereo player with the most essential features. RCA's SGT 250 accepts only CED-type discs and allows the user basically to sit back and watch television. It affords easy repetition of scenes and easy advance to later portions of a program or movie—via remote control. Each disc contains up to two hours of programming (one hour per side—you must flip all these discs over manually to see side 2). The SGT 250 is mainly a machine to play TV shows and movies; it's very easy to use, perfect for most viewing situations, and is built by RCA, one of the nation's most dependable manufacturers of electronic equipment. It sells for about $450. (You can buy discounted CED players for less than $300 if you shop around.)

RCA's SelectaVision VideoDisc Player, the SFT 100. (Photo courtesy RCA Consumer Electronics)

The VHD system is being sold by the greatest variety of manufacturers. Quasar's Video Disc Player is typical. It looks very much like the RCA unit and accepts discs of up to two hours

WHAT'S HAPPENING INSIDE YOUR MACHINE: LASERDISC

1. Every Laserdisc is pressed from a mother "stamper" into reflective vinyl. After the disc is stamped with picture, sound, and synchronization data, it is coated with a clear protective layer.

2. You actually place the disc in position in the player and close the cover to start it spinning.

3. The stylus is a laser beam, which is focused by a lens that sits *underneath* the videodisc. The entire laser assembly begins at the center of the disc and reads outward (exactly the opposite of a standard audio record player).

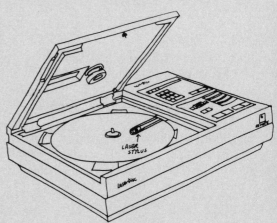

4. The laser is focused through a lens and points up toward the *bottom* of the disc.

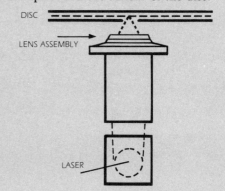

5. The laser reads information from microscopic pits imbedded in the disc's surface. Since the laser does not actually ride the grooves, it can scan the entire disc's surface in seconds, by simply moving in the track.

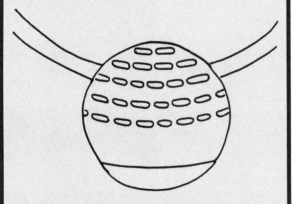

6. After collecting picture and sound information, the disc machine circuitry translates the electronic impulses to television signals, which can be seen on any TV set.

in caddies (of a different size and design from the CED discs, unfortunately). Each disc's contents may be accessed by either time (e.g., ten minutes from the start of the disc), or chapter code (e.g., Chapter 3). You can preprogram up to five segments for playback, by using a simple numerical keypad, either on the unit itself or via wireless remote control. You can display time and/or chapter numbers on the machine, and on the TV set if you like. This, plus high-speed picture search, fast and slow motion, still frame and pause, and stereo sound, make the Quasar VHD a formidable competitor of the RCA system.

Quasar's VHD machine allows for single-frame access, slow motion, and a variety of special features. (Photo courtesy Matsushita Electric)

Magnavox's Model 8000 was the first commercially available videodisc player. Released on a limited basis in 1978, it remains the most inexpensive LaserVision player available. It features a still frame that can be stopped either in forward or reverse, slow scan in either direction (best used to show a succession of still frames at a

Magnavox's Model 8000.
(Photo courtesy Magnavox)

constant slow-motion rate—a gymnast is fascinating to watch in slow motion), and the normal play speed. The machine will also scan an entire side of a disc in a mere twenty-six seconds, in either forward or reverse (this scan is visual). An "index" feature will display current chapter number or frame number (frame #00000 through about #55000 or so), in white block letters in the upper left corner of the screen. Laserdiscs can hold up to two hours of programming, one hour per side. The Magnavox 8000 plays only Laserdiscs, and lists for $699 ($749 with remote control as model 8005). The picture quality is excellent, and so is the stereo sound.

Pioneer makes two top-of-the-line Laserdisc players; Magnavox now makes a full-feature player as well. The popular Pioneer VP-1000 lists for $749 (available for less from discounters). An optional remote control for the unit costs about $50 more. The Pioneer VP-1000 looks like a futuristic record player with a space-age control panel. Like the Magnavox, it has a variable-speed slow scan (from thirty frames every second to a single frame every five seconds),

a three-times normal speed fast visible scan, and a superfast (invisible) scan in either direction. A still frame, with advance in either direction, is also standard. The reason for the added price is a numerical keypad, which allows individual frame or chapter access by number. Use the SEARCH button to see chapter or frame numbers on the TV screen, choose an appropriate number, press SEARCH again, and you'll see your desired sequence in seconds. The remote controller duplicates the entire keypad (with the exception of the switch, which controls the speed of the slow scan, which must be preset on the mother unit) on a hand-held device. The remote controller is battery-operated and is about the size of a deck of playing cards. It must be used with an unobstructed view of the player. Pioneer's upgraded LD-1100 is sleekly designed to complement Pioneer audio components, and contains all VP-1000 features plus a noise-reduction system for CX encoded discs. Pioneer makes a basic LV player as well.

Two final notes about videodiscs. First, for all systems, you should know that you will hear the

Pioneer's LaserDisc Player is a full-featured machine, which can be operated by wireless remote control.
(Photo courtesy Pioneer Video)

disc's soundtrack only when the disc is played at normal speed. Sound automatically cuts out in all special-effects modes. Second, most discs will play just one hour per side, or two hours per disc. Certain of the longer programs played in the extended play (CLV) mode on a Laserdisc machine will limit the number of features you can use while playing that particular disc (e.g., variable slow speed cannot be used). This is not the case with other systems.

The decision among machines should be based on your personal preference, but, more important, on the number and desirability of programs available for use on your system. Remember, a videodisc system can do nothing but *play* discs. It is important that you have as much choice as possible, now and in the future, when setting out to buy disc programs. When you buy a disc player, you will start a library of discs. Be sure enough titles are available to keep you happy. (In an effort to entice new buyers, extraordinary numbers of discs have been released—a pattern likely to continue through the mid-1980s, or at least until economic reality takes root in the home video business.)

Talk to a few local retailers and gather impressions about the three systems. You may hear stories about limited availabilities in your area, about technical problems that have surfaced with certain discs or players, about one format's plans to increase the size of its library dramatically. Your retailer has everything to gain by telling you what he knows—once you buy a disc player, he wants you to keep returning to buy discs.

Perhaps the single greatest drawback of the videodisc is its inability to do anything except play back store-bought software. There are those who believe that video playback is inexorably linked to video recording, and that both are necessary for a truly flexible media room. For these practical souls, there are videocassette recorders.

You'll need more information to make your decision between cassettes and discs, and you'll find it in the next chapter.

CHECKLIST: HOW TO BUY A VIDEODISC PLAYER

A. The first questions deal with the differences between videocassette recorder/players and videodisc players.

1. Do you wish to buy a machine that will record programs for later viewing?
   a. Yes
   b. No
2. Do you wish to record your own original productions using a video camera?
   a. Yes
   b. No
3. Do you wish to buy either a VCR *or* a videodisc player, or are you likely to buy both machines in the foreseeable future?
   a. Either one or the other
   b. Both machines
   c. Already own a VCR, am thinking about a disc player as well

B. The second group of questions deal with the way that you watch television.

4. Are you perfectly happy with TV/cable TV right now (choice a) or do you believe that you will use (or do use) additional video equipment to supplement standard television programming (choice b)?
Once again, to review:
   a. Happy with current TV/cable programs
   b. Want more than current TV/cable
5. Do you enjoy playing videogames, interacting with images on a TV screen?
   a. No
   b. Yes

6. If you own a VCR, enter choice "b" if you have *ever* rewound a tape to see an "instant replay" of a particular program sequence. Enter choice "a" if you just use the VCR to watch programs straight through, or just use the "pause" control. (If you don't own a VCR, go to question #7.)

7. (Do not answer if you own a VCR.) When you watch a program or a movie on TV, do you change channels as you watch, or do you screen the entire program straight through?
    a. Change channels
    b. Watch straight through

8. Do you think interaction between you, your children, and computers is to be encouraged in the home?
    a. Yes
    b. No

C. The final questions are about your own specific needs in a videodisc player.

9. Do you plan to use your videodisc player primarily as a record player that shows movies and complete programs (choice b), or as a machine that can play games and teach as well as show movies (choice a)?

10. Will you pay more for features that allow interaction between you and your disc player?
    a. Yes
    b. No

SCORING

Draw a scoring grid on a sheet of paper (graph paper will be easiest), with 3 columns across and at least 12 lines down. It should look something like this:

	VCR	CED	INTERACTIVE
1.			
2.			
3.			
4.			
5.			
6.			
7.			
8.			
9.			
10.			
TOTAL			

Each of the questions you answered in the checklist has a value. Some questions may have values in all three colums, but others may have values only in one column.

On question 1, score 10 points in the VCR column if you answered "a" and 5 points in the CED and Interactive colums if you answered "b."

Score 10 points in the VCR column for an "a" answer on question 2, 10 points in the other two columns if you answered "b."

On question 3, the "a" answer is worth 10 points in the VCR column, and 5 points in each of the other columns. A "b" answer scores 10 points in all three columns. A "c" also scores 10 points in all three columns.

Question 4's "a" answer scores 3 points in the CED column, none in any other; the "b" answer scores 3 points in the VCR column, 5 points in the CED column, and 10 points in the Interactive column.

If you answered "a" on question 5, score 3 points in the VCR column and 10 points in the

CED column. If you answered "b," score 10 points in the Interactive column.

If you own a VCR, score 10 points in the Interactive column if you answered "a," or 10 points in the CED column if you answered "b."

If you don't own a VCR, don't score anything for question 6. Score question 7 instead.

If you answered "a" on question 7, score 5 points in the VCR column, 10 points in the Interactive column. If you answered "b," score 7 points in the CED column.

An "a" answer on question 8 scores 10 points in the Interactive column, 7 points in the VCR column, and 2 points in the CED column. A "b" answer scores 2 points in the VCR column, and 10 points in the CED column.

Question 9's "a" answer places 10 points in the Interactive column, 5 points in the CED column, and 3 points in the VCR column. Choice "b" scores 5 points in the CED and VCR columns, but only 2 points in the Interactive column.

The final question, 10, scores 5 points for an "a" answer in the CED column, 2 points in the VCR column, and 10 points in the Interactive column. A "b" answer scores 10 points in the CED column.

Now total your scores. If you scored the VCR highest, you should probably look at VCRs as well as videodisc machines before you make a final purchase (unless, of course, you already own a VCR). If you scored highest on the CED column, look at the machines made by RCA and other companies which make CED players (see chart on page 48). If you scored highest in the Interactive column, be sure to read the descriptions of both interactive videodisc systems in this chapter carefully—your choice will be either in LaserVision format sold by Pioneer and others, or the VHD format sold by JVC, Panasonic, Quasar, and GE.

AUTHOR'S NOTE: VHD ceased operation in early 1983. No players were ever sold in the United States or Canada. Plans for a Japanese release are still going ahead, but we will not see a VHD player here for several years, if at all.

■ 4 ■

VIDEOCASSETTE RECORDERS

Videotape is a common term these days, the standard medium for hours of television programming seen day in and day out. Created some twenty-five years ago for the then-youthful television industry, this magnetic recording medium has dramatically altered not only how we watch television but what we watch as well.

Early television producers were faced with two ways to present their productions: live or on film. Live television, now revered as a mass-media theater experience, was more often a showcase of sloppy production. More important, live TV did not allow subsequent screenings of expensive productions. The use of film permitted reruns and editing, but the cost of film stock and developing, and the time required for the processing, made it imperfect for the immediacy of television. (Film was also a Hollywood medium, and in the early days Hollywood and TV were bitter enemies.) By the mid-1950s, film was used for hours of programming, but it was clear that television required a new medium, one that allowed instant and unlimited playback of recorded material, and the ability to edit quickly and cheaply. That medium was videotape.

Videotape has since changed the course of television in several dramatic ways. This change is most apparent on news programs, where the old promise of "film at 11" (meaning that an event covered by a film crew just before the six o'clock news would be processed and finally ready for screening by the time the eleven o'clock report was on the air) is no longer part of the language. About half of all prime-time shows are now taped, or "prerecorded," as are all soap operas, game shows, talk shows, and even many commercials. The popular *PM Magazine* (also known as *Evening Magazine* in some cities) and other TV magazine programs have been created due to the relatively low cost of remote videotape production. There are those who believe that videotape may eventually eliminate the use of film on TV. Filmmakers express contrary opinions, arguing that film's ability to reproduce true-to-life color and texture will keep it alive as a parallel medium for years to come.

Videotape, like its cousins audiotape and computer data tape, is actually a long, thin strip of Mylar whose surface has been coated with metal particles. Electrical impulses are exposed to the tape's particles in the tape machine at contact points known as "heads" (also "recording heads," "playback heads," and "tape heads"). When the tape's surface touches the head, the metal particles are arranged, or recorded, in what amounts to a special code. And since the tape is moving at a constant speed, the illusion of motion is created when the invisible "frames" are played back in rapid succession. The code can be read, or decoded, by another contact point, the playback head, and is eventually changed to sound (audiotape), data (computer tape), or sound and picture (videotape).

The television networks were the first to use videotape on a regular basis, mainly because they were the only ones who could afford to buy and maintain the machines. Through the 1950s, 1960s, and most of the 1970s, the networks and most of their affiliated local stations used 2-inch videotape. By the early 1980s, most had converted to the less costly, more versatile 1-inch tape, with the comparatively cheap ¾-inch format (described below) used in certain instances as well. One-inch is the format most often used by broadcasters today.

Schools and businesses usually use ¾-inch tape in videocassettes, introduced by Sony in 1969 as the U-Matic. Some picture quality was exchanged for huge cost savings, as ¾ inch, not 1 inch or 2 inch, became the dominant format in non-broadcast television. These U-Matic ¾-inch cassettes were originally intended for home use, but the cost of even these machines proved to be too high for the consumer market.

Due to further reduction in tape size (and loss of picture quality), you can now buy a home video recorder for as little as $500. Although you will be able to see some difference between the network's 1-inch or 2-inch originals and your home recordings, you will find that ½-inch Beta and VHS tape provides sufficiently clear and colorful pictures, and adequate sound, to satisfy most home-viewing situations. When one considers the cost comparisons, the home videocassette recorder is quite a bargain indeed.

2-inch professional broadcast VTR	$65,000
2-inch tape (1 hour)	$350
1-inch professional broadcast VTR	$75,000
1-inch tape (1 hour)	$200
¾-inch industrial VCR	$2,500
¾-inch tape (1 hour)	$40
½-inch home VCR	$500
½-inch tape (1 hour)	$8

(All prices quoted are approximate, indicative of the most basic units available.)

One-inch VTR. (Photo courtesy RCA)

Two-inch VTR. (Photo by H. Blumenthal)

¾-inch VCR. (Photo courtesy U.S. JVC Corporation)

This is Panasonic's low-cost PV-1270 ½-inch VHS recorder/player. (Photo courtesy Panasonic Company)

Manufacturers have been eyeing the consumer video market for well over fifteen years. JVC, Sony, Panasonic, Ampex, Hitachi, and RCA are among the companies that regularly supply broadcast professionals, so their entry into the home video market is a logical extension of their activities. Makers of audio/high-fidelity equipment, 35mm photography gear, and TV sets have entered the home video recording market as well.

Sony was the first to succeed in the home videocassette field, with the introduction of Betamax in 1975. Sony's original idea was unique: the recording machine would be part of a new kind of television set. The revised format, with a separate recorder/playback machine sold as a "Betamax," was the one that caught on. The original marketing concept was based on time-shift viewing, where a viewer could preset the Betamax's timer, automatically record a program when it was on the air, and watch the recorded version of the program when convenient. It was an idea whose time had come. Sony's Betamax was not an overnight sensation, but reactions were promising when it was introduced in 1975.

At about the same time, movie studios started taking notice of what might eventually become a new home video industry. Lots of memos were written, but nothing much was done until a few years later. By the end of the decade, each of the movie studios had created its own label, selling (and later renting) recent and classic films, and had begun discussions about made-for-video programs.

Shortly after Sony introduced Betamax, the Japanese company JVC (an aggressive subsidiary of Japan's Matsushita, which exerts more direct control over its Panasonic and Quasar divisions) introduced its new VHS (short for Video Home System) in America. Manufacturers chose sides and started a selling competition that continues to this very day. At present, Beta (née Betamax) machines are sold by Sony, Zenith, Toshiba, Sanyo, and Sears. VHS, the more popular of the two formats, is sold by Panasonic, RCA, JVC, Quasar, Magnavox, Sharp, General Electric, Mitsubishi, Hitachi, Akai, Sylvania, Curtis-Mathes, Philco, Fisher, Canon, Minolta, Olympus, Kenwood, and J. C. Penney. The differences between VHS and Beta are mainly in the size of the cassette and in the mechanics of the tape path, as illustrated on page 64.

You should be aware of a few other tape formats besides Beta and VHS that may become popular in the near future. Remember that these tape formats are incompatible; each requires its own machine. Europeans have long enjoyed a Philips product that looks like a VHS cassette, with a side 1 and a side 2, for twice the amount of recording on each cassette.

The newest format has cassettes identical in size to an audiocassette. Used mainly for portable VCRs (see Chapter 5), this Japanese system, sold by Technicolor in the United States, allows for easily portable recording machines because of its size, with some additional loss of picture quality. JVC is developing a VHS-compatible mini-cassette system to permit an equivalent amount of portability.

Other formats, as you might imagine, are in the works. Most are smaller, with longer record/play time. Floppy or rigid computer discs may also replace tape in some systems. (Several still-picture cameras that record images on discs for viewing on TV are described in Chapter 11.)

For the present, probably until the mid-1980s, VHS and Beta are the *only* videocassette formats you should buy for normal use in home or office. Other formats may come and go, but there are two significant antiobsolescence factors already built into these formats: (1) a huge amount of available software (which represents a large investment by videocassette labels) and (2) the great number of people who already own VHS or Beta VCRs—a group not likely to be topped by owners of a competitive format for years.

There is little difference in performance between Beta and VHS. A technical difference,

dealing with the way the tape winds around the record and playback heads, makes the systems incompatible. The cassettes themselves are of different sizes as well: a Beta cassette is roughly 4 inches by 6.25 inches, while a VHS cassette is roughly 4 inches by 7.5 inches. Both use ½-inch tape, and both housings are about 1 inch thick. You cannot use VHS tape in a Beta machine, nor vice versa, and you cannot use either in your school or business ¾-inch U-Matic machine. These cassettes are all different sizes, requiring their own distinctive machine formats.

Beta and VHS cassettes are very nearly the same size. It is the way that the tape is threaded in the machine that varies between formats. (Photo by H. Blumenthal)

BUYING A VCR

Whether you are buying a VHS or a Beta machine, it's wise to look at all available units, from the simplest record/playback machines, featuring the most basic tuner and timer, to full-featured machines with picture manipulation ca-

WHAT'S HAPPENING INSIDE YOUR MACHINE: VIDEOCASSETTE RECORDERS

1. The VHS table model (above) and the Beta portable with tuner/timer (below) will both record signals from the air, from cable, or from cameras. The tuners, which send a particular signal to the tape, are just like standard television tuners. The timers are essentially digital alarm clocks. (*Photos courtesy Panasonic and Toshiba*)

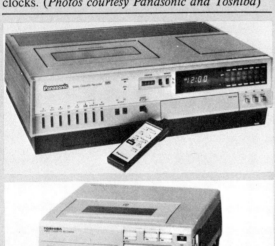

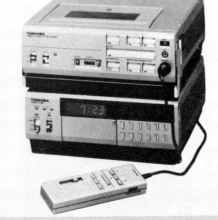

2. The principal difference between Beta and VHS is the way in which the tape is threaded. Take a good look at the two cassettes pictured and you'll see that the VHS wrap looks like the letter *M* and the Beta wrap looks like a sideways letter *U*. In both cases, the tape makes contact with the head assembly (the double circle just above the center of each cassette). The head drum spins as the tape passes, so contact with the heads is very brief (even at the slowest tape speed).

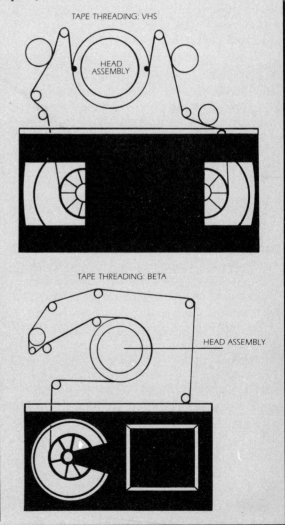

TAPE THREADING: VHS

HEAD ASSEMBLY

TAPE THREADING: BETA

HEAD ASSEMBLY

3. The VHS cassette diagram is placed in perspective, with a cutaway view of a VHS machine in operation. Notice that the head assembly (the darkened drum just above the cassette itself) is tilted slightly.

4. This tilt allows the heads to touch a slightly greater surface area on the tape (rather like angle-cutting vegetables to increase the surface area exposed to cooking). The increased surface area makes for better picture quality; this is a system that originated in broadcast television.

5. When you play back a tape, the audio, video, and synchronization signals are received by the heads and then translated into TV signals by the machine's electronics. An RF carrier is used to transport the signals from machine to TV.

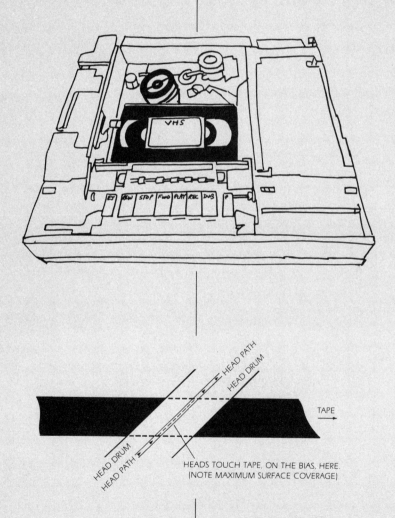

HEAD PATH
HEAD DRUM
TAPE
HEAD DRUM
HEAD PATH
HEADS TOUCH TAPE, ON THE BIAS, HERE.
(NOTE MAXIMUM SURFACE COVERAGE)

pabilities—e.g., fast scans and still frames. The basic systems don't change much from year to year, but special features are added regularly. The newest RCA VHS machines, for example, have an EXPRESS RECORD function, which tells the machine to record the next 30, 60, 90, or 120 minutes. Earlier machines could do the same job, but programming the timer is a little more involved than pressing a single EXPRESS RECORD button a couple of times.

If you are buying a full-feature machine, you will get everything available in the most basic (or, in industry lingo, "leader") models, plus some special convenience features. Since the full-featured, or "high-end," VCR is the one the manufacturers most want to sell, the latest models are always crammed with features that are just a little bit better than last year's model (EX-PRESS RECORD is a perfect example). If you are buying a full-featured machine, the *best* machine on the market, expect that its sovereignty will last only until the new product line is released. Full-featured machines don't really become obsolete any faster than the less expensive models, but the psychological factor of not having every feature possible may make your machine seem substandard after a while.

About VCR Manufacturers

As you shop, you will no doubt recognize a certain physical similarity among machines. It should be no surprise that many VCRs are built by the same (Japanese) manufacturer (Hitachi and Matsushita do most of the work) and later modified for the secondary manufacturer, who sells it to the stores. A manufacturer who makes products for other manufacturers is called an "OEM," or "Original Equipment Manufacturer." OEMs are common in some electronics industries, oftentimes generating both greater product availability and lower prices. It's always

a good idea to try and find out who the OEM was for a particular piece of equipment and, if possible, to buy the equipment *from* the OEM. The reason: service. Companies who simply sell an OEM product may or may not stock parts after they drop the item, but the OEM is likely to continue servicing users for a longer period of time. (This is not always the case, but it frequently is a rule of thumb worth discussing with the salesperson.)

Another bit of advice: Think twice before buying a heavily discounted VCR—it may be a discontinued item. (This can be a good situation if you're looking for last year's model to save a few dollars, but a very bad situation if you want to buy the best machine, and you find yourself with last year's flop.) Service for discontinued items can be inconsistent (certain to be a problem in the VCR category, where service is a *necessity* several times during the life of a machine).

When you buy a VCR, you are buying far more than a machine. You are buying a relationship with a manufacturer. You will probably visit your local service center at least twice during the life of your VCR, most likely to replace the record and/or playback heads, whose life expectancy is only about three years.

As a rule, one manufacturer's authorized service centers will not fix a machine made by somebody else. When buying a videocassette recorder, it is always a good idea to find out where you can get it serviced before you buy it.

VCR Features

Back to the matter of purchasing. All videotape machines are priced according to the number of features they offer. Generally, the higher prices will bring the greatest flexibility: high number of preset recording times, better tuning systems, remote control, fast scan, slow scan, and still frame/advance. Some machines offer only two heads (both heads record and play back); the better machines offer four heads (two record and two play back). Most features work flawlessly, but some are marginal. Still frames, for example, are notoriously "jittery," on both VHS and Beta machines. They're nothing like the nearly photographic quality of videodisc stills. Tape scanning is also inferior to disc scanning: it too is jumpy, oftentimes filled with interference. Ask about stereo recording and playback. Be sure to check on the number of features available on the remote control as well; every playback, scan, and still function *should* be operable via remote. Compare wired with wireless remote controls for significant price variations.

As you're shopping, ask about middle-range VCRs, which contain only a limited number of features. It may be wise to consider a mid-range unit before spending top dollar, since you may give up a feature or two in exchange for a substantial cost saving.

While you are shopping, particularly in the summertime, you are likely to see this year's XYZ-1000 (a made-up name) in some stores, and next year's XYZ-1100 in others. Manufacturers tend to add a feature or two every year, and change some external design, but chances are the two XYZ units are very similar. Compare prices and you'll probably find that the older model is less expensive, especially if the store is trying to clear out old stock. It pays to know the history of the model you're interested in buying for just this reason. Ask around at different stores, and compare salespeople's stories. Be sure that you're buying a model discontinued for its age and not for its quality—then shop around to save up to $100.

Each of the features available for videocassette machines is an advertising point for manufacturers, and there is a tendency to call a feature by a particular trade name. One machine's "Speed Scan" might be another's "Fast Scan 3x," and so forth. The best way to find out about these features, and the few differences between them, is

to shop around and compare (with hands-on experimentation, if at all possible). The actual names and descriptions of these features change too quickly to commit them to book publication with any hope of accuracy.

Tuners and Timers

All tabletop VCRs (as opposed to portable, or "convertible," VCRs, which are described in the next chapter) contain both timers and tuners. The tuners are usually high-quality electronic push-button systems, although some low-cost models still feature rotary tuners. (For more about tuners, see page 31.) A tuner tells the machine which channel to record, and may be used either by flipping the VCR into the record mode manually, or by using a preset program-record mode in concert with a timer.

The simplest timer will allow you to preset the machine to turn on at a given time, record a program, and then turn off at a given time. A digital clock is first set with the actual time of day, then the "start time" of the program you wish to record, then the "stop time" when the program ends. Only a single channel's offerings can be preset for recording using a "24-hour, single-day timer," as there is no provision for changing channels except by hand. You must leave the machine preset to the channel you wish to record.

The most advanced timers will allow a preset programming of some eight programs on up to eight different channels, within the course of fourteen consecutive days. You can record a new program every day at a different time, or you can record the same show daily, skip a weekend, and continue the process on the following Monday. (This last example is a favorite of soap opera fans whose daytime jobs don't normally allow regular-time viewing.)

Unfortunately, there are two problems sometimes encountered with preset recording, problems not always made clear when you first buy the machine. You can preset up to eight shows, but the total running time of the longest tape available (circa 1982), at the slowest speed, is only eight hours. You cannot, therefore, tape ten daily, hour-long soap operas, unattended, because you must change tapes after hour #8. The second problem is more serious. Until recently, all VCR tuners were built for standard broadcast television. Some VCR makers sell cable-ready VCRs with 105 or more channels, and others sell VCRs with fewer channels (not necessarily the *right* channels for your area). Ask careful questions of the salesperson, and consult your cable system before you buy a cable-ready VCR (or a cable-ready TV set for that matter).

If your VCR is not cable-ready and you wish to record a program from cable TV, you can do so. Simply connect your cable tuner to the RF IN jack on your VCR (more on how to do this on page 134). One problem: You have only one cable tuner, so you can tune to only one channel at a time. You'll have to decide whether to feed that cable signal to your VCR or to your TV set.

Some accessory items are sold to eliminate the need for rewiring if you wish to watch cable while recording from broadcast television, or vice versa.

If your home is wired for cable and you want to preset channel changes for later recording, you must use a cable-ready VCR to do so.

Consult Chapter 10 for more information about the hows and whys of connecting VCRs, sets, and cable TV.

Tape Speeds

Regardless of how you're receiving your signal, you will probably be using your VCR to make your own recordings. This process is simple enough, but you should be cognizant of different tape speeds before you start.

There are three VHS speeds: SP, LP, and SLP, which will play 1 times, 2 times, and 3 times normal speed on a given cassette. A 120-minute cassette will record and play for 2 hours in SP, 4 hours in LP, and 6 hours in the SLP speed.

Beta speeds are slightly different. They are as follows: x1, which runs a 2-hour cassette for 2 hours; x2, which runs the same cassette for 3 hours and 20+ minutes; x3 for a 5+-hour run. The longest cassettes, which run 5+ hours at x3, are labeled "L830."

In both formats, the fastest speeds, the ones that use the *most* tape in a given period, will reproduce the best pictures. One more note on speed: Some special features (e.g., still frame) will not be operable at certain speeds. There is no dependable logic to this; it just varies with different model manufacturers. Double check to be sure you know what you are buying.

The checklist on pages 70–71 will help you select the right VCR for your needs.

There is no single "best" VCR available. Each of the machines described below is among the best in its class. Use these machines as benchmarks; compare them with any machine you may buy.

Panasonic's low-end leader VHS, the PV-1280 (previous models include the PV-1100, PV-1200, PV-1210, and PV-1270), is a good example of an inexpensive VHS table model. It records 2, 4, or 6 hours on T-120 cassette, offers 1-day, 24-hour program ability, two mechanical tuners (one UHF, one VHF), an automatic fine tuner (AFT), a mechanical counter, and a remote pause control (connected by a wire to the VCR). The machine can be connected to a TV set via RF cable or to a monitor (or another machine for dubbing) by audio and video connectors. The PV-1280 is a simple, straightforward machine of-

Panasonic's full-featured PV-1770 VHS recorder/
player with wireless remote control.
(Photo courtesy Panasonic Company)

fering only the essentials of home video recording and playback for a relatively low price, but it
is not without features, including visual speed
search and AUTOSTART/AUTOSTOP (similar to
RCA's EXPRESS RECORD). It's generally available, at a discount, for about $600–$700, although the list price is considerably higher. Keep
your eyes out for discounts in this range, particularly in last year's models. (By the time you
read this, the 1280 will be old news, and other
models will have taken its place.)

Panasonic's top-of-the-line PV-1780 is an example of the best consumer VHS model available. It can tune 105 channels, including almost
every cable channel (double check in your area
to be sure), but there are only fourteen tuning
push buttons, so you'll have to choose fourteen
favorite channels (a definite improvement would
be a push-button digital 0–9 keypad). In the SP
and SLP (not the LP) modes, you can visual-
scan at twice normal speed, see slow-motion pictures at variable speeds, and isolate still frames
and step them forward one by one. OmniSearch,
at either 5 times normal speed in SP, and 9
times or 15 times in LP and SLP, is available as
a visual search with some limited interference at
all three speeds in both directions. The PV-1780
has four heads (not two as in most machines)
and automatically rewinds when the tape is over.

It can record up to eight events over fourteen
days in the programmed mode, on up to eight
different channels, and it has stereo/Dolby
sound.

Sony's least expensive Betamax VCR, the
SL-5000, has a good many features; more, in
fact, than most comparably priced VHS
machines. Fast search (forward), known here as
BetaScan, is standard in two of the three playback speeds. There's a freeze-frame as well as a
pause. All of this, plus push-button tuning and
one day/one event programmability make this a
fine starter unit if you want to buy a Beta
machine (price $700–$800).

At the top of Sony's Beta line is the SL-5800,
with four-event/fourteen-day programmability.
BetaScan works in forward or reverse, and is

Sony's low-cost Beta table model.
(Photo courtesy Sony Corporation)

Sony's full-featured Beta machine with remote controller. (Photo courtesy Sony Corporation)

CHECKLIST: HOW TO BUY A VCR

There are three principal types of VCR designs, in both Beta and VHS formats, with several variations among these categories. Each one is designed for a distinctive purpose:

1. *Basic* tabletop VCR
—Records and plays tapes at all speeds
—Can be preprogrammed within 24-hour period
2. *Full-feature* tabletop VCR
—Records and plays tapes at all speeds
—Permits still frames, fast scans, and slow-motion viewing
—Permits preprogrammed recordings beyond 24-hour period
3. *Portable* VCR and tuner/timer
—Records and plays tapes at all speeds
—May allow still frames, etc. (depending on model and manufacturer)
—Permits recording and playback anywhere; battery operation option

The checklist on p.71 is easy to use. On the left, you will find all available features. Place a check to the left of the features you consider essential.

The six colums on the right are a rundown of features for six popular VCRs, including a basic tabletop, a mid-range tabletop, a full-feature tabletop, a basic portable, a full-feature portable, and a portable without a tuner. (Panasonic's 1982 product line provides the means for comparison; features will vary with other manufacturers.)

Once you've checked the features you need, count the number of checked items in each column. The machine with the *lowest* factor is probably best suited to your needs.

You'll find more about factors after the checklist.

There are two steps in using this checklist. First, eliminate any machine that is incapable of serving your needs (e.g., if you must have portable operation, eliminate all tabletop models). Second, subtract the number of features you need from the total number available to find the factor. The machine with the lowest factor is probably best suited to your needs.

You may use the blank space to the right of the chart to check off the features of machines not listed on this chart.

augmented by a 3X scan, still frames, variable-speed slow motion, and an electronic tab marker for finding specific spots on a playback tape.

Both the SL-5000 and the SL-5800 (and two in-between machines, the 5400 and 5600) play Beta I speed tapes, but will not record at this "old and slow" speed. Speeds Beta II and Beta III are now the standard.

BUYING BLANK TAPES

When you set out to buy blank tapes, you'll find a dozen makers of Beta and almost two dozen makers of VHS stock. Prices for the longest tapes start at about $10, ranging up to a high of about $25. The price difference is frequently justified, because the best tape will deliver not only

	Basic PV1270	Mid-range PV1470	Full-Feature PV1770	Full-Feature PV4500	Basic PV3200	Port. Only PV4100
——Use with any TV set	✓	✓	✓	✓	✓	✓
——2–4–6-hour record/playback	✓	✓	✓	✓	✓	✓
——1 day/1 pgm unattended recording	✓	✓	✓	✓	✓	
——VHF, UHF tuner	✓	✓	✓	✓	✓	
——Remote pause	✓	✓	✓	✓	✓	✓
——Memory counter	✓	✓	✓	✓	✓	✓
——Audio/video in/out	✓	✓	✓	✓	✓	✓
——105 channel cable ready		✓	✓			
——8 event/14 day/unattended recording		✓	✓	✓		
——Visual fast forward/reverse		✓	✓	✓		
——Still frame		✓ *	✓ **	✓ *	✓	✓ **
——Full-feature remote control		✓	✓	✓		
——Four heads (for heavy use)			✓			✓
——Wireless remote control		(costs extra)	✓			
——Variable speed slow motion			✓ **			
——Double speed			✓ **			
——Frame-by-frame viewing			✓ **	✓ *		✓ *
——Battery operation				✓	✓	✓
——Portable use				✓	✓	✓
——Use with camera	✓	✓	✓	✓	✓	✓
——Remote AC operation				✓	✓	✓
——Use in car				✓	✓	✓
——Stereo/Dolby sound				✓		
Total available features	9	14	19	18	14	15
Total features of interest to you	?	?	?	?	?	?
(Subtract to find the factor)						
FACTOR (lowest is best)	?	?	?	?	?	?

*In 6-hour SLP mode only.
**In 2-hour SP or 6-hour SLP mode only.

fine pictures but minimal wear on your machine's heads as well. Cheap tape is more likely to damage your heads than expensive tape. It is best to buy tape only from the name manufacturers, who care about quality control. TDK is just about the best tape you can buy, with Fuji and Maxell in the same league. These products are generally the most expensive—and worth it.

Next in quality, and certainly adequate, are the tapes sold by the VCR manufacturers. JVC, Memorex, Panasonic, RCA, Quasar, and other tapes are all acceptable, and sometimes discounted.

Tapes that are heavily discounted are suspect. Some are truly inferior, while others are simply fakes. Beware of boxes with logos like TOK (in-

A sampling of some recommended VHS blank tapes. (Photo by H. Blumenthal)

stead of T*D*K) and so forth. Consult video specialty stores for the latest technical comparisons on blank tapes.

A few manufacturers, TDK in particular, have introduced Super High Grade tapes at slightly higher prices. These are primarily made for the serious videophile, the one who spots every imperfection, who holds technical quality in high esteem. TDK's Super High Grade (HG) tape costs a few dollars more, but there are many enthusiasts who will accept nothing less than the best.

One final note about buying tapes: There are two foreign television systems, called PAL and SECAM (our own is called NTSC); each requires its own custom videocassette machine. Each system's technical recording and playback system is different, so tapes recorded on one system cannot play on another. The blank tapes, however, *are* interchangeable. This is important for two reasons: first, you cannot buy prerecorded PAL or SECAM tapes overseas and expect them to play in your U.S.-model VCR, and second, you *can* buy blank videocassettes overseas for use in your machine. Unfortunately, the tape speeds are different, so a VHS T-180 tape, for example, will play only a few minutes longer than our own VHS T-120 cassettes.

For more about the PAL and SECAM TV systems, see pages 154–55.

Maintenance

As for the care and storage of your tapes, common sense is the rule. Extreme heat (from a radiator or even an amplifier hot from long hours of use) and extreme cold (winter window drafts) are not good for the fragile metal particles on the tape. Direct sunlight is bad, and so is dust. Keep your tapes upright, like books in a bookshelf (bookshelves are very good places to store cassettes), or in one of the many custom tape-storage cases available in video specialty stores. Your machine should be treated with the same respect, and should be kept covered (there are several commercial covers available) if your place gets dusty or full of dog hairs during shedding season.

Cleaning your VCR is chancy at best, because its component parts, mainly the heads, are very fragile. *Never* try to clean the inside, except with one of the kits described in Chapter 10 (and even then, please be very, very careful). It's best to bring your VCR to a service center every year or two for a cleaning and maintenance check.

■ 5 ■

PORTABLE VCRS AND CAMERAS

Shortly after the home VCRs were established, manufacturers started thinking in
terms of lightweight portable VCRs that
could be used with a lightweight television camera to create original programming: video home
movies. The average tabletop videocassette recorder, however, weighed in at about thirty
pounds, hardly the perfect weight for portable
use.

The weight problem was solved by splitting the VCR into two component parts: the
recorder/player in one unit and the tuner/timer
in another. The recorder/player is for home or
field use—it weighs under ten pounds. Mated
with the tuner/timer home base, the recorder/
player will work as well as any standard one-
piece VCR.

You won't save any money by purchasing the
paired components. A tuner/timer and recorder/
player will cost about $1,000, just slightly more
expensive than a comparable tabletop model
VCR. You do gain flexibility, however.

When you first set out to buy a VCR, you'll
probably be most interested in the machine's
ability to play prerecorded tapes and to record
TV programs for later viewing. Making your
own programs, home movies, and Hollywood
productions are likely to be low on your list of
priorities.

But then your child joins the Little League,
and you want to capture the moment for posterity. You ask around at the office and borrow a
video camera for the weekend. Suddenly you feel
like a movie director. *You* decide what to shoot,
what portions of life your audience will see,
what will become the permanent record. Everybody says your camerawork is "as good as anything on TV." Just for fun, after the game you
take the camera on a drive through the neighborhood, dropping in on friends for "interviews."

You're hooked!

Actually, it's very easy to become hooked, because the cameras are so simple to operate, and
good pictures are so easily achieved.

Now that you've played with the camera,
you're probably going to go out and buy one.
After all, you already own the portable VCR.

Before we move on to an explanation of how
to buy a video camera, there are a few oddities
about portable VCRs (sometimes called "convertible VCRs") that you should know. The

The magic of a portable VCR and camera becomes obvious when kids are around—a wonderful improvement on home movies.
(Photo courtesy General Electric Television Division)

most vexing is the battery pack, which replaces the heavy power supply that feeds the tabletop units. You *must* use either the battery pack (good for about an hour on each charge), an optional AC power supply (a box about half the size of the portable VCR), your car's battery (tapped via the cigarette lighter using the proper adapter—either 6-volt or 12-volt depending on your car), or the power supply in the tuner/timer, which plugs into AC house current.

If you're shooting at home, you can usually juggle the cables to tap the power in the tuner/timer. (Accessory cable extenders make this job easier.) If you're shooting at somebody else's place, or at another indoor location like a wedding reception hall, the optional power supply, which is smaller, lighter, and more portable than the tuner/timer, may be a better choice. You

may recharge the battery pack by connecting either the tuner/timer or the AC adapter with power on, and the VCR power switch in the "off" position. A "charging" indicator will light on the power supply when you are charging batteries.

If you are shooting outdoors, away from civilization, your needs will be different. Obviously, you should take along as many fully charged batteries as possible. Additional batteries, however, are not cheap, and even the best of them will keep you going for only two hours. Realizing just how bothersome this whole battery situation can be, manufacturers created a car-battery tap. With the car's cigarette lighter and the proper adapter, you can use the car's DC power either to recharge the VCR's batteries or to power the unit directly. The latter situation is not ideal, because the car must be running while you're shooting (which is noisy, wasteful, and frequently disruptive to most shooting situations).

Aside from the aspect of power, you will find the connection pattern between tuner/timer, recorder/player, and TV set a little more complicated than with a standard VCR. Take some time to read the connection information on page 134; once you understand the flow of signal from machine to machine, you should have no trouble at all with hookup. The instructions that come with each unit are helpful, but it's best to have the salesperson show you what to do before you leave the store.

You can, of course, use your VHS or Beta portable just as you would a standard VCR. You can record programming off the air, play it (or any other prerecorded tape) at your convenience, even set the timer for preset recordings from specific channels. You lose absolutely nothing essential in buying a portable VCR system. You may, however, sacrifice a feature like fast visual scan, because of the extra weight such a mechanism might add to the recorder/player unit. If you need special features, shop around. Different manufacturers sell different configurations.

The single greatest concern when buying a portable VCR is weight. Compare all weights so that they include both the battery and a tape cassette, and *try each one on as a shoulder pack before you buy*. Eleven pounds may not sound like much as the salesperson is describing the unit, but remember that you'll be carrying that VCR at the same time you're carrying a five-pound camera, perhaps for as long as an hour or two without much of a break. Weight is a very important consideration, especially if you're of only average strength, or if you plan to use the system when traveling.

Tuners, incidentally, vary considerably in quality. Since most portables are sold together

Panasonic's PV-4500 portable VHS videocassette recorder/player, alongside a tuner/timer unit. The recorder is available without the tuner/timer from the manufacturer.
(Photo courtesy Panasonic Company)

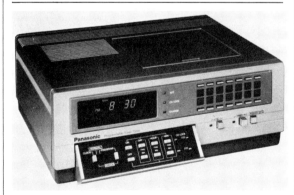

Here's a better look at the Panasonic tuner/timer unit, with the timer controls revealed.
(Photo courtesy Panasonic Company)

with compatible tuner/timers (few are sold separately), it is wise to review the capabilities of these units also. Timer capabilities vary as well.

BUYING A VIDEO CAMERA

Buying a camera is more complicated than buying the VCR, because you must be concerned not only with electronic gimmickry but with photographic excellence as well. A television camera is a fragile device, far easier to damage than most consumer items available today.

A television, or video, camera has three basic parts: the lens, the electronic pickup tubes, and the viewfinder. Take a good look at "What's Happening Inside Your Video Camera" on page 77. It will tell you everything you need to know about the technology before you buy.

Note that the chart and all material in this book deal only with color cameras. You can buy a black-and-white version for a few hundred dollars (as opposed to nearly $1000 for color), but these cameras are not very useful for everyday situations (they're mainly for industry and home security). Consult your local retailer for information regarding black-and-white cameras—and be sure to read up on color cameras in this book, because the information about lenses, viewfinders, and other features will be relevant to any TV camera you buy.

Television camera lenses are similar to the lenses used on still-picture cameras. Zoom lenses are the most versatile (and the most common), allowing the photographer ("videographer") to keep the camera in one place while zooming into a portion of an overall scene. A 6:1 zoom will let you magnify the picture six times, so that you can stand at one end of a basketball court, make a wide shot of all action, and then zoom in to the backboard on the far side of the court, filling the screen with its image. Or you can sit on your

Six still pictures show the difference between a 1:1 and a 6:1 zoom.

WHAT'S HAPPENING INSIDE YOUR VIDEO CAMERA

1. Obviously, the very first thing that happens when you turn on the camera is that it "sees" a picture with its lens. This image is focused on the faceplate of the picture tube. This faceplate is chemically treated, so that it will react to light by sending out weak electrical impulses.

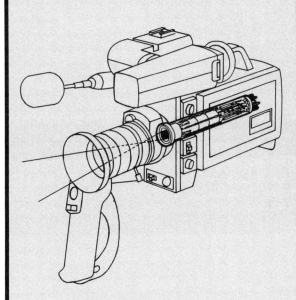

2. The back of the picture tube, now energized with weak electrical impulses, is "read" by a scanning electron beam. The scan "paints" the entire surface of the picture tube thirty times each second. The result of the scan is a video signal, which can be recorded on videotape, seen on a monitor, or, when attached to an RF carrier signal, seen on any TV set.

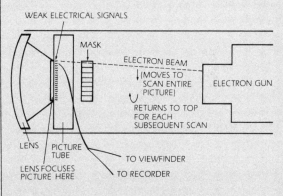

WEAK ELECTRICAL SIGNALS

MASK

ELECTRON BEAM
↓(MOVES TO SCAN ENTIRE PICTURE)
∪ RETURNS TO TOP FOR EACH SUBSEQUENT SCAN

ELECTRON GUN

LENS | PICTURE TUBE

LENS FOCUSES PICTURE HERE

TO VIEWFINDER

TO RECORDER

3. Most video cameras are designed with a monitor built into the viewfinder. The video signal, therefore, is split between the viewfinder and the recorder.

4. Microphones are built into most home video cameras. The microphone receives all audio signals and changes the physical sound waves to electrical energy. This electrical audio signal travels in synchronization with the video signal to the portable recorder.

5. Since the camera viewfinder is a monitor, it can be used to screen videotape playbacks. There is no speaker, however, so you must listen to the audio track with either an earplug, a headset, or a supplementary speaker.

front lawn and fill the frame with your neighbor's living-room window. A 3:1 zoom will allow you half as much magnification power, so that you can cut the distance between you and your subject only by two thirds. A 12:1 zoom will give you twice as much magnification as a 6:1 zoom. As of 1982, most of the better cameras have 6:1 zoom lenses (ask around for possible improvements). It is best to buy the most powerful zoom you can find, because your camera will be able to get the closest shots—and closeups are what television is all about.

Today's home video cameras are usually sold with permanently attached lenses. Video will follow the 35mm photography industry in allowing videographers interchangeable lenses for flexibility on future units. Front-of-lens attachments for closeups, filtering, special effects, and increased telephoto distances are already available for some video cameras. Wide-angle lenses (great for landscapes) and super-zooms (to get a shot of the quarterback even though you're in the top row of the stands) are two good reasons to buy an interchangeable-lens camera.

Zooms may be operated by hand, and if you're steady, manual operation is one way to keep both camera weight and price down. If you're not as steady as you'd like to be, don't buy a manual zoom—buy a power zoom instead. The Panasonic PK-751 (pictured above right) offers a power zoom at either fast or slow speed via push buttons with a manual override. I find that each has its uses, and that the power-zoom option (which adds a little weight) is usually necessary for good camerawork.

The Panasonic zoom lens's focal range begins at about a foot, and will allow sharp focus to infinity. In order to get even closer, there is a "macro" option on the lens itself—push button, followed by a twist of one of the lens rings—and this feature allows focusing as close as two inches. Think of the macro and the zoom as two separate lenses built into the same physical lens tube, because you cannot smoothly switch from

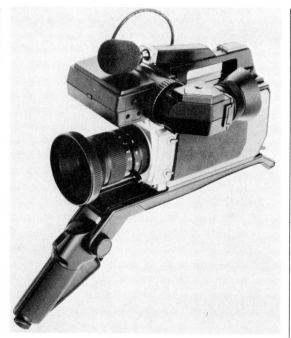

Panasonic's PK-751 camera.
(Photo courtesy Panasonic Company)

one mode to the other without jerking the camera and totally losing focus.

If you would like to know more about lenses, read a book about 35mm photography. Your local photography store will be happy to recommend titles.

A television camera is far more complicated than a still camera in the way that it takes pictures. As detailed on page 77, the lens focuses images on camera pickup tubes, which translate pictures into electronic information. To reproduce colors accurately, the camera must be given a reference color every time lighting conditions change. Video cameras are designed to "lock" to white, and most will "white balance" automatically when you point the camera at a white card (or T-shirt) and press the WHITE BALANCE button on the camera. It is most important that this is done every time lighting conditions change (sunny to cloudy, dusk to morning light, a move from beneath a tree to an open field) to ensure accurate relationships between colors and contrast. Under normal circumstances, no color "tweaking" should be needed—the white balancing will do it all.

Most cameras automatically adjust for the available light in each shooting situation by processing pictures for average or normal contrasts. If there is a very bright object in an otherwise dark picture, the camera will attempt to equalize the bright area by darkening the object, and by lightening everything else. If the picture is generally bright with a very dark spot, the camera will again equalize everything for so-called normal contrast relationships. If your picture is generally dark, the camera will allow as much light to reach the pickup tubes as it can. For most shooting situations, this saves the work of presetting the f/stops—the amount of light reaching the camera tube.

In other situations, the automatic control may be totally counter to the effect you're trying to achieve.

Let's say that you're shooting at noon, in peak light, or on a bright, beautiful, sunny day. The camera will take its automatic reading and darken everything to compensate for the extreme brightness. If you're planning to shoot a white sailboat against this beautiful sunlit sky, you'll probably see a slightly darkened sky, and a grayish sailboat, almost in silhouette. The camera is working properly: it is adjusting everything in the picture so that it fits into the normal or average range. An automatic iris is, therefore, a good feature, but only if you can override its brightness control under extreme conditions.

(A basic photo book of recent vintage will also explain how f/stops control the amount of light that reaches the film and how automatic cameras work. There are parallels.)

There is one more essential part on every video camera: the viewfinder. As with still cameras, you can buy two types: those whose viewer is a

small telescope adjacent to the lens itself and those that use a series of mirrors to see precisely what the lens and the camera pickup tubes are seeing. The latter is always best, because it accurately shows the videographer what is being recorded.

Through-the-lens (sometimes abbreviated TTL) viewfinders are best if they are electronic, in effect mini TV screens that monitor everything the lens sees. An electronic viewfinder traditionally uses a 1.5-inch screen, with a magnifying glass for easy reading. (Nonelectronic TTL viewfinders are also available, at a lower price, but they're much more difficult to use.)

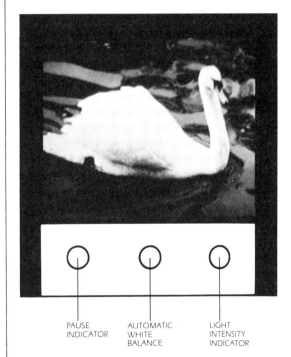

PAUSE
INDICATOR

AUTOMATIC
WHITE
BALANCE

LIGHT
INTENSITY
INDICATOR

Through a camera viewfinder.
(Photo by H. Blumenthal)

Cameras are generally manufactured with built-in microphones as well. You may bypass the built-in mike by plugging a microphone of your own directly into the back of the camera or into the VCR itself. You can buy a wireless microphone (actually a small transmitter and receiver) for home video use as well.

Your camera is connected to the portable VCR by a thick cable. This cable carries the necessary power from VCR to camera, and also carries the picture from the camera to the VCR. The very same cable is also used to transmit the start/stop controls (there is a button on the camera that can be used to pause the machine) and to carry other push-button messages as well.

Panasonic's PK-801 is a good example of a versatile home video camera. It looks like a movie camera with a big lens and a big carrying brace, but it is heavy, so is easiest to use with a shoulder support.

In the picture on page 78 you can see the principal working parts of Panasonic's camera: the zoom lens, the electronic viewfinder, and the built-in microphone. The push-button controls, intelligently placed for most shooting situations, are the key to this system's top-notch design. (Unless you are left-handed—there are some concessions made to lefties, but finding a perfect lefty camera is as much of a challenge as finding other left-handed devices in our right-handed world.)

The trigger on the brace's handle is a VCR pause remote control, used to stop the tape for the few minutes between action. (The VCR should not be left in PAUSE for more than a few minutes. If you anticipate a break, stop the tape.)

An automatic iris switch is located on the side of the camera. It can be left on for most shooting situations, but may be set manually at various positions when you want to override the normal and show special lighting or effects.

Directly above the iris control is a color temperature correction switch. Since outdoor light is usually bluish, and indoor light is usually orangy, you must tell the camera where you are shooting so that colors will be reproduced properly. An improper adjustment may be used for special effects or for shooting indoors under fluorescent lights, which are usually bluish like the outdoors.

Under the lens, you'll find a pause switch (for use when the camera is off its brace—on a tripod, for example). You will also find the automatic white balance switch here, which should be pressed every time lighting conditions change.

Panasonic's electronic viewfinder is particularly good for several reasons. First, it can be adjusted to sit on the left side of the camera if you're right-handed, or on the right if you're left-handed. Second, the black-and-white picture tube is very clear and easy to see, made even more so by a magnifier. Third, three indicator lights just below the screen remind you to make all adjustments for good pictures. The left lamp will glow green when you are recording and will be dark when you are not recording. This lamp is connected to a similar lamp in the front of the camera, so that your subject will also know when you are recording (called a "tally light"). The center lamp will glow red if you've not yet adjusted the white balance or will glow green if you have made the adjustment. The right lamp will go on if there's not enough light to record good images.

This camera's power zoom can be operated manually, with a small handle or by push buttons. Two power-zoom speeds are available: one that will cycle a full 6:1 zoom in 6 seconds (fast) and another that will do the same in 10 seconds (slow). Both are useful.

On the back panel of the camera are five controls, used for professional-style techniques. A FADER switch will automatically fade the picture in at the start of a scene, and/or fade it out at the end. A STAND-BY switch will extend battery life in the field. Use STAND-BY when you've stopped shooting for a few minutes; it will cut

The back panel of a Quasar top-of-the-line home video camera offers controls for more professional productions. (Photo by H. Blumenthal)

the power to the viewfinder and other power-consuming parts of the camera. In low-light situations the automatic gain control (AGC) maintains the best possible colors and contrast ratios under less than perfect lighting circumstances. If you're shooting in normal or bright light, the AGC should be *off*.

There is also a color control knob on the back of the camera to add green or violet tint. This control is most useful when your recording is being monitored by a color set on the premises. Portable monitors are made for just this purpose. (See page 34 for more about monitors.)

The fifth item on Panasonic's back panel is an outlet for a remote controller, which allows operation of the VCR from the camera itself. The remote controller is an optional accessory.

Aside from minor points about the shoulder grip, which is adjustable and remarkably well balanced, and about some very specialized features common only to this camera, this description of Panasonic's camera should give you a good basis for comparison when you shop for a camera.

Newer cameras also include character generators that can print time and date information on your tape. The very same character generator prints step-by-step instructions on the viewfinder.

YOUR OWN PRODUCTION

Now let's go out and shoot. Be sure to read every step for the clearest picture of what's happening.

1. Make all the proper connections, according to the instruction book (with some help, if you need it, from Chapter 10 in this book).
2. Press the RECORD and PLAY buttons on the VCR at the same time. The tape will start to move. Look into the viewfinder on the camera. It should be glowing a bright gray. Then press the PAUSE button on your camera to pause the VCR until you are ready to shoot.
3. Now (and not before), remove the lens cap from the camera. In a second or so, you'll see a picture in the viewfinder. Focus the picture by twisting the focus ring (see diagram in your camera's instructions) on the lens until you see a picture that pleases you.
4. Tell the camera whether you're shooting indoors or outdoors by flipping the appropriate switch.
5. Point the camera at something white (but never, never at a direct light source like a lamp, a bulb, or the sun), and press the AUTOMATIC WHITE BALANCE button. A sheet of white typewriter paper or even a white T-shirt will do just fine.
6. Make the other adjustments. Tell the camera whether you'll need automatic iris, automatic gain control, and so on.
7. Point the camera at your subject, and press the PAUSE (to release) again to start recording. You will see the tape moving in the VCR.

8. Choose your subjects carefully, make your moves slowly and gracefully, and pause the VCR (using the button on the camera) whenever you want to stop, even just to think or steady yourself for a moment.

9. Once you've made the recording, press STOP on the VCR, REWIND the tape and press PLAY. You will see the program you just recorded on the electronic viewfinder (without sound) or on a monitor (with sound). If you are working only with the viewfinder, use an earplug to hear what you've picked up.

10. Practice often. You'll see marked improvements each time you shoot. Experiment with the camera and with all its controls—that's the best way to learn how to handle a camera. Videography really can't be learned from a book. The only way to become a good videographer is to shoot, critique the results, and shoot some more. (You can, of course, record over productions you do not want to keep.)

BUYING YOUR CAMERA

When you set out to buy your camera, start by looking for one made by the manufacturer who made your VCR. You need not buy a camera only from that maker, however. Technical compatibility is no problem, but manufacturers have not standardized the connecting cables. Some cable adapters require special boxes and *more* adapters to connect properly. Be sure you buy everything you need. Cameras made by VHS manufacturers will work with Beta machines, and vice versa, provided you can get the proper cables. If your retailer does not stock special cables, contact Comprehensive Video Supply (148 Veterans' Drive, Northvale, N.J. 07647) for a catalog of cables and other video accessories.

There is a final note about videotape formats, one of particular interest to users of portable equipment. Technicolor sells a Japanese portable recorder/player (from the manufacturer Funai)

Both Canon and Technicolor sell a featherweight videotape recording system, using cassettes that are considerably smaller than VHS and Beta tapes. (Photo courtesy Canon)

that weighs only 7 pounds, which is considerably lighter than any VHS or Beta portable on the market. This VCR uses a smaller tape format (the videocassette looks just like an audio-cassette) and produces slightly inferior pictures. For those who travel, the machine is a godsend since it is so light. Technicolor also sells a cam-

One-piece camera and VCR units will become increasingly popular in the near future. This electronic news-gathering (ENG) camera/recorder was designed for professionals, but consumer units are planned as well. It combines camera and recorder into a single compact unit through use of a special $\frac{1}{2}$-inch tape cassette, a new high-precision VTR mechanism, and a three-tube color camera. (Photo courtesy Matsushita Electric)

CHECKLIST: HOW TO BUY A COLOR VIDEO CAMERA

Buying a camera is very much a matter of comparing features, but personal comfort is also a major concern.

When you first consider buying a camera, go to a store and try a few on for size (literally). Weight will be the major difference between cameras. You will also find that the location of controls will be more convenient on some cameras, less on others (particularly if you are left-handed). Viewfinder designs vary as well.

Standard operating equipment for a video camera includes an electronic viewfinder, a built-in microphone, and color recording. (There are cheaper cameras without these features, for specialized uses.)

Once you're comfortable with a physical design, then consider features. Simply check below the ones you feel you will need, and make your selection accordingly.

First, in the basic category:
____ 6:1 zoom lens
____ Stand-by switch to save power
____ Color temperature switch
____ Automatic white balance
____ Color preference adjustment dial

Next, in the mid-range category:
____ Side-mounted viewfinder
____ Fade in/fade out control
____ Optional remote VCR control
____ Automatic gain control for low-light shooting
____ Motorized zoom

In a slightly higher range:
____ Automatic indoor/outdoor correction
____ Macro lens
____ 12:1 lens
____ Automatic iris
____ On-screen graphics (date, time, step-by-step instructions)

Finally, in the expensive range:
____ Interchangeable lenses (available on some models)
____ Two motorized zoom speeds
____ High-quality (semiprofessional) camera tube

AUTOFOCUS

All manufacturers offer their own individual groupings of features for marketing reasons. Check the features most important to you; those that are expensive in one product line may be standard in another. Show the list of features that you want to the salesperson, and then try every camera that suits your needs.

More shopping hints:

1. If you already own a portable VCR, bring it to the store and hang it over your shoulder while you test cameras. Feel the weight; see how steady you can be for extended periods. If you don't own a VCR and you are buying an entire system, *choose the VCR first*; then choose the camera for comfort as well as features.

2. Ask the store if you can borrow the camera for a few minutes to shoot outside. Record and playback on your chosen VCR, and then look at pictures from at least three different cameras inside the store. (Plan on no less than an hour for camera shopping—you *must* be comfortable with the camera before you buy the unit.)

3. The difference between 5–6 and 8–9 pounds may not sound like much, but it is. Carry the heaviest camera for about fifteen minutes, and make sure that you can remain steady. If you're a little shaky, try a lighter camera (even if you must eliminate some features).

4. If you're planning to shoot meetings or other sedentary activities, buy a tripod. (Most camera makers sell a tripod under their own name.)

era and a tuner/timer as accessories for this VCR. Keep an eye out for the new mini-cassettes that will bring smaller VHS-compatible portables.

In a related development, Sony has shown a small-format recorder/camera, about the size of today's regular video camera. It uses still another tape format, but is not expected to be available for a few years. Other manufacturers are working on similar schemes.

ACCESSORIES

Portable VCR and camera owners are served by a wide array of products that encourage professional production. Many are direct copies of professional models. Not all videography products are as widely advertised as products in other categories, so it's wise to ask about what you need.

Most major manufacturers who sell cameras also sell tripods. With proper screws and flanges, almost any *heavyweight* still-camera tripod can be used for a video camera as well. Tripods are a necessity for good videography; they allow anyone to hold the camera steady, even for long periods of time. When buying a tripod, consider its ability to support the weight of a video camera

(up to 10 pounds) first. Next, inspect the tripod's swivel head, and try it with a camera mounted on top. You should be able to move the camera smoothly up and down (called a "tilt" in TV lingo), and left and right ("pan"); with some practice, you should be able to tilt and pan simultaneously. Feel the fluidity of movement—that's the difference between a cheap tripod and an expensive one. Plan to spend up to $100 for a good video tripod with rubberized feet. If you're planning to use the tripod in a multiple-camera setup in a studio or a classroom, consider a more expensive tripod with wheels, so that you can move the tripod while the camera is shooting (this move is called a "dolly," as in "dolly left" or "dolly back").

Other camera supports include a back brace (which uses your body for support and generally ties in with a VCR backpack—excellent for news-style shooting) and a chest brace (not always comfortable—try before you buy).

For more versatile shooting, there are several lens kits available for most (but not all) cameras. If you're planning to go beyond birthday parties and back-yard barbecues, it's usually wise to ask about lens attachments (for closeups, etc.) before you buy the camera.

You can also buy special lighting and microphones for most portable video systems.

HOW TO BUY
TAPES AND DISCS

Although the retail prices of videocassette and videodisc machines may seem to be competitive with one another, there is a very great difference between the prices of programs on cassettes and programs on discs. An example illustrates the point: *Jaws,* a top-grossing movie, sells for about $65 on cassette, but for only $25 on disc—and the Laserdisc version is stereo!* *The Graduate* costs about $60 on cassette, and only $20 on RCA SelectaVision videodisc. So you can figure a 50 percent savings on discs versus cassettes, and sometimes even more.

In favor of cassettes, beyond the obvious recording capability of the machine itself, is the vast number of cassette programs already on the market. Thousands are now available, as opposed to the several hundred for each of the individual disc systems. Many of the movies available on cassette or disc also play on pay TV and on broadcast television, so you can build your own library for the cost of blank tapes. (More about the legalities of off-the-air recording later in the chapter.)

*Stereo videocassettes are now beginning to surface as well.

There is no apparent pattern as to when a new movie will be released for broadcast television, for pay TV, for cassette, or for disc. Some are released on videocassette and on disc on the same day that they hit the theaters (the Lily Tomlin–Jane Fonda–Dolly Parton comedy *9 to 5* was the first of these simultaneous releases). Most hit films are now released on tape or disc within a year of theatrical release (long before they'll appear on NBC, CBS, or ABC, and at about the same time they appear on pay TV's HBO or Showtime, or The Movie Channel services). There is no way to predict a film's release date for retail sale on tape or disc; it is best just to be patient and check with your local video store periodically for news about specific titles.

When a new film is released on cassette or disc, it is frequently sold on the movie studio's own label. Warner, Paramount, Columbia Pictures, MCA/Universal, Twentieth Century-Fox, MGM/UA and Disney have their own labels. Older films follow more convoluted distribution paths, because libraries have been bought and sold by studios and distributors since the film industry began. Films not made by a studio may appear on any label. Smaller companies, notably

The Nostalgia Merchant, sell older titles as a result of unusual business deals, where a studio's distribution contract for a specific film may not have included its eventual sale in the home video marketplace. There are older films no longer protected by copyright, and these public-domain movies are often released by more than one of the smaller labels. Some films may never become available in the home video marketplace at all, because of either contractual limitations or a perceived lack of consumer interest in the property.

You will find the greatest selection of films and special programs on cassettes and discs in a video specialty store. This is a relatively recent kind of retail outlet, one of America's great new franchise opportunities. You're likely to find them in shopping malls and in business districts nationwide. Video stores typically sell videocassettes (both blank and prerecorded), videodiscs, and, frequently, videogame cartridges. All these items are considered "software," sold like books or records, complete with their own top-ten sales list. Some video specialty stores stock VCRs, disc players, and giant screens as well.

Department stores usually sell the most popular cassettes and discs in their TV or record department. As more people buy machines, and video software becomes a bigger business, you will probably be able to buy cassettes and discs either in the book department or in a newly arranged electronics department (which is likely to contain calculators, electronic games, small computers, and other high-tech paraphernalia) in every department store.

Your local appliance discounter will probably be the cheapest place in town to buy video hardware and software, because these discounters buy in quantity. The high-volume concept usually precludes stock of the more obscure titles.

In most stores, you will be able to choose between the purchase and rental of videocassettes (and sometimes discs as well). Every rental plan is different, but you can be sure that a week's rental will be cheaper than a purchase—and your rental fee will usually (but not always) be applicable to the purchase price, should you decide to buy. A weekend rental is likely to be roughly the cost of two movie admissions. Weekday rentals are sometimes discounted, because Mondays and Tuesdays are traditionally slow traffic days for retail stores.

If there is no video store near you, you can buy programs by mail. When dealing with any mail-order operation, be sure that you understand the payment and delivery contract completely, and be sure to include hidden prices (like shipping) when you compare different plans.

Keeping up with new releases and with the mail-order services is easy. Video store specialists are the most knowledgeable, partially because it is their business, but mostly because the store managers are as interested in the new program releases as you are.

Consider also the video specialty magazines for current information about both software and hardware. For about $2.00 an issue (less with monthly subscriptions), you can have the most up-to-date information about the video field.

Video Review is specifically written for people who own videocassette recorders, cameras, and videodisc machines. Each issue is crammed with program reviews, technical equipment reviews of everything from small screens to cameras, and feature stories about new VCR developments, things to tape from TV schedules, and how-to tips for your own video productions, generally from professionals. Several columns round out the magazine, including one on videogames, a Q&A service, and previews of future releases. The reviews of individual programs and movies are particularly good, written objectively by respected critics. *Video Review* is published by CES Publishing, 325 East 75 Street, New York, New York 10021, and is generally available on newsstands for $1.75 (1981 price). Subscriptions are $15 a year.

Home Video is a well-organized monthly re-

(Reprinted by permission of Video Review)

port on the entire video industry, from the use of video in new Las Vegas slot machines to reviews of hardware and software products. Regular features include "Video Times" (miscellaneous items from all corners), "VideoCast" (things to watch and record on cable, public, and network TV), "VideoTapes/Discs" (reviews of new releases, including a list of the top-ten sellers and renters), "Video Wares" (new hardware), and a Q&A column. This magazine's strong suit is its crisp informational style, very newsy, very much concerned with keeping current. You can find *Home Video* on most newsstands. Write to their subscription department, P.O. Box 2651, Boulder, Colorado 80321. The magazine is published by United Business Publications, 475 Park Avenue South, New York, New York 10016. Single copies cost $1.75; a year's subscription costs $13.97.

Video magazine, the oldest of the video publications, is a product of Reese Publishing, 235 Park Avenue South, New York, New York 10003. *Video* covers a wide variety of topics, not just about video recording and playback, but, in a broad sense, about television viewing and its myriad variations. You'll find feature articles about cable television, personal computers, media environments, special people in video, almost anything relevant to the new media. Extensive product reviews of both hardware and software are regular features, as are numerous reader-service columns. A single issue of *Video* costs $1.75, and an annual subscription, $15, with discounts available.

Both *Video* and *Video Review* publish annual

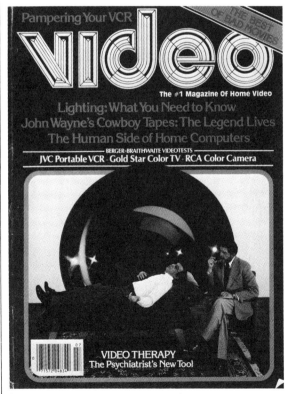

(Reprinted by permission of Video)

guides to hardware, and these are fine reference works. Each is available on newsstands through the wintertime.

As for guides to available software, there is a company called National Video Clearinghouse in Syosset, New York, that catalogs all new entries in a master computer and publishes guides at regular intervals. You can buy their *Video Tape and Disc Guide to Home Entertainment* at most bookstores ($7.95). The listings are culled from a massive computer data base with well over 30,000 entries, which is periodically published as *The Video Source Book.* A sample page appears on the following page.

The NVC master directory, The Video Source Book.

National Video Clearinghouse offers nine guides to videotapes and discs for consumers.

For more information about these books, write to the National Video Clearinghouse, 100 Lafayette Drive, Syosset, New York 11791, or visit a well-stocked bookstore for the guides. These are the premier guides to software; there are none better.

Building your video library will be largely a matter of personal choice, but the choices are easier when you know what's available. Videocassette and disc programs are hardly limited to movies—you will find sports classics, performance and entertainment specials, Broadway productions, instructional shows, assorted pornography, video versions of non-fiction books, and children's programming, to name a few topics. You will certainly be able to record some of these off the air (assuming the commercials don't bother you), and from cable, but most are more

Sample pages of
The Video Source Book.

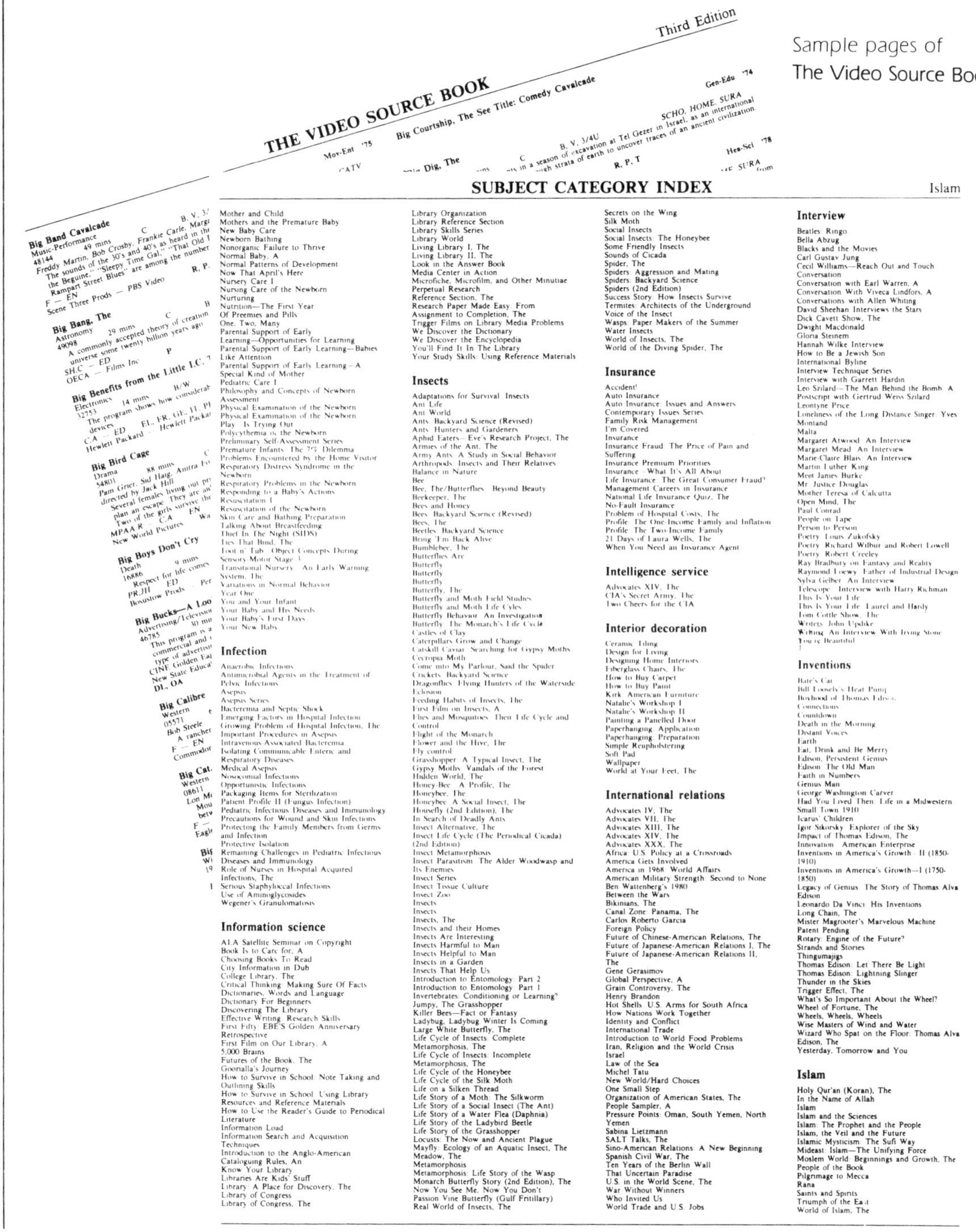

SUBJECT CATEGORY INDEX   Islam

Big Band Cavalcade C B V. 3/
Music-Performance 49 mins Margi
48144 Freddy Martin, Bob Crosby, Frankie Carle, the
the sounds of the 30's and 40's as heard in the
Beguine."—"Sleepy Time Gal."—"That Old f
Rampart Street Blues" are among the number
F — EN — PBS Video
Scene Three Prods

Big Bang, The C B
Astronomy 29 mins
40098 A commonly accepted theory of creation
universe some twenty billion years ago
SHC — ED P
OECA — Films Inc

Big Benefits from the Little I.C. H/W
Electronics 14 mins
32253 The program shows how consideral
devices ED EL, FR, GR, IT, PI
C A Hewlett Packard
Hewlett Packard

Big Bird Cage
Drama 88 mins B
54801 Starring Sid Haig, Anitta Fo'
Pam Grier, Sid Haig, directed by Jack Hill
Several females living out pri-
anal an escape. They are se
Two of the girls survive the
MPAA R CA EN
New World Pictures

Big Boys Don't Cry
Death 8 mins
18686 Respect for life comes
PR.JH ED Pet
Benustow Prods

Big Bucks—A 1,00
Advertising/Television 30 min
48785 This program is a
commercial and s
type (il Golden Lie)
CINE Golden Eag
New State Educat
DI, OA

Big Calibre
Western e
05571 Bob Steele
A ranchei
F EN
Commodor

Big Cat
Western
08611
Lost Mi
Mou
hero
F
Eagle

Bi
W
19

Infection

Anaerobic Infections
Antimicrobial Agents in the Treatment of
Pelvic Infections
Asepsis
Asepsis Series
Bacteremia and Septic Shock
Emerging Factors in Hospital Infection
Growing Problem of Hospital Infection, The
Important Procedures in Asepsis
Intravenous Associated Bacteremia
Isolating Communicable Enteric and
Respiratory Diseases
Medical Asepsis
Nosocomial Infections
Opportunistic Infections
Packaging Items for Sterilization
Patient Profile II (Fungus Infection)
Pediatric Infectious Diseases and Immunology
Precautions for Wound and Skin Infections
Protecting the Family Members from Germs
and Infection
Protective Isolation
Remaining Challenges in Pediatric Infectious
Diseases and Immunology
Role of Nurses in Hospital Acquired
Infections, The
Serious Staphylococcal Infections
Use of Aminoglycosides
Wegener's Granulomatosis

Information science

ALA Satellite Seminar on Copyright
Book Is to Care for, A
Choosing Books To Read
City Information in Dub
College Library, The
Critical Thinking: Making Sure Of Facts
Dictionaries, Words and Language
Dictionary For Beginners
Discovering The Library
Effective Writing: Research Skills
First Fifty: EBE'S Golden Anniversary
Retrospective
First Film on Our Library, A
5,000 Brains
Futures of the Book, The
Guenalla's Journey
How to Survive in School: Note Taking and
Outlining Skills
Resources and Reference Materials
How to Use the Reader's Guide to Periodical
Literature
Information Load
Information Search and Acquisition
Techniques
Introduction to the Anglo-American
Cataloguing Rules, An
Know Your Library
Libraries Are Kids' Stuff
Library: A Place for Discovery, The
Library of Congress
Library of Congress, The

Mother and Child
Mothers and the Premature Baby
New Baby Care
Newborn Bathing
Nonorganic Failure to Thrive
Normal Baby, A
Normal Patterns of Development
Now That April's Here
Nursery Care I
Nursing Care of the Newborn
Nurturing
Nutrition—The First Year
Of Premies and Pills
One, Two, Many
Parental Support of Early
Learning—Opportunities for Learning
Parental Support of Early Learning—Babies
Like Attention
Parental Support of Early Learning — A
Special Kind of Mother
Pediatric Care I
Philosophy and Concepts of Newborn
Assessment
Physical Examination of the Newborn
Physical Examination of the Newborn
Play: Is Trying Out
Polycythemia in the Newborn
Preliminary Self-Assessment Series
Premature Infants: The 7% Dilemma
Problems Encountered by the Home Visitor
Respiratory Distress Syndrome in the
Newborn
Respiratory Problems in the Newborn
Responding to a Baby's Actions
Resuscitation I
Resuscitation of the Newborn
Skin Care and Bathing Preparation
Talking About Breastfeeding
Thief In The Night (SIDS)
Ties That Bind, The
Tool n' Tab: Object Concepts During
Sensory Motor Stage 1
Transitional Nursery: An Early Warning
System, The
Variations in Normal Behavior
Year One
You and Your Infant
Your Baby and His Needs
Your Baby's First Days
Your New Baby

Insects

Adaptations for Survival: Insects
Ant Life
Ant World
Ants: Backyard Science (Revised)
Ants: Hunters and Gardeners
Aphid Eaters— Eve's Research Project, The
Armies of the Ant, The
Army Ants: A Study in Social Behavior
Arthropods: Insects and Their Relatives
Balance in Nature
Bee
Bee, The/Butterflies: Beyond Beauty
Beekeeper, The
Bees and Honey
Bees: Backyard Science (Revised)
Bees, The
Beetles: Backyard Science
Bring 'Em Back Alive
Bumblebee, The
Butterflies Are
Butterfly
Butterfly
Butterfly, The
Butterfly and Moth Field Studies
Butterfly and Moth Life Cycles
Butterfly Behavior: An Investigation
Butterfly: The Monarch's Life Cycle
Castles of Clay
Caterpillars Grow and Change
Catskill Caviar: Searching for Gypsy Moths
Cecropia Moth
Come into My Parlour, Said the Spider
Crickets: Backyard Life Cyles
Dragonflies: Flying Hunters of the Waterside
Eclosion
Feeding Habits of Insects, The
First Film on Insects, A
Flies and Mosquitoes: Their Life Cycle and
Control
Flight of the Monarch
Flower and the Hive, The
Fly control
Grasshopper: A Typical Insect, The
Gypsy Moths: Vandals of the Forest
Hidden World, The
Honey-Bee: A Profile, The
Honeybee, The
Honeybee: A Social Insect, The
Housefly (2nd Edition), The
Insect: A Study of Deadly Ants
Insect Alternative, The
Insect Life Cycle (The Periodical Cicada)
(2nd Edition)
Insect Metamorphosis
Insect Parasitism: The Alder Woodwasp and
Its Enemies
Insect Series
Insect Stories
Insect Tissue Culture
Insect Zoo
Insects
Insects
Insects and their Homes
Insects Are Interesting
Insects Harmful to Man
Insects Helpful to Man
Insects in a Garden
Insects That Help Us
Introduction to Entomology: Part 2
Introduction to Entomology: Part 1
Invertebrates: Conditioning or Learning?
Jumpy, The Grasshopper
Killer Bees—Fact or Fantasy
Ladybug, Ladybug Winter Is Coming
Large White Butterfly, The
Life Cycle of Insects: Complete
Metamorphosis, The
Life Cycle of Insects: Incomplete
Metamorphosis, The
Life Cycle of the Honeybee
Life Cycle of the Silk Moth
Life on a Silken Thread
Life Story of a Moth: The Silkworm
Life Story of a Social Insect (The Ant)
Life Story of a Water Flea (Daphnia)
Life Story of the Ladybird Beetle
Life Story of the Grasshopper
Locusts: The Now and Ancient Plague
Mayfly: Ecology of an Aquatic Insect, The
Meadow, The
Metamorphosis: Life Story of the Wasp
Monarch Butterfly Story (2nd Edition), The
Now You See Me, Now You Don't
Passion Vine Butterfly (Gulf Fritillary)
Real Mystery of Insects, The

Library Organization
Library Reference Section
Library Skills Series
Library World
Living Library I, The
Living Library II, The
Look in the Answer Book
Media Center in Action
Microfiche, Microfilm, and Other Minutiae
Perpetual Research
Reference Section, The
Research Paper Made Easy: From
Assignment to Completion, The
Trigger Films on Library Media Problems
We Discover the Dictionary
We Discover the Encyclopedia
You'll Find It In The Library
Your Study Skills: Using Reference Materials

Secrets on the Wing
Silk Moth
Social Insects
Social Insects: The Honeybee
Some Friendly Insects
Sounds of Cicada
Spider, The
Spiders: Aggression and Mating
Spiders: Backyard Science
Spiders (2nd Edition)
Success Story: How Insects Survive
Termites: Architects of the Underground
Voice of the Insect
Wasps: Paper Makers of the Summer
Water Insects
World of Insects, The
World of the Diving Spider, The

Insurance

Accident!
Auto Insurance
Auto Insurance: Issues and Answers
Contemporary Issues Series
Family Risk Management
I'm Covered
Insurance
Insurance Fraud: The Price of Pain and
Suffering
Insurance Premium Priorities
Insurance - What It's All About
Life Insurance: The Great Consumer Fraud?
Management Careers in Insurance
National Life Insurance Quiz, The
No-Fault Insurance
Problem of Hospital Costs, The
Profile: The One-Income Family and Inflation
Profile: The Two-Income Family
21 Days of Laura Wells, The
When You Need an Insurance Agent

Intelligence service

Advocates XIV, The
CIA's Secret Army, The
Two Cheers for the CIA

Interior decoration

Ceramic Tiling
Design for Living
Designing Home Interiors
Fiberglass Chairs, The
How to Buy Carpet
How to Buy Paint
Kirk American Furniture
Natalie's Workshop I
Natalie's Workshop II
Painting a Panelled Door
Paperhanging: Application
Paperhanging: Preparation
Simple Reupholstering
Soft Pad
Wallpaper
World at Your Feet, The

International relations

Advocates IV, The
Advocates VII, The
Advocates XIII, The
Advocates XIV, The
Advocates XXX, The
Africa: U.S. Policy at a Crossroads
America Gets Involved
America in 1968: World Affairs
American Military Strength: Second to None
Ben Wattenberg's 1980
Between the Wars
Bikinians, The
Canal Zone: Panama, The
Carlos Roberto Garcia
Foreign Policy
Future of Chinese-American Relations, The
Future of Japanese-American Relations I, The
Future of Japanese-American Relations II,
The
Gene Gerasimov
Global Perspective, A
Grain Controversy, The
Henry Brandon
Hot Shells: U.S. Arms for South Africa
How Nations Work Together
Identity and Conflict
International Trade
Introduction to World Food Problems
Iran, Religion and the World Crisis
Israel
Law of the Sea
Michel Tatu
New World/Hard Choices
One Small Step
Organization of American States, The
People Sampler, A
Pressure Points: Oman, South Yemen, North
Yemen
Sabina Lietzmann
SALT Talks, The
Sino-American Relations: A New Beginning
Spanish Civil War, The
Ten Years of the Berlin Wall
That Uncertain Paradise
U.S. in the World Scene, The
War Without Winners
Who Invited Us
World Trade and U.S. Jobs

Interview

Beatles: Ringo
Bella Abzug
Blacks and the Movies
Carl Gustav Jung
Cecil Williams—Reach Out and Touch
Conversation
Conversation with Earl Warren, A
Conversation With Viveca Lindfors, A
Conversations with Allen Whiting
David Sheehan Interviews the Stars
Dick Cavett Show, The
Dwight Macdonald
Gloria Stienem
Hannah Wilke Interview
How to Be a Jewish Son
International Byline
Interview Technique Series
Interview with Garrett Hardin
Leo Szilard—The Man Behind the Bomb: A
Postscript with Gertrud Weiss Szilard
Leontyne Price
Loneliness of the Long Distance Singer: Yves
Montand
Malta
Margaret Atwood: An Interview
Margaret Mead: An Interview
Marie-Claire Blais: An Interview
Martin Luther King
Meet James Burke
Mr. Justice Douglas
Mother Teresa of Calcutta
Open Mind, The
Paul Conrad
People on Tape
Person to Person
Poetry: Louis Zukofsky
Poetry: Richard Wilbur and Robert Lowell
Poetry: Robert Creeley
Ray Bradbury on Fantasy and Reality
Raymond Loewy: Father of Industrial Design
Sylva Gelber: An Interview
Telescope: Interview with Harry Rasky
This Is Your Life
This Is Your Life (Laurel and Hardy)
Tom Cottle Show, The
Writers: John Updike
Writing: An Interview With Irving Stone
You're Beautiful

Inventions

Bate's Cat
Bill Lossely's Heat Pump
Boyhood of Thomas Edison
Connections
Countdown
Death in the Morning
Distant Voices
Earth
Eat, Drink and Be Merry
Edison, Persistent Genius
Edison: The Old Man
Faith in Numbers
Genius Man
George Washington Carver
Had You Lived Then: Life in a Midwestern
Small Town 1910
Icarus' Children
Igor Stravinsky: Explorer of the Sky
Impact of Thomas Edison, The
Innovation: American Enterprise
Inventions in America's Growth— II (1850-
1910)
Inventions in America's Growth—I (1750-
1850)
Legacy of Genius: The Story of Thomas Alva
Edison
Leonardo Da Vinci: His Inventions
Long Chain, The
Mister Magrooter's Marvelous Machine
Patent Pending
Rotary: Engine of the Future?
Strands and Stories
Thingumajigs
Thomas Edison: Let There Be Light
Thomas Edison: Lightning Slinger
Thunder in the Skies
Trigger Effect, The
What's So Important About the Wheel?
Wheel of Fortune, The
Wheels, Wheels, Wheels
Wise Masters of Wind and Water
Wizard Who Spat on the Floor: Thomas Alva
Edison, The
Yesterday, Tomorrow and You

Islam

Holy Qur'an (Koran), The
In the Name of Allah
Islam
Islam and the Sciences
Islam: The Prophet and the People
Islam, the Veil and the Future
Islamic Mysticism: The Sufi Way
Mideast: Islam—The Unifying Force
Moslem World: Beginnings and Growth, The
People of the Book
Pilgrimage to Mecca
Rana
Saints and Spirits
Triumph of the East
World of Islam, The

easily (if more expensively) acquired by purchase or rental.

Though the number of available programs will increase, particularly in the non-movie areas, you will find the author's recommended starter list for your library beginning on page 165.

THE LEGALITY OF TAPING OFF-THE-AIR PROGRAMS

When you first buy your VCR, you will no doubt try recording programs off the air. Strictly speaking, this is against the law. All television programs (and commercials) are protected by copyright and cannot be duplicated for any reason without the written permission of the copyright holder.

Sony has been battling in the courts for years, hoping to win an exception to the law for "time-shift viewing," but it has met with only limited success.

As of mid-1982, recording off-the-air or off-the-cable programs was against the law. Making copies of programs sold on videocassettes was also against the law. Since this law is virtually unenforceable, it's best to let your conscience guide your recording activities. It seems likely that blank tape will soon be sold with a surcharge, whose proceeds will be divided among copyright holders.

■ 7 ■

CABLE, SATELLITES, AND PAY TV

Millions of Americans (roughly 200 million, in fact) watch television. And they don't have to pay a nickel for the privilege (directly, that is). As a rule, Americans have never paid hard cash for broadcast entertainment or information. Instead, we've patronized the advertisers who pay for precious minutes of network and local sponsorship. This is a happy example of capitalism at its generous best, with the masses receiving billions of dollars' worth of programming without paying directly for any of it.

American broadcasting has been supported by advertising since its inception in the 1920s, when a real estate promoter in Jackson Heights, New York, first paid a radio station to broadcast a commercial message. Radio advertising became a big business where companies sponsored entire programs like *The Kraft Music Hall*, *Texaco Star Theater*, and *Colgate Sports Newsreel*. As radio listeners, Americans learned to associate product names with certain programs and stars, which was precisely what the sponsors were after. This continued with TV. To this day, we associate Hallmark Cards with the prestigious *Hall of Fame* theater specials, and, somewhat less

overtly, we associate Mobil with PBS programs like *Masterpiece Theatre*. Although advertisers rarely sponsor whole shows today, the system still works, satisfying sponsor, program network, and most viewers.

One missing link in this chain, in a small town in Pennsylvania, has already caused a great deal of anxiety among broadcasters. A mountain blocked the local television signals and thus brought about the invention of cable television. The story, probably apocryphal in part, goes something like this:

It seems that an appliance dealer in a small mountain valley town in Pennsylvania, circa 1950, was not selling any television sets. The townspeople were not buying, not because of any doubt in television's formidable future, but because a mountain blocked their town from a nearby city's transmitters (television signals travel in straight lines and cannot be received if something big and bulky is in the way). The appliance dealer got a bright idea. He bought a very large antenna and erected it *on top* of the mountain. He then ran a cable from the antenna to his shop, attached it to the usual antenna terminals on his set, and was able to watch TV like

STEP-BY-STEP GUIDE: HOW CABLE TELEVISION WORKS

1. Most national cable networks distribute their programming via satellite. There are several communications satellites currently stationed above the United States, but RCA's SATCOM I is used by most major cable networks.

3. Satellites are only one of several distribution systems that serve the cable operator. Local TV signals and stations from nearby cities are collected by using a very tall antenna (when a hill is available, the antenna is placed on the hill so that it can "see" more broadcast antennas). All broadcast channels received are then assigned cable channel numbers (which may or may not correspond to their broadcast designations) and distributed via cable to subscribers.

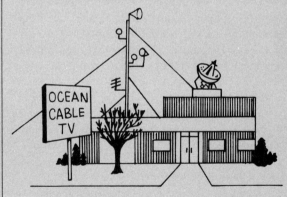

2. Multiple-channel cable operators generally have at least one earth station (also called a satellite receiver or a "downlink") on the premises. This dish receives network programming from the likes of Home Box Office, ESPN, WTBS, and other cable networks. The local cable operator then assigns each network a cable channel.

4. The cable operator distributes programming via coaxial cables, usually along existing roadways, through a complex series of trunk and subtrunk lines and line amplifiers (to keep the signal strong miles from the point of origin, or "head-end"). A typical cable network looks a lit-

tle like a river system, beginning very strong and gradually branching (smaller branches are no weaker thanks to amplifiers). Eventually, the signal reaches the home or office.

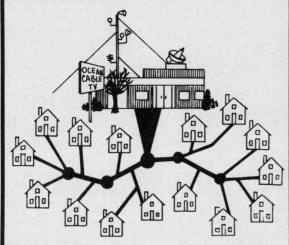

5. Each house is literally wired to the head-end. Special hardware is required to tune the cable channels. This hardware is correctly called a converter box and may be offered in either push-button, dial, or digital keypad format.

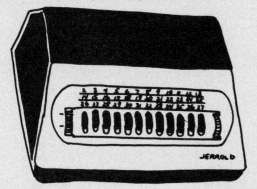

6. Cable television now offers well over 100 channels in many cities. Two-way television systems, like Qube, allow users to pass messages back "upstream" through the cables, to the head-end's computers. (See "How Qube Works," page 101.)

the rest of America. He decided that this could be a money-making venture and invited people who bought TV sets in his shop to connect to his antenna cable for a monthly fee. Cable television, also known as Community Antenna Television (or CATV), was born. (It was also known as MATV, for Master Antenna TV.) A similar tale is told about an Oregon appliance dealer with mountain problems. You may choose your myth.

It wasn't long before entrepreneurs realized that this idea had possibilities beyond towns with mountains. An antenna posted high in San Diego, for example, could pull in Los Angeles stations from 100 miles or so up the coast. San Diego became one of the fastest-growing cable markets for just this reason—people wanted to see more television channels. People in small cities with only one TV channel suddenly could receive all three networks for a nominal monthly fee. The investment in the antenna and the connecting cables, amplifiers, and such wasn't very steep, and so small cable companies sprouted in cities and towns of every size. Through the 1950s, 1960s, and most of the 1970s, cable television in America was almost always a "Mom-and-Pop" affair, frequently run from the back of a warehouse or, in some cases, a garage.

Cable's uneven growth and essentially small-time mentality made it a matter of little concern for government leaders. Some cities simply granted the exclusive right (or "franchise") to cable a community to the first people who wanted to do so. Some cities granted these franchises with the understanding that a dozen channels would be made available, while others awarded franchises with hardly any conditions at all. There were few enforced regulations governing this fragmented industry, because nobody paid much attention.

Periodically, the Federal Communications Commission (the government agency that regulates the radio, television, and telephone industries) would step in and make a rule or two, occasionally favoring a broadcaster who was miffed about a cable operator making a profit by simply rebroadcasting a station. And then there were the rules that favored the cable operator, who was simply expanding the area served by the broadcaster. Reading the FCC rules on cable through the sixties and early seventies shows a marked confusion on the part of everyone involved. Nobody seemed to understand what cable could be or whether or not it would become a significant force in American television.

But by the mid-1970s, cable was becoming very significant, a prime utility in many markets. The FCC made a few more rules, this time favoring comparatively unrestricted growth for the industry. Major corporations like Warner Communications and Time, Inc., took an interest. "Multiple System Owners" started buying the smaller, privately held cable systems, "Mom and Pop" operations in towns and cities across the U.S. Large communications companies, many of whom had toyed with cable in the past, established divisions to ride what cable marketeer Ron Castell dubbed "the franchise trail."

Local governments have long enjoyed the right to issue franchises for the construction and operation of local utilities. Cable, because it requires the physical wiring of a community, is often considered such a utility. Logistics usually dictate that a utility be constructed and maintained by a single company, whose franchise is granted as a monopoly. The cable franchise, which has a contract requiring renewal every fifteen years or so, can be an extremely lucrative right, particularly for a company that intends to operate many such franchises, in different cities, as a network. This factor, combined with the likelihood of profit built into a monopoly, made cable franchises extremely desirable in the late 1970s and to this day.

Local governments are usually aware of the value of their franchises, and so they ask that anyone interested in building a cable system submit a franchise bid. This bid is far more than a mere budget. A franchise bid is a promise to build a large-scale cable system, to charge community members as little as possible for the service, and, in most cases, to build a few television studios in schools, churches, and government buildings in the spirit of good community relations. The bid is usually supported by the best political handshaking and public-relations schemes money can buy, and is executed by special task-force teams that travel from city to city, hoping to win as many franchise awards as possible.

Once the franchise is won (usually by a large multiple-system owner [MSO] like Warner-Amex Cable Communications or Cox Cable or ATC, in partnership with a local company), the construction begins. After a year or two of building, the company must provide all that it promised in the franchise proposal—or risk losing the franchise altogether. Most of the franchises now being awarded promise an eventual selection of about 100 channels, with half to be activated during the first year or two of service. Most of these services are "basic," provided to the subscribers in exchange for payment of a flat monthly fee (usually $10–$25, depending on the city and the number of basic channels and services provided). These basic services must include all local stations available via normal television, and may include a few distant commercial stations received via either satellite, high antenna, or microwave links; an assortment of information/data channels (newswires, sportswires, weather maps, time/temperature, etc.); and a commercially sponsored sports network (ESPN, owned by Getty Oil, is one of several). Other entertainment and information channels may be included in the basic package as well. The chart on pages 96–98 details many of the services generally available as basic cable on systems around the country.

In addition to the basic cable services, an operator may decide to provide "pay television" services. A pay-TV channel requires that the subscriber pay an additional monthly fee for a specific service (e.g., HBO, which is split between the local cable operator and the pay-TV network). A listing of pay-TV networks is included in the chart on pages 96–98.

An operator may also decide to group channels in "tiers," offering the basic services as Tier 1 for a low price, more basic services plus a pay-television service as Tier 2 for a higher price (Tier 2 usually includes all that appears on Tier 1), and Tier 3, offering all of 1 and 2's channels, plus additional services, for a still higher price. On a tier system, you probably won't pay a specific fee for, say, Home Box Office, but you will pay for the overall group of channels in the tier that *includes*, for example, Home Box Office. Cable operators design their own tier configurations. Services do vary.

It is the local cable operator who decides which channels are to be offered. Most pay-TV channels cost the operator a per-subscriber fee, which is split with the network. If the split is a favorable one, the operator is likely to offer the channel. Basic cable channels are usually available for a small per-subscriber fee, but the operator cannot charge subscribers directly for basic cable services—these are subsidized by the monthly fee and, in some cases, by commercials. Since your basic monthly charge pays not only for programming but also for the cable company's salaries, equipment, and offices, your system's basic package may not be nearly as good as the offerings in the next town. Operating costs vary among the systems, and so do the amounts of money charged for using a network (based on the number of subscribers and other considerations).

The power to decide which channels should be available resides in the hands of local cable programmers. They may choose to offer an adult film channel rather than a religious network, or

vice versa. There is reason to question whether the operator should mold community standards or simply reflect its personality. It is important to remember that you as a subscriber are *paying* for everything you watch, and that you as a member of a community have a right to raise objections if you don't like what you're seeing. Unlike broadcast television, which is programmed from on high, your local cable office probably isn't more than a fifteen-minute drive from your home. The individual can, and should, have a great deal to say about what is shown on cable TV. If everyone in your PTA votes not to pay bills until a children's channel is added, your cable operator will certainly respond. (It is not just money at stake, don't forget—it's the good standing in the community when franchise-renewal time comes around.) Whether your system has 20 channels or 120, you have a right to choose what you see. That choice is what television's future is all about.

Many media observers genuinely believe cable TV to be the future of television. Cable will eventually provide more than 100 channels in nearly every American city, channels programmed internationally, nationally, regionally, and locally. If all goes as planned (and as promised in many franchise proposals), most schools will have their own channels, as will town councils, local arts groups, and many major corporations.

The cable medium has been severely criticized, however, for several inherent drawbacks. The process of wiring everybody's home, for example, is a wasteful, cumbersome process. Cable television currently requires that all users be connected by an actual wire (or by an advanced technology that replaces wire with either lasers or guided light waves). In most cities and suburbs, these cable connections are easily made, usually at reasonable prices. In rural locales, though, where houses may be acres or even miles apart, the cost of servicing the community can be prohibitive. The sheer cost of miles of the

CABLE CHANNELS

Every month or so, a large corporation makes an announcement about an exciting new cable network in the works. Most of these networks die on the drawing board, never to be heard from again. In this highly competitive world of new television, launching a network is a complicated and costly affair. It is extremely likely, therefore, that this list of major cable networks will be in need of revision almost immediately after the publication of this book. But use it as a guide to what's available, and feel free to ask about any network that sounds interesting—your cable operator should be familiar with all the available networks.

If you want to find out more on your own, the home-base city is listed with each entry. Companies owned by larger corporations are so designated.

All channels are basic services, provided without extra charge to subscribers, except those specified as "pay service."

ABC/ARTS (N.Y.C.) (ABC/Hearst). A culture channel, featuring the best of fine-arts programming.

ABC/"DAYTIME" (N.Y.C.) (ABC/Hearst). Hearst Publishing (*Cosmopolitan*, *Good Housekeeping*) takes its women's service information to the airwaves, offering new programming every day.

AP NEWSCABLE (N.Y.C.). News, sports, features, etc.

BRAVO! (Long Island, N.Y.) (Rainbow/Cablevision). A culture channel, with many foreign films. Pay service.

CABLE HEALTH NETWORK (N.Y., L.A.) (Viacom, *et al.*). Personal- and public-health programming for both the consumer and professional medical audiences.

CABLE NEWS NETWORK (Atlanta) (Ted Turner). 24-hour-a-day news channel (the first of its kind), featuring in-depth interviews, medical, women's, financial, and consumer news, as well as the standard headline reports.

CINEMAX (N.Y.C.) (Time, Inc.). 24-hour movie service, mostly recent, with some classics. Pay service.

CNN HEADLINE NEWS (Atlanta) (Ted Turner). An expansion of CNN, concentrating on headline news.

CONTINENTAL BROADCAST NETWORK/CBN (Virginia Beach, Va.). A wholesome blend of entertainment, talk, and information programs, including children's and inspirational shows and movies, and, recently, a lot of classic TV sit-coms. Formerly "Christian Broadcast Network."

C-SPAN (Washington, D.C.). Coverage of House of Representatives proceedings, as well as other public-interest programs.

THE DISNEY CHANNEL (Connecticut, L.A.) (Westinghouse, Disney). Family and children's programming.

THE ENTERTAINMENT CHANNEL (N.Y.C) (RCTV, which in turn is owned by RCA and Rockefeller Center). Almost half this channel is BBC programming (formerly a PBS staple). The rest of the schedule is movies, original entertainment events, and some children's programming. Pay service.

ESCAPADE/THE PLAYBOY CHANNEL (Long Island, N.Y. and L.A.) (Playboy, Rainbow Program Services). On certain hours *Playboy* magazine takes to the air with original programs for the adult audience and adult films.

ESPN (Bristol, Conn.) (Getty). 24 hours of sports programs, for the sports fanatic. From scholastic to professional, everything from volleyball to the Canadian Football League; some documentaries and interview shows on sports as well.

HOME BOX OFFICE (N.Y.C., L.A.)

(Time, Inc.). First-run movies, big-name performances, specials, documentaries, sports programs (Wimbledon coverage, *Inside the NFL*, *Race for the Pennant*), and series (including a *Consumer Reports* program). This is the top pay-television service.

MODERN SATELLITE NETWORK
(N.Y.C.). A compilation of documentaries, corporate presentations, and almost any other kind of program you can think of on an astonishing array of topics.

THE MOVIE CHANNEL (N.Y.C.)
(Warner-Amex Satellite Entertainment Corp./ WASEC). 24-hour movie service, with both new and classic films.

MTV/MUSIC TELEVISION (N.Y.C.)
(WASEC). A 24-hour pop-music channel, with a video disc jockey playing videotapes of the top songs. Some concerts and music documentaries as well.

NICKELODEON (N.Y.C.) (WASEC). A children's channel, featuring the award-winning original series *Pinwheel*. For preschoolers through teenagers, there's something for all children on Nickelodeon—and it's noncommercial (and nonviolent).

PLAYCABLE (N.Y.C.) (General Instrument/ Jerrold, Mattel, Inc.). You must own a Mattel Intellivision videogame unit to use this channel. See page 110 for more about Intellivision. Fifteen games are available 24 hours a day, for a subscription fee.

PRIVATE SCREENINGS (N.Y.C.). Adult films.

PTL (Virginia Beach, Va.). One of the nation's most popular cable services. PTL stands for "Praise the Lord." As with CBN (above), very handsomely produced religious programs.

REUTERS FINANCIAL/SPORTS NEWS
(N.Y.C.). Delayed NYSE and AMEX quotations during business hours; at all other times, this is a sports scoreboard and source for sports headlines (text only).

REUTERS IDR (N.Y.C.). A professional service (quite expensive) that delivers up-to-the-minute financial information at the touch of a button. Instantaneous access to stock quotations, foreign exchange rates, etc. Ask your cable operator about this service; it is not often publicized to consumers, but is offered in many of the larger cities, primarily to company offices.

REUTERS NEWSVIEW (N.Y.C.). A text service, where news stories are printed on the screen. Topics here include hard news (national, international, some regional), along with daily horoscopes, pet-care tips, vacation and travel information, consumer insights, etc.

SATELLITE NEWS CHANNEL (Stamford, CT) (Westinghouse/ABC). A 24-hour news service, headline-oriented, for cable subscribers.

SATELLITE PROGRAM NETWORK
(Omaha, Neb.). Miscellaneous programming.

SHOWTIME (N.Y.C., L.A.) (Viacom). Similar to HBO, with a broader spectrum of programs, including comedy series, numerous Broadway shows, and many interesting off-beat films. Pay service.

SPOTLIGHT (L.A.) (Times-Mirror, Cox Cable). An entertainment channel, mainly movies with some specials as well. Pay service.

UPI NEWSTIME (N.Y.C.). This service shows black-and-white newspaper photos, while a radio-style reporter reads news stories 24 hours a day.

USA NETWORK (Glen Rock, N.J.) (Madison Square Garden and Time, Inc.). Numerous sporting events, including *Thursday Night Baseball*, Madison Square Garden sporting events (ECAC, NIT, many more), plus the *English Channel* (a compilation of programs from British TV), *Calliope* (award-winning children's films), *Night Flight* (late-night rock concerts and movies), and daytime women's service programming.

THE WEATHER CHANNEL (Chicago) (Landmark). A 24-hour weather report, created by John Coleman of *Good Morning America* fame, featuring a staff of over fifty meteorologists.

WGN (Chicago). An independent Chicago TV station, notable for the original *Bozo the Clown* show (still running, and still a favorite of younger children), as well as Cubs baseball, Bulls basketball, and almost 60 hours of movies every week.

WOR (N.Y.C.). Knicks and Nets basketball, Rangers and Islanders hockey, Mets baseball, NASL soccer, and plenty of terrific movies and syndicated series. A superstation.

WPIX (N.Y.C.). Yankees baseball, lots of other sports and syndicated programming. Another superstation.

WTBS "THE SUPERSTATION" (Atlanta). The original "superstation," and still the best, with 80 hours of movies every week, plus Braves baseball, Hawks basketball, many other sports. Some original variety specials and series as well.

Nearly all the above channels are delivered to the operator via satellite.

There are a few other types of channel that you may be interested in seeing on your local cable service.

The cable operator is required to offer all channels available via standard broadcast television in your area. This usually means NBC, CBS, ABC, and as many as three PBS channels, as well as any non-network stations. The operator may also offer "distant signals," from nearby cities, by using a special antenna or a microwave link. (If you live in Milwaukee and want to see Chicago sports, you might ask your cable operator about offering select Chicago stations. It is not uncommon to make such a request: in New York City, cable subscribers demanded Boston

Red Sox baseball, and the cable company responded to their requests by making a deal with the Boston organization.)

The cable operator is also likely to have promised some locally originated programming in a franchise agreement. Local programs may come from schools, libraries, churches, universities, amateur theaters, even shopping malls. Many cities have individual channels assigned to the police department, to each elementary, junior high, and high school, and to every college, library, and hospital, with studios and equipment provided by the cable company to produce programs for those channels.

Then there is the matter of information. Most cable companies have an electronic typewriter that will print letters on a TV screen (called a "character generator"). The possibilities for local text channels are endless. Some communities have their own weather channel programmed by local college students or by a computer service, local news headlines, hourly program guides, classified ads (for which the cable operator can charge, as the newspapers do), housing listings, and related services. Market-basket channels, where a local shopper compares prices for a prescribed list of items at several local stores, are also popular.

Finally, and often forgotten, is music. Cable television connections can also be used for the transmission of sound, of radio. If radio reception in your area is not perfect, or if you simply want more radio stations (again, available via large antenna or microwave link), your cable operator should be able to provide them for a nominal charge. Cable radio channels are received on a radio (not a TV), and the radio must be connected to the cable in order to receive them.

physical cable itself, and its related installation expenses, along with the amplifiers needed to keep the signals strong over long distances, frequently adds up to a losing proposition for the cable operator. If you live in a thinly populated area, it is possible that you will never have cable television.

Cable TV's future is equally shaky in communities where several franchises have been awarded—one for each section of a city or town. In Columbus, Ohio, for example, four different cable systems can be found within a few square miles, and the competing companies are always trying to buy one another out. It is generally good business for a single operator to service an entire community. In terms of future potential, an operator's zeal for serving one fourth of a city will be understandably limited.

Cable's future becomes even more convoluted when one considers the problems in upgrading current systems. Most systems more than ten years old were built with twelve channels, to match the 2–13 channel positions on VHF tuners (so that no additional tuner was needed). These systems are hardly impressive by today's standards, and so many twelve-channel operators are contemplating (or already building) upgraded systems. Upgrades are usually initiated as the result of promising business plans, based on subscriber revenues that new channels and services could generate. Many cable systems will upgrade in the near future, but some will wait to see the results of similar upgrades in neighboring cities.

For subscribers, it's tough to understand why upgrades take so long. If you can see twelve channels, you are probably waiting for twenty-four. If you've got twenty-four, and know that a friend in another city has thirty-six, you're bound to wonder why your system is inferior. And with 100+ channel systems now being built, it is harder still to comprehend the logical reasons for cable's uneven growth.

THE FUTURE OF CABLE

I believe that the true success of cable TV is only partially based on the delivery of entertainment channels. In order to become an indispensable aspect of American life, it must offer an amalgam of vital *services* that will secure its status as a household utility.

One of the first high-visibility showplaces for multiple-channel, multipurpose cable television and all its related services was Qube, now a successful cable system concept operated in several cities by Warner-Amex Cable Communications. In the late 1970s, Warner Cable (now Warner-Amex) tested Qube in Columbus, Ohio, where subscribers were given a much-publicized glimpse of things to come:

—Thirty channels of cable television, including ten "pay per view" channels

The first-generation Qube home terminal unit, which allowed selection of thirty different channels. The five black buttons on the right are used to register interactive responses. (Photo courtesy Warner-Amex Cable Communications, Inc.)

—Mini-keyboards used to communicate with a central cable system's computer

—Watchdog security services tied to local police, fire, and health-care facilities

Specially wired for these unique ventures (the new services required an enhanced cable to be run from the head-end, or cable headquarters, to all homes), Qube of Columbus successfully tested concepts that would later be standard on newer systems in Cincinnati, Pittsburgh, St. Louis, Dallas, and the Chicago suburbs.

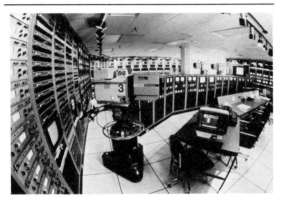

A large-scale cable head-end, the technical headquarters of Warner-Amex's Pittsburgh operation. The bank of machinery on the left side is used for audio processing. The back wall is filled with ³/₄-inch VCRs and monitors. In the front, on the table, is the computer terminal that routes all the signals in the head-end to the proper channels at the proper times. The bank of monitors in the center of the room allows technicians to watch all channels at one time. (Photo courtesy Warner-Amex Cable Communications, Inc.)

Pay-per-view, an idea in existence since the pioneer days of television, permits viewers to watch a single program and pay for only that show (a movie might cost $3.50, for example). The computer keeps track of what is watched by whom and sends bills at the end of every month.

Qube's mini-keyboard is the tool used by individual viewers, who can interact, for example, with a TV teacher (keyboard button 1: "Slow down, you're going too fast for me"; 2: "Please repeat that last explanation"; 3: "I understand"). These responses are generally solicited by a live on-screen instructor who stops his lesson periodically to interact directly with his audience. The very same buttons can be used, again in response to a prompt on-screen to buy concert tickets ("Register the number of tickets you want by touching button 1, 2, 3, 4, 5 now") or to vote on a local issue ("The mayor is doing 1: a fabulous job; 2: a good job; 3: an adequate job; 4: a so-so job; 5: an abominable job. Touch now"). Early

The latest Qube console, like most cable controllers, uses a digital keypad. It is capable of accommodating up to 110 videochannels. (Photo courtesy Warner-Amex Cable Communications, Inc.)

HOW QUBE WORKS

Although there were two-way cable television systems before Qube's introduction in 1977, Warner-Amex Cable's Qube is generally recognized as the first major two-way system actually in operation in the United States.

Qube is essentially a combination of cable television and computer technology, used daily by thousands of viewers in Columbus, Cincinnati, and Pittsburgh, and in the suburbs of St. Louis, Dallas, and other cities around the country.

At the simplest level, Qube offers a few dozen cable television channels. In this respect, Qube is very much like any other cable-TV system built since the mid-1970s.

What makes Qube unique is its computer connection. A viewer tunes to a channel that is offering an interactive program and holds a console in his/her hand, ready to touch a button when a prompt appears on the screen. Thousands of viewers are likely to be watching such a program at the same time.

Let's say that the question on the screen involves a quiz game:

"What is the capital of South Carolina?"
"Touch the button whose number corresponds with the correct answer."

1. Charleston
2. Charlestown
3. Charlotte
4. Columbus
5. Columbia

"Touch now."

About a second after the "Touch now" signal appears, a computer operator in Qube's studios issues a command for the polling computer to check the responses in all participating homes. This poll actually monitors all homes on the Qube system, whether they are watching the program or not. In this particular poll, the game players' responses are collected and sorted in seconds, and points are added to the scores of all correct players' homes.

The poll does not simply gather game data. Every poll (one is taken every six seconds) collects information on which channel is being watched, whether the console is working properly, and, if there is a Qube security system in the household, that all security checks are in the "normal" position.

Back to the South Carolina question for the moment. As a viewer, you would have touched one of the five selections on cue, and you would be sitting at the edge of your seat to see whether your "Charleston" answer would give you enough points to win the free movie tickets. The host of the interactive program returns, and tells the viewers that number 5, "Columbia," is the correct answer. At the same time, a small light (called a "message lamp") on the home console glows for a few seconds in all homes that answered correctly (the lamp is computer-controlled, and the instruction to turn the lamps on is sent out within seconds).

Qube is basically a cable system whose signals travel not only "downstream" (from the cable station to the households) but "upstream" as well. For the present, the upstream flow is data, collected by periodic polling of the entire community. In the future, that data may well be accompanied by pictures and sounds originating in the home. That, along with a vast number of wonderful concepts in education, home security, information, and entertainment, is the future not only of Qube but of cable television in America.

Qubes used only five buttons for these communications; more recent Qubes and other interactive cable consoles use a 0–9 telephone-style keypad to register interactive responses as well as channel selections.

Subscribers to some Cox Cable systems may be offered INDAX, an interactive cable system with an emphasis on data—be it stock trading, banking, or shopping at home.

Full computer keyboards will expand television's potential dramatically when connected to cable. Most large corporations are exploring this connection as a means of fast information transfer, both within the office and to and from the outside world. The process is not a simple one, and its implications are both expensive and mind-boggling, particularly when you consider the possibilities of a kitchen-table keyboard terminal replacing the workaday world of socialized employment.

Cable TV is one of two communications systems that are capable of linking your home to a central computer, your local McDonald's hamburger restaurant, or your office. Unfortunately, cable television is still developing and operates in different cities in a very uneven fashion. The second cable communications system is already in place and has been dependably serving nearly every man, woman, and child in America for generations. With some upgrading, the telephone company could expand their voice and computer-data network to show pictures, with sound, to all telephone users. Ma Bell is a network, but cable completely lacks a national structure. Recent changes in the structure of AT&T will allow the new American Bell some entry into the future world of teletext (see page 159), but AT&T's involvement in cable TV, except in its role as a common carrier of channel signals, is likely to be limited. AT&T and American Bell will figure prominently in the future of communications in America—as to where and how, it is too early to guess.

The role of new technologies in cable is still being tested in scattered systems around the country. Personal computers connected to cable can provide viewers with convenient, low-cost information. Near Dallas, this information takes the form of a daily newspaper, which appears on the TV screen, story by story. *The Des Moines Register, The Buffalo Courier-Express,* and *The Phoenix Republic* are among the dozens of newspapers that have cooperated with cable operators in newspaper text delivery on TV screen via cable. They are exploring cable as a means to stay alive in the explosive information age, an age in which, ironically, the sheer costs of paper, ink, and unions have already driven many of our best dailies out of business.

Electronic banking, shopping by television, and even working at home are all in various stages of development, and are likely to be offered to cable subscribers by decade's end.

Games may well clear the path for cable delivery of inexpensive computer programs to American households. Using Mattel's Intellivision videogame system (see page 110) and a specially designed connection box, cable viewers can play videogames without buying the individual cartridges. The game programs are stored in a central PlayCable computer, and you simply choose one by number. A dozen game programs are available at all times, transmitted as a small part of one channel's signal (a computer program is data that can easily be added to a sound-and-picture TV signal) without being visible on the TV screen. If you subscribe to PlayCable (assuming, of course, that your local cable operator offers the service), you'll pay a flat monthly fee for the unlimited right to play the month's dozen-plus games at your convenience. You actually use the cable system for less than a second, to select the game you want and to enter the game program into the accessory box's memory. If PlayCable is a success, the games-only menu will be expanded to include computer programs on topics ranging from exercise to conversational French. PlayCable is a prime example of a cable/computer connection at work. There will be plenty of others.

The 100+ channel cable systems are now being designed for a 50/50 mix of regular television programming and computer-related data channels. The first fifty or so will show network and local TV, pay TV, movies, sports, educational programs, and so forth. The second fifty will be information channels, offering now-standard newswires, weather maps and forecasts, sports scoreboards, consumer market-basket comparisons, and community bulletin boards, along with a wealth of financial, municipal, and industrial communications data services. It is very likely that teletext and videotext services, where single pages of informational text can be accessed by topic or by number (see Chapter 11), will appear on these channels as well.

SUBSCRIPTION TELEVISION AND LPTV

Most of the services currently offered by cable, or planned for cable's future, can be accomplished by a combination of satellite, microwave, and existing over-the-air television channels. Consider the widely ignored terrain of UHF (Channels 14–83), some seventy channels that can be received on every American television set manufactured since the early 1960s. Most cities have a UHF station or two, but nowhere is UHF used to its full potential. Because of its limited coverage area (a VHF station can serve a larger area than a UHF station with equal power), UHF stations have not been programmed very aggressively. There is a catch-22 problem here: Nobody watches UHF because nothing's on, and nothing's on UHF because nobody watches it. Until now.

Entrepreneurs, noting the success that Home Box Office and Showtime have enjoyed by filling a channel with new movies and specials, have taken a second look at UHF. A new concept called over-the-air subscription television, or STV, was born. Any broadcast channel (UHF or VHF) can be made into an STV channel, which scrambles the broadcast signal so that it cannot be viewed without a "de-scrambler," which is supplied for a monthly fee by the local STV company. Every major city will have at least one STV channel before the end of this decade, and many will have three or four. Los Angeles has long been served by two competitive STVs: ON-TV and SelecTV. Other cities have STV stations under similar brand names.

Piracy of STV signals is apparently common, since a wily engineer can build a de-scrambler box for under $100. Piracy is, of course, against the law.

Unused television channels also hold great promise for local interest groups and corporations in a mode known as "Low Power Television," or LPTV for short. If you are within the relatively small area served by an LPTV outlet, you may be able to see special-interest programs about religion, medical training, or dozens of other topics. LPTV applications in specific cities are now under consideration at the Federal Communications Commission; construction will begin shortly.

SATELLITES

Beyond the commonplace world of earthbound UHF and VHF television float the communications satellites. There are more than a dozen of these satellites now hovering 22,300 miles over the United States. They are in a "geosynchronous orbit," meaning that they move at precisely the same speed that the earth spins on its axis, so that these satellites seem not to move at all relative to the ground.

The concept of a communications satellite is fairly simple. A signal is transmitted from an earth antenna (called an "earth station" or an "uplink") to one of a few dozen transponders, which receive the earth signal and retransmit it to a receive-only earth station. Since one satellite can retransmit a few dozen signals, the antenna or "downlink" receives a variety of channels, which may be tuned in, one at a time.

Since a downlink looks more like a giant dish than a TV antenna, it is nicknamed a "dish." If you point your dish (or a cable operator points his dish) toward one satellite, to receive, say, Home Box Office, Showtime, Cable News Network, WTBS the Superstation, and so forth, the dish cannot receive signals from other satellites. The dish must be physically moved (they are usually quite large, so a motor actually does the moving—all you do is flip a few switches) to receive another satellite's offerings.

The cable network idea first came into its own when HBO discovered that they could reach lots of cable operators if they transmitted via satellite, and provided the cable operators with downlinks. The idea worked, and now every cable network is distributed via satellite. The broadcast networks use satellites for some program distribution as well. When a network transmits a signal to a satellite, it is basically relaying that signal to various cable systems, which assign the signal a channel number and pass it on to their subscribers on that channel.

However, it is possible for anyone to buy a downlink, and theoretically anyone can watch whatever he or she likes from these satellites without paying a network or a cable operator for the privilege. (This has not yet been tested in court.) For rural dwellers miles from the nearest town and hopelessly forgotten by the local cable franchise, a satellite dish may be the answer to limited reception. For a media fanatic, a home satellite receiver is the greatest gadget ever invented.

There are several commercial suppliers of home satellite rigs, each of whom markets primarily by mail (most video specialty stores lack the space necessary to demonstrate an antenna larger than a car's).

There are essentially three parts to your downlink. The first is a giant dish, likely to be at least 10 feet in diameter. This dish must be perfectly mounted and aimed at the proper satellite or it will not operate at all. Generally speaking, the larger the dish, the clearer your reception will be. Inside the dish sits a small antennalike device (see page 105) called a feedhorn.

The second component is an amplifier, which connects directly to the feedhorn. The amplifier increases the strength of the signals you receive. It connects directly to the third component, the tuner, which sits safely indoors beside your television set.

This tuner is not unlike the TV tuner you have been using for years, but the channel designations are different—tuning in a satellite is rather like searching for distant AM stations on the car radio in the middle of the night. You continually fine-tune until the signal is loud and clear.

A fourth component may be needed to translate the type of signal coming from the satellite into something that can be seen on standard TV sets. That component is called an RF converter (see page 39 for more about RF). If you own a VCR, you can pipe the signal through its RF converter and avoid the purchase of an additional electronic box. If you don't own a VCR, or its use is inconvenient, an RF converter should cost about $100.

Hooking everything up is theoretically easy, but one does not just unpack a few crates and start watching satellite TV. The basic setup steps are reasonable, but the dish itself is as big as a Volkswagen, and so a little cumbersome.

The best place to set up the dish is the south side of your house or lot, where it will be able to see satellites to the east and to the west without obstruction. If you live on the East Coast, you

STEP-BY-STEP GUIDE: HOME SATELLITE RECEPTION

1. There are a handful of satellites currently in geosynchronous orbit above North America, each with an extraordinary array of television programming (and data and audio programming). In order to receive that programming, you must aim your home satellite dish at a particular longitude and latitude, carefully focusing the feedhorn for perfect reception.

2. Once you've spotted the satellite (WESTAR 3, for example, which carries CNN, news from three networks, and a few cable channels), you must amplify the incoming signal with a line amplifier and then tune to any one of twenty-four available transponders, or satellite channels. Fine tuning can be an inexact process if your tuner is less than perfect.

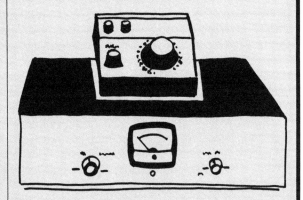

3. You are now receiving audio and video signals, which can be plugged directly into a television monitor. An RF converter (available by passing the signal through any VCR) will be necessary if you want to watch your satellite channels on a standard television set. (*Photo courtesy Downlink*)

can also use the west side of your house; vice versa if you live on the West Coast. You should avoid having a house (or a very substantial tree) blocking the line of sight from dish to satellites. Reception will be best in the center of the continental United States, and worst in the extremes of Florida, New England, Southern California, and Washington state. In areas where reception is difficult, plan to use a larger antenna dish to correct the problem. Once you've picked a site (which should be conveniently out of the way, because you're going to lay a cement base), you must first align the dish on a precise north-south axis, and then start to hook up.

Plan to use an area about 12 feet square for the overall satellite dish and base assembly.

Once you've positioned the dish (according to the installation instructions), you will set the antenna's feedhorn. This is attached by cables to the amplifier, then to the tuner, which is connected to the RF converter (or VCR), which is connected to your TV set. When you flip the switch on your VCR from TV to CAMERA, activating the RF converter, and adjust the face of the dish, you should eventually see a picture on the TV screen. Finely adjust the dish for a better picture, and then pour a cement base to fix the position permanently.

Note that the satellites are about 4 degrees (about $1/100$ of a circle) apart in the geosynchronous orbit, with an arc of about 50 degrees (about $1/7$ of a circle) from the easternmost satellite to the westernmost above the U.S. Your satellite dish mush face exactly the position of a given satellite in order to receive the signals properly. In order to move from the popular SATCOM I (home of HBO, among others) at 135 degrees longitude to WESTAR I at 99 degrees, you must move the dish 36 degrees, or the equivalent of $1/10$ of a circle. On a rainy night (rain does not affect reception in most cases), it's nice to know that a remote-control motor is doing all the work.

The prices on satellite receivers, including all the necessary accessories, begin at $4000–$5000 and run as high as $10,000+.

One drawback to satellites and their receivers should be noted. When your satellite receiver/tuner selects a channel from a particular satellite, this channel is the only one that can be seen throughout the house. In individual cases, this is no problem. But if you're planning to split the cost of a dish with your next-door neighbor, or, worse yet, with seventy other tenants in an apartment complex, *you will all have to watch the same channel at a given time.* At present, only one channel's signal is amplified, so only one can be seen on TV at a time. Although receiver technology is improving, this remains a problem as of 1982 and should be investigated before you buy a system.

Several specialized manufacturers sell satellite receivers both by mail and via regional distributors. Each of these manufacturers predicts that prices will fall slightly and that waiting periods of a year or more are likely when the trend toward home satellite receivers takes hold.

(Chapter 11 discusses the next step in direct-to-home satellite reception, with a proposal being considered by the FCC regarding new TV channels designed expressly for homes that buy a new —and inexpensive—satellite dish.)

■ 8 ■

VIDEOGAMES

A videogame is, in essence, a small computer that is designed to play games with you on your television screen. It is a "special-purpose computer," in that it only knows how to play games using custom programs in cartridge form.

The idea of a videogame dates back to the early 1970s, when two key events occurred. A creative engineer named Nolan Bushnell developed a coin-operated game called Pong, the first successful videogame. It was an electronic Ping-Pong game, where each player controlled a racquet or paddle (actually, a white dash), hoping to outmaneuver an opponent in ball-handling (actually "blip-handling" is a more accurate term—the "ball" was nothing more than a small white dot on the screen, which sounded a beep whenever it made contact with a paddle). Pong and its inevitable spinoffs (Pong Doubles, Super-Pong, etc.) were the first successful videogames, made by a new company (originally called Szygy) whose name would soon be changed to Atari. We'll be back to Atari in a moment.

At about the time Bushnell and company came up with Pong, a New Hampshire firm, Sanders Associates, headed by Ralph Baer, came up with a game system that could be played on any television screen. The revolutionary machine was called Odyssey, and it was the first *home* videogame. Sold by Magnavox, Odyssey didn't look much like the videogames of today, but they sure had the right idea. There were no on-screen graphics per se, only a white blip (close relative to the Pong blip). Odyssey used thin plastic overlays, which were attached to the screen, to play games like tennis, hockey, cat-and-mouse (hide-and-seek), football, roulette, and Simon Says. All games were based on the blip's ability to dance around the screen in a path prescribed by program cartridges. The cartridges were inserted into a special slot in the machine—precisely the design adapted by Atari, Mattel, and other videogame manufacturers some three or four years later. The blip's motion was always coordinated with the on-screen plastic overlay, so that you'd actually see a tennis ball (the blip) travel on a fairly realistic court (the overlay). It was a clever notion, but not one that was accepted readily by the public.

Atari, in the meantime, was introducing new games to the coin-operated arcade market as quickly as they could produce them. Other man-

The first videogame cartridge system for the home—Magnavox's Odyssey. (Photo courtesy N.A.P. Consumer Electronics Corp.)

Pong was one of the first home videogames, the beginning of a revolution in home entertainment. (Photo courtesy Atari, Inc.)

Atari's VCS, or Video Computer System, is the only way to play games like Asteroids at home. Note the cartridge (it says ASTEROIDS on the edge), which can be replaced by other game cartridges. (Photo courtesy Atari, Inc.)

ufacturers, including some traditional pinball and target-game makers, followed suit. Pong and its family of related games became fixtures in bars, bowling alleys, shopping malls, airline terminals, and just about every other public gathering place short of churches. America was Pong-crazy in the mid-1970s, and the time was right to introduce—you guessed it—a home version.

First came Pong, then SuperPong, then Super-Pong 10 and UltraPong, each a low-cost, special-purpose machine capable of playing only Pong-type games. The various Pongs were fun, but gimmicky and easily forgotten after a few weeks of play. Units that played only a single game were another false start in home videogames.

About two years later, Atari introduced a new product, priced higher than almost any other successful toy or game in retail history ($150). Called the Video Computer System, Atari's new videogame system was designed to attach to any television set and to accept any of a promised wealth of game program cartridges. This is the basic game system that Atari sells to this very day—with great success. And for very good reasons.

Atari's design of a cartridge system that could be programmed, instantly, to play different games was a shrewd marketing decision. The company would first introduce a game in the coin-operated format, and if the game was successful, it would then issue a home version. This was precisely the pattern of release for Breakout, Asteroids, Missile Command, and Atari licenses like Pac-Man and Space Invaders (for which Atari owns home rights—both were Japanese games originally, licensed to Atari competitors for U.S. coin-operated formats). As Atari continues to flourish in the arcade business, so will it in the field of home videogames.

The basic mechanics of Atari's popular Video Computer System (not to be confused with the same company's personal computer, which uses a similar cartridge-type program for many of its games and other applications, or the newer Atari 5200 unit, which uses still another cartridge size) are threefold. First, you must have a television set, and it is best if that set is a color set with a screen larger than 5 inches. You will find that an old color set will suffice, because the accuracy of the colors doesn't matter much with a videogame. The screen size is important because you must have a reasonable distance between, for example, the invading force and your missile bases in the game of Space Invaders; otherwise the game will be nearly impossible to play. A giant projection screen will work equally well (and the giant image really enhances the fun of the game), but the texture of play may change slightly due to its size. A black-and-white screen will do, but you'll lose a lot of the fun.

The second item you'll need is a console, a special computer that contains the logic of how a videogame works. Controllers, either in joystick, paddle, or push-button format (see photo), attach directly to the console. The Atari joystick controller is basically an 8-position switch, used mainly to guide action toward any one of the eight compass points (N, NE, E, SE, S, SW, W, NW), with a red button used principally to "fire." The Atari paddle controller is essentially a steering wheel, used in car races and in games

The Atari videogame system uses three different kinds of controllers: joysticks (left), keyboards (center), and paddles (right). (Photo courtesy Atari, Inc.)

involving a racquet (like Breakout). The Atari push-button controller is a keypad, laid out like a telephone push-button dialer. The videogame console also has a series of switches, controlling game difficulty and allowing you to select individual games from multigame cartridges and to reset any game to start. A slot in the top of the console is used for the insertion of game cartridges (plastic boxes open at one end); the opening allows the cartridge's internal electronics to make contact with the console's electronics. The cartridge contains a computer program, which includes specifics on how the screen display is to look, what the colors will be, how the console is to interpret the information that you are "inputting" by moving a joystick or twisting a paddle, what to place on the screen as a result of those interpretations, the speeds at which all of this is to occur, and so forth.

You need an individual cartridge to play each game or group of games. Some Atari cartridges contain only a single game, while others include variations on the basic format—a one-player version, a two-player version, a version where certain screen elements are not seen or where more invaders are added, etc.—or a few additional games. The number of games and variations in a cartridge is usually determined by the complexity of the basic game's computer program and the expense involved in mass-producing it. Cartridges vary slightly in price, partially because of the amount of computer technology used, partially for marketing reasons.

Atari's Game Program cartridges can be used only in their VCS game unit. You will find that cartridges are not interchangeable among any of

(Photo courtesy Atari, Inc.)

the videogame systems on the market, primarily for reasons of electronics, but also for reasons of size (only Atari cartridges, and cartridges made by other manufacturers for the Atari system, will fit into the mouth of a VCS).

The Atari VCS lists for $199.95, but it is available for less than $150 from discounters. Its 50+ cartridges generally cost $20–$30 each (some slightly higher). Many of the cartridges allow a dozen or more variations. Space Invaders contains 112 variations in all. In an electronic world where boredom is an eventual certainty, Atari's multiple-game and multiple-variation cartridges, and the increasing number of Atari-style cartridges made by other vendors, make that system very desirable—especially since the cartridges and the console unit are considerably less

expensive than those sold by Atari's principal competitor, Mattel.

Atari is not the only company that makes cartridges for the Atari VCS. Activision, a company started by some former Atari game designers, also makes some terrific games for the VCS and may well begin creating games for other systems as well. Parker Brothers sells two Atari-type games for the VCS; Imagic, Coleco, Mattel (under the name M Network), and Games by Apollo sell several as well. A review of the best games for the Atari VCS appears on pages 172–73.

Atari shares its lead in the videogame market with Mattel, a top name in both the toy field and in the realm of hand-held electronic games. Mattel Electronics' Intellivision is more expensive than the Atari system, but the higher price is justified because the unit plays more sophisticated games and shows them in a more colorful, engaging manner.

Intellivision is a tabletop console, not unlike

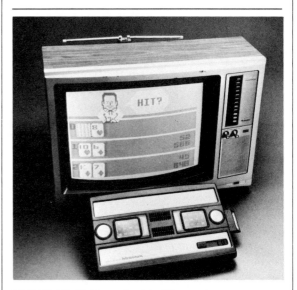

Mattel's Intellivision plays terrific sports games.
(Photo courtesy Mattel Electronics)

Atari's VCS, designed so that all switches are on a pair of multipurpose, hand-held controllers. The controllers are permanently connected to the console by telephone-style cords. Each controller contains a pressure-sensitive keypad and a flat disc control that acts just like a joystick. Every Intellivision cartridge comes packed with a thin plastic overlay, which slides directly over the keypad (see photo). This is a clever idea—

The Major League Baseball overlay is placed over the keypad, so that you can actually touch the man who is to catch the ball. (Photo by H. Blumenthal)

the plastic Baseball overlay shows a baseball diamond, and you actually touch the player to whom the ball is to be thrown or the fielder who is to make a play. Two additional buttons on the right side of the controller (repeated on the left side of the controller for the left-handed) are used in many of the games as well. These buttons are used in baseball to "bat" or to "bunt," in other games to "fire," and so forth.

The graphics of Mattel's Intellivision are better than those of the Atari VCS (although neither is particularly realistic). You will pay about $250 ($100 more than the Atari) for those

graphics and for other improvements resulting from Mattel's more powerful computer. Mattel, incidentally, calls its game console a "master component," because it also serves as the first half of a home computer, whose second half is called a "keyboard component," for obvious reasons. (The keyboard availability is limited to certain regions.)

As for the games on Intellivision, each cartridge is usually designed with only a single game, and many are designed only for two-player competition. The sports games are already classics, each new one better than what went before. Mattel, Coleco, and several other companies make game cartridges for Intellivision, priced at about $30 each. All cartridges are packed with keypad overlays and with instructions (which *must* be read—the games can be a little complicated). You will find a review of the best Intellivision games on page 174.

Since Atari and Mattel dominate the videogame market, you should compare all aspects of each system before you buy. The chart on page 112 should aid you in that comparison. (Note: This chart was created as of summer 1982, to be used only for general comparisons. Both companies will have already released new games by the time this book is published. Still, it does provide some interesting and helpful contrasts. Consult your dealer for updates.)

Atari has further complicated the videogame competition with a new, advanced system called Atari 5200. Introduced for Christmas 1982, Atari 5200 has a powerful computer, capable of far more colors, more detailed graphics, and a wider range of realistic sound effects.

Atari 5200 is used with a new kind of controller, which is capable of enhanced joystick, paddle, and keypad action. Note that Atari 5200 requires its own cartridges (they're larger than those used in Atari's VCS and personal computer systems). The initial group of 5200 games included improved versions of Pac-Man, Space Invaders, Star Raider, and excellent versions of

CATEGORY	ATARI	MATTEL
System price	$199.95	Under $300
Cartridges	$19–$45	$30–35 (some less)
Graphics	Good	Very good
Sound effects	Good	Very good
Available cartridges as of 12/1/82	Over 400	About 100
Average games per cartridge	About 20	3
Best sellers	Space Invaders	Football
	Asteroids	Baseball
	Circus Atari	Space Battle
	Missile Command	
	Pac-Man	
Ease of operation	Excellent	Excellent
Cartridge availability	Excellent	Excellent
Time required to learn games	5 minutes	10 minutes
New cartridge introductions		
1977	8	None
1978	12	None
1980	18	19
1981	4 + 12 (from Activision)	6
1982	Hundreds, from about a dozen companies Imagic, Coleco, Parker Brothers, Games by Apollo, etc.	10–15, plus many more from other companies

(Photo courtesy Atari, Inc.)

(Photo courtesy Mattel Electronics)

Atari's exciting new 5200 Home Entertainment System. (Photos courtesy Atari, Inc.)

Football, Baseball, and Soccer. System price: about $300.

One further development will take videogame players by storm—games that talk! Mattel Intellivision now offers an add-on module for speech. Special speaking games like Space Spartans and Bomb Squad, as well as talking versions of the system's most popular games, are in the works. The Atari 5200 will offer talking games in the near future as well.

There are other contenders in the videogame race. Running third is the company that started it all: Magnavox, with a system called Odyssey 2. This is another cartridge system that requires its own (incompatible) cartridges. The graphics aren't nearly as good as the ones on the Atari and Mattel units, which is unfortunate, because many of the Odyssey 2 games lose their appeal as a result of lackluster on-screen presentation. Still, games like Quest for the Rings make Odyssey 2 an interesting system. Controllers are joystick only, but the console itself contains a pressure-sensitive typewriter keyboard, making Odyssey 2 look more like a personal computer than a videogame. Odyssey 2 is a versatile system, with a reasonable price tag (under $150) and a good assortment of games (including some being made by Imagic and other companies).

An inconsistent pattern of machine and cartridge availability makes Astrocade difficult to recommend. The system itself, originally sold by Bally, the pinball manufacturer, is designed to work either as a videogame or as the beginning of a computer system (you can buy an excellent "learn to program" cartridge and instruction book for use with its built-in calculator keypad). Like the Mattel system, the Astrocade game unit is designed to fit into a larger computer system's keyboard housing, making it even more desirable. Astrocade is priced competitively with the Mattel unit. Nearly all the Astrocade games are good, and some are excellent.

The toy maker Coleco is the most recent entry into the videogame hardware business. Their new ColecoVision system looks a little like Intellivision, but it is far more versatile. ColecoVision can play its own cartridges (eight to start, including Donkey Kong, Zaxxon, Venture, and a game based on the Smurf characters), and it can play all Atari VCS cartridges as well (adapter required). The controllers contain 0–9 keypads, 12-position joysticks (compared to Atari's 8 positions), and a dial called a Speed Roller. The graphics and sounds are first-rate, making ColecoVision a prime contender in the videogame market—it's priced competitively with Intellivision. All of the Coleco cartridges have been designed for sale in three formats, so that you can buy a separate version of every Coleco game for either Atari's VCS, Mattel's Intellivision, or the ColecoVision system. Coleco is covering all bases in this rapidly expanding market.

You are likely to encounter a few other video-game systems in your travels, notably one made (and discontinued) by Fairchild. Don't buy a discontinued videogame system—*ever!* Regardless of the price and regardless of the manufacturer, a discontinued system will be impossible to service, and almost totally useless, because of the lack of available cartridges. Similarly, nix on game systems that play only one or two games—cartridges are the only way to keep your game system active in the years to come (you *will* get tired of a single game). There are a few foreign game systems that appear once in a while, but most are not as good as our own, and are made even less desirable by limited cartridge availability.

Insofar as overseas purchases go, you will certainly find that American-made cartridges are very expensive in Europe and elsewhere. Mattel cartridges are the same all over the world, be-cause the differences among television systems are addressed in the master components. Neither Atari consoles nor Atari cartridges can be used without modification outside the United States, Canada, and a few other "NTSC" countries (see page 154). Beware of game systems bought in other countries, as they may not work at all on American television sets.

Here in the States, you can buy the Atari and the Mattel systems at most department stores and appliance discounters. The Atari system is sold as a Sears system, and a Sylvania Intellivision is available as well. The products are identical. Mail-order buying is no problem for videogame consoles, and no problem for cartridges—just shop for the best price and deal with a reputable organization.

As for keeping current, the best way to find out about the latest cartridges is to find a friendly retailer who likes to play the games as much as you do. Failing that, check *Video* and *Video Review* magazines for their regular columns about videogames or see a new magazine called *Electronic Games*. Most of the new cartridges are released between July and November, just in time for the Christmas season.

■ 9 ■

PERSONAL COMPUTERS

All the devices covered up to now in this book have been mainly concerned with receiving or replaying programming created by somebody else (with the exception of video cameras, of course). As you become familiar with personal computers, you will see that program playback is only one side of video. A personal computer is best used actively—to run programs, and to create your own. The user does not require previous computing experience— loading a program is just a little more complicated than loading a videocassette. And writing programs isn't much harder, provided you have the interest and the patience.

A couple of definitions will help you begin to understand what computers are all about:

Computer: A single chip, the size of a child's fingernail, containing elements that process commands supplied in the program. The computer chip is generally connected to other electronic parts and circuits, to an input device (like a keyboard) and an output device (like a TV screen) in order to communicate with the outside world. The console that houses the circuitry, the chip, the keyboard, and sometimes the screen is also called a "computer."

Program: A list of commands and instructions that utilize mathematics and logic to cause a computer to act in a prescribed way.

ABOUT PROGRAMS

You will find that there are many prerecorded programs on the market. The most popular programs are games, including both the mental and the action/arcade variety. There are business, bookkeeping, tax preparation, real estate analysis, accounting, and word-processing programs available as well—leading a list of hundreds of programs custom-written for every popular computer on the market.

The programs available in computer stores or by mail are generally longer, more complicated, and more efficient than those you could write yourself. Each is a list of commands, written in logical order, to be read and interpreted by a computer as instructions. In the case of games, store-bought programs are likely to include flashy graphics, intriguing variations, and flaw-

Microsoft's Olympic Decathlon is a series of ten sports simulations that can be played on an Apple or TRS-80 personal computer.
(Photo courtesy Microsoft)

less play. Some are written by clever amateurs, but most are written by pros. Household and business management programs, written by professionals, are generally designed to be easy for anyone with no training whatsoever to use.

It is beyond these applications that the magic of having one's own computer really emerges. A fully equipped personal computer becomes an automated typewriter called a word processor for about $1000, including a special computer. Businesses can eliminate many bookkeeping chores by using the very same computer that teenagers use to do math homework or to play mystical adventure games in the style of Dungeons & Dragons. There are already programs available that will teach you how to fly a plane, control the resources necessary to maintain a small kingdom, increase your typing speed and efficiency, monitor the energy output of household appliances—and tell you dirty jokes. Some programs simply type words on the TV screen; many offer full-color animated graphics.

Each of these programs, these lists of instructions, is sold in one or more recorded formats.

Audiocassettes (which record computer data as what sounds like beeps and gurgles) are the least expensive, but also the least efficient. Some programs for selected computers are available on videogame-style (PROM) cartridges. The most popular program-storage format is the floppy diskette, a record played on a high-speed recorder/player. Each diskette holds enough programming and data for personal computing needs.

Computing at home began as a hobbyist phenomenon. Bright young engineers purchased integrated circuits, display screens, keyboards, and other electronic parts and built their own small computers. These early computers looked very complicated, required special scientific codes even for the simplest of operations, and were generally reserved for the scientifically minded.

In a garage that is now legend, two California college dropouts created a small computer that anyone could use. It was called the Apple. And it was the first small computer designed for the average person to use for common household and business tasks. Using money scraped together by selling their VW bus and a calculator,

The best computer programs actually prompt the user as to the action to be taken. This program is Atari's Touch Typing. (Photo by H. Blumenthal)

Steven P. Jobs, then twenty-one, and Stephen G. Wozniak, twenty-six, developed the first computer that could seriously be used in the home or office. Radio Shack, a company best known for hobbyist electronics and low-cost consumer items, introduced their TRS-80 home computer a short time later. These two companies dominate the home computer market to this day, selling more than half of all personal computers.

Both Apple and Radio Shack have created new products to compete in a field since entered by several other major companies, including Atari, IBM, Texas Instruments, Commodore (the third-largest seller of personal computers), and, most recently, Osborne, Xerox, and even Timex. In all cases, simplicity of operation combined with the power to accomplish complicated tasks has been the key selling point.

With almost no training at all, anybody can load a program into a computer. Computers are very much like videogames in that regard—aside from some operating instructions, they are essentially blank slates until a program is loaded into an electronic working space known as a computer's internal memory. The programs recorded on diskette or cassette are then duplicated in the computer's memory using a few simple steps. The routine varies with each system, but this Atari step-by-step is fairly typical. (The following assumes that the cassette player, computer, and TV set are properly connected.)

1. Turn on all three pieces of equipment (in a specified order).
2. Insert the program cassette. Press PLAY.
3. Type the letters CLOAD (short for cassette load) on the computer keyboard. Press the RETURN key.
4. The cassette should start moving (if not, tap the RETURN key once more). Allow one to five minutes (sometimes longer) for the computer to "gurgle" while its memory is being filled with the program. You'll know that the program is loaded when the TV screen displays the word READY.
5. To start using the program, type the command RUN.
6. The program will remain in the computer's memory until you turn the computer power off. (The program will remain on the cassette tape forever, or at least until it is erased.)

Loading a program from a floppy disc is more complicated, and also varies from computer to computer. You can learn the procedure in about five minutes for any machine.

Once a program is loaded, you generally need only follow the prompts on the screen. For example, in the Letter Perfect word-processing program that I am using to write this book, I see a "menu" as soon as the program is loaded. I choose the EDITOR mode, which allows me to compose new text. And when I'm ready to PRINT what I've written, I simply return to the menu, choose the PRINT command, and watch my printer generate the words I've just written onto manuscript paper.

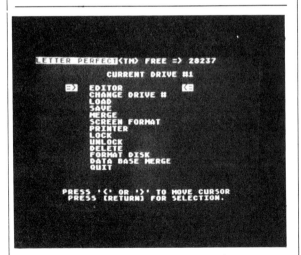

In order to write or edit text on my word processor, I would press RETURN to choose the EDITOR mode on this computer menu. (Photo by H. Blumenthal)

If the program was a game, like 3-D Tic-Tac-Toe, I would enter the first move to start the game.

And if the program was a mortgage-and-loan analysis, I would simply wait for the explanation page to appear and follow on-screen instructions as to how and when I should enter today's interest rate, the amount of the loan, and so forth.

Let's use a sample routine to demonstrate how a program works. It is a step-by-step affair, performing A before going on to B, B before C, and so on.

This particular example is a flashcard drill for children learning to divide by the number 9.

Each numbered step you see here in English is shown with its programmed equivalent in a computer language called BASIC. The program itself is in all upper-case letters; the explanations are in italics.

GOZINTO

10 REM GOZINTO GAME (*This just identifies the program*)

20 DIM A$ (5) (*Allows a name up to 5 letters*)

30 PRINT "HI THERE, WHAT'S YOUR NAME?": INPUT A$ (*Prints message, accepts inputting of name*)

35 PRINT (*Skip a line*)

40 PRINT A$: PRINT "I HOPE YOU LIKE GAMES" (*Print name, followed by message*)

45 PRINT "THIS ONE IS CALLED GOZINTO" (*Print message*)

50 PRINT (*Skip a line*)

60 PRINT "DO YOU WANT AN EXAMPLE?" (*Print message*)

70 PRINT "TYPE 1 IF YES" (*Print message*)

75 PRINT "TYPE 2 IF NO" (*Print message*)

80 INPUT B (*Accept entry of a number, label the entry "B"*)

85 IF B=1 THEN GO TO 500 (*If B is 1, the program skips ahead to line 500 in the program*)

90 IF B=2 THEN GO TO 100 (*If B is 2, the program just continues in order. This line is not actually needed in the program*)

100 PRINT "TELL ME HOW MANY TIMES 9 GOZINTO 27"; INPUT C (*Print message, accept entry, label it "C"*)

110 IF C=3 THEN PRINT "VERY GOOD, A$." PRINT "LET'S TRY ANOTHER GOZINTO" (*If C is 3, print the message including the name*)

120 IF 3>C<3 THEN GO TO 150 (*If C is larger or smaller than 3, skip to line 150 in the program*)

130 PRINT "I'M SORRY," A$ (*Print message and name*)

150 PRINT "THAT'S NOT THE RIGHT ANSWER. WHY NOT TRY AGAIN?" GO TO 100 (*Print message, skip back to continue from line 100*)

200 PRINT "HERE COMES THE SECOND GOZINTO" (*Print message*)

210 END (*We'll stop here. Note that if you'd entered 1 on line 85, you would have skipped this line entirely*)

500 PRINT "OKAY, HERE'S AN EXAMPLE. TELL ME HOW MANY TIMES 9 GOZINTO 18. I'LL GIVE YOU THE ANSWER." (*Print message*)

510 PRINT "THE NUMBER 9 GOZINTO 18 TWO TIMES, BECAUSE 2 TIMES 9 EQUALS 18" (*Print message*)

520 PRINT "NOW YOU TRY ONE" (*Print message*)

525 PRINT (*Skip a line*)

530 GO TO 90 (*Skip back to continue from line 90*)

And so on.

The logic that guides this program is very common. The commands used are typical of what you'll see in many computer programs. The command to print something on the screen is PRINT. The command to jump out of the program's numerical order is GO TO (as in "Go to step 8"). There is an IF . . . THEN command, as in "IF Suzy answered 3, THEN PRINT 'Suzy, you're so clever.'" All these are BASIC commands, used in the most common of personal computing languages, BASIC. (Other languages include PILOT, PASCAL, LOGO, FORTRAN, COBOL, and LISP.)

Programming a computer can be an absorbing creative process, initially requiring little more than a logical, clear-thinking mind and a few hours of reading and practice. It is said that the best programmers are not necessarily engineers or scientists, but chess players and musicians, whose sense of natural logic seems to parallel the programming mentality. Until you reach the advanced levels, your innate sense of logic will carry you through most programs you care to write. Be forewarned, however, that the process of programming a computer is time-consuming and tedious as well as addictive for many people. Programming is best learned by actually using a computer, preferably in conjunction with a textbook (or, better yet, with a teacher). One of the best books about programming in the BASIC language is called *Basic Basic* (published by Hayden Publishing, Rochelle Park, New Jersey). The book is most effective when used in conjunction with *The BASIC Workbook* from the same publisher. Each of these books offers generalized lessons, which must be modified for the computer you intend to use. Your computer store will be able to recommend programming instruction books written specifically for your computer system.

BUYING YOUR COMPUTER

Now to the matter of buying that personal computer, the most intriguing of all media room equipment.

You'll start with a television screen, which presumably you already own. A black-and-white set is sufficient, but color sets are better if you're using an Apple, an Atari, a TI, a Radio Shack Color Computer, or Commodore's MAX, VIC 20, or 64, because you'll be able to see the color graphics, and made-for-computer monitors are

The Apple II Plus desk-top computer is one of the world's most popular, and most versatile, computer systems. (Photo courtesy Apple Computer, Inc.)

best. These monitors cannot display TV pictures; they are exclusively for use with computers. Try not to go below a 7-inch screen, because the computer's display is tough to read on smaller sets. Hookup is as easy as any videogame—in fact, you can use precisely the same connections. Some computers, notably the Radio Shack Model I and III, the Osborne, the Xerox SAM (520), and the Commodore PET and CBM systems, come with their own display screens.

Your keyboard console usually contains not only a full-scale typewriter keyboard (plus a few specialty keys) but a series of integrated circuits containing those magical silicon chips we've heard so much about. Among these circuits are devices that are programmed to do arithmetic, to display images on a TV screen, to understand the pulses generated each time you touch a key on the keyboard, to communicate with other parts of the computer system, and to make the computer work as a single integrated system. There are also integrated circuits, or "IC"s, for available working memory (or RAM, for random-access memory), erasable with the input of

The silicon chip sits inside this integrated circuit. Several ICs are used to create a circuit board. One or more circuit boards are used to construct a computer. (Photos by H. Blumenthal)

can usually be upgraded. Machines like the Apple II and the Atari 800 usually start at about 16K, and can be upgraded to 48K, which is sufficient for most home uses. The largest desktop computers, like the IBM Personal Computer, can be upgraded to accommodate several hundred thousand characters of memory. You will find some programs that cannot be run on your machine with less than a certain amount of memory, meaning that the length of the program itself may be greater than the space available in the computer's RAM. Most personal computers are sufficiently versatile with 40K–64K RAM.

Beyond RAM, for reasons of available memory space and permanent storage (remember, RAM is wiped clean whenever the computer is shut off), you'll want to use accessory memory devices like diskettes or cassettes. When I write a chapter of this book, I can generally fit it, along with the word-processor software, in the 48K of memory space I have in my Atari 800. This Atari can accommodate roughly one chapter of this book, about 18K of operating instructions and word-processing software. A few of the chapters in this book, however, have been just a little longer, and I have seen the message MEMORY FULL on my screen. In order to complete the chapter, I must divide it into two parts. I load the first part onto a floppy diskette, which stores every word for future use. I can now erase this part from the computer's memory, which gives me the full working space once again, and start the second part of the chapter. When I have completed the second part of the chapter, I will store that on a floppy diskette as well, for future use (and for future editing, as you will see shortly).

Notice that I have chosen to use a floppy diskette to store programs instead of an audiocassette. The reason is a practical one: audiocassettes take a very long time to record and play back data, and simply don't hold very much information. Floppy diskettes allow faster loading, hold lots of information, and permit fast access

each new program and completely cleared each time you turn the computer power off. On most computers, you can increase the RAM by adding RAM cards or cartridges. Smaller computers generally offer about 8000 characters of memory (represented in computerese as "8K RAM"), but to individual entries.* Any old audiocassette player will work with your computer, and you probably won't have to buy a new one if you've got one lying around (although a new machine costs only about $30). A disk drive, one bought specifically for your computer system, will cost about $500. Individual diskettes are a bit more expensive than blank cassettes, but in fact they are more economical, because a diskette holds more information than a cassette.

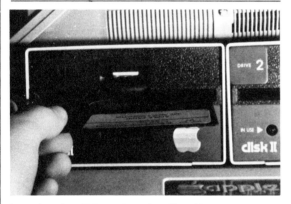

Inserting the diskette into the disc drive.
(Photo by H. Blumenthal)

On the left, dot matrix characters. On the right, characters printed by a typewriter.
(Photo by H. Blumenthal)

After you buy a personal computer, an audiocassette recorder, and a disk drive, you may find that the temporary display allowed by a TV screen needs to be enhanced by a more permanent display system. A computer printer is a $500+ addition that will turn your personal computing system into an even more valuable tool. The most useful printers use 8½-inch-wide paper (some wider) and will print dot-style letters as well as dot graphics. (A sample of this dot letter, more correctly called a "dot matrix,"

appears on this page.) For another $1000 or so, you can buy a printer that will print "formed characters," like those you see on an office typewriter.

A printer reproduces all the letters and numbers that appear on your TV screen, although not in strict line-by-line style. Most personal computers allow only 40 characters per line, whereas most printers can print more than twice that amount across an 8½-inch page.

A separate device, called a "plotter," will reproduce graphics (e.g., pie charts or bar graphs). Plan to spend well over $1000 for a plotter. Some of the newer dot matrix printers will reproduce screen graphics as well.

Some printers and plotters will not be able to work with your personal computer unless you add an interface, which essentially translates data so that various pieces of equipment can understand one another. Different computers have different interface requirements—be sure to ask about interfacing when you buy a printer, a plotter, or a "modem."

With a "modem," you can connect your computer to a telephone data network. Plan to spend about $150 or so for the modem, and about as

*You can store several programs, or data entries, on a single diskette or audiocassette.

A telephone receiver fits neatly into the modem. (Photo by Clark Dunbar; courtesy Atari Inc.)

much for the interface, if your computer needs one (some computers are built with this RS-232C Interface; others are not).

Computer accessories, known in the trade as "peripherals," can be seen at your local computer store. Look in the Yellow Pages for names like ComputerLand.

There are about a dozen consumer-oriented personal computer systems currently available, most starting in the $300–$1500 range. Each begins with a keyboard/console unit, connected to (and sometimes in the same box as) a cassette player. A fully equipped system, with disk drive, modem, and printer, will cost $2000–$5000.

If you are not already experienced with computers, it is wise to concentrate on the following brands: Apple, Atari, Radio Shack, Commodore, IBM, Xerox, APF, Osborne, Texas Instruments, Timex, Panasonic, and Quasar. Each of these systems is designed with a general user in mind, and most offer a sizable library of easy-to-use software, able to be mastered without too many hours of reading.

In the "under $400" category, there are several machines available, limited by memory space. These are designed for the beginner, mainly for education, games, a limited amount of home management (checkbook balancing, budgets, etc.), and as terminals for a data network (with a modem, of course). In this category: Commodore's MAX VIC 20, Atari's 400, the Radio Shack Color Computer, the Radio Shack Videotex, Texas Instruments TI 99/4A, and the Sinclair ZX-81 (a.k.a. the Timex computer).

Starting at just over $500 are the most versatile personal computers: the Apple II and Apple II Plus, the Atari 800, APF's Imagination Machine, Commodore's 64, and a few others that can be connected to your television set for full-color graphics. Radio Shack's TRS-80 Model I and Model III are both in this general price category, as is the Commodore PET line, but none uses a home TV screen (each comes with its own monochromatic screen). A full line of accessories is available for each system, all of which are incompatible with other systems. Take a look at the Osborne I as well. It's a big portable computer that comes with a disk drive, a screen, and hundreds of dollars worth of software for only $1799. It's not for everyone, but it might be quite a bargain for you.

The top-of-the-line category of desk-top computers is mainly for businesses. Systems made by IBM, Xerox, Hewlett-Packard, and Commodore for serious business applications are just too large and too costly for most home situations (and entertainment programs like games are tough to find for these solemn devices). The Apple III, which can play most Apple II programs, offers the best of both worlds.

You should also be aware of hand-held computers, sold by Panasonic (and Quasar, which sells the very same machine) and by Radio Shack. These are miniature computer systems, to be used alone or in conjunction with mini-printers, cassette storage, and even minimodems. Panasonic's LINK and Quasar's HHC ("Hand-Held Computer") are designed to fit into a standard-size briefcase. It's terrific for the salesman on the road and for the executive who likes

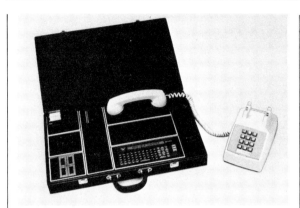

The Quasar Portable Computer System fits in a brief-case. (Photo courtesy Quasar Company)

to keep in touch. For home applications, however, HHCs are not yet appropriate, because of limited program availability.

THE COMMODORE VIC 20: AN INEXPENSIVE COMPUTER

For most home uses, you will probably buy either a low-priced or a medium-priced personal computer.

Commodore's VIC 20 is a particularly good example of a low-priced unit, usually available for less than $300. The VIC 20 is a perfect starter machine. It's physically smaller than most typewriters and appears to be little more than a keyboard. But it is a powerful little machine, and even the most uninformed amateur will understand its many uses within two hours of unpacking. A clearly written instruction book, leading the newcomer step-by-step through color graphics, sounds and music, calculations, and essential program commands, is the key for beginners.

The keyboard is a little intimidating at first, because each key can be used in up to four different ways—single keys display graphic symbols

and colors as well as alphanumerics. Example: Hold down CTRL (a shiftlike key) and the number 8 to get yellow characters. CTRL-7 changes the characters to blue. Several other special-function keys further reduce normally complicated routines to simple keystrokes.

The VIC 20 itself really is a starter computer, but one designed to accomplish a great many functions. It comes with PET BASIC, has nine 4K RAM, and is expandable to 32K. An optional modem, cassette player/recorder, and even plug-in game and program cartridges can be purchased to expand this $299 special into a second-level system (which may raise the system's price to the level of an Apple II or Atari 800). If you treat this as a system for games, for learning computer basics, and for connection to data services, you will be very happy with it. For word processing and most business applications, though, you'll probably want to look at more sophisticated systems.

AN ALL-PURPOSE HOME COMPUTER: THE ATARI 800

I believe that small computers are quickly outgrown and that one of the better consumer-oriented personal computers like the Atari 800 is a better choice, even for beginners. This machine is made to handle rigorous technical applications, but its design is simple enough for anybody to understand. The 800 requires no experience with electronics; any modifications that a user must make can be done with videogame-style cartridges. This is unlike the Apple, where one must actually remove integrated circuits and handle fragile electronic circuit cards to install, for example, disc drives. Best of all, the instruction books for the Atari are written by adults, for adults. Unlike the insipid cartoon simplicity that typifies other manufacturers' manuals, inevitably making an adult feel like a corrected child if he or she does not understand a poorly explained concept or direction, the simplicity and clarity of the Atari manuals are real. Just follow the instructions carefully, and you should have no problem with most of the common start-up procedures.

The Atari can be hooked up in minutes. Within the first half hour, there is no reason why you should not be playing Star Raider, one of the top Atari computer games, loaded into memory by the insertion of a cartridge. Other game cartridges include Basketball, 3-D Tic-Tac-Toe, Computer Chess, Missile Command, Pac-Man, Space Invaders, Asteroids, and Super Breakout. Each of these is played with an optional joystick controller, the very same one used in the Atari VCS videogame system (see page 109).

Other cartridges for the 800 include a four-voice music synthesizer called Music Composer and a color-screen painting system called Video Easel. There is also a cartridge called TeleLink, to be used when you are connected with a data network, and a BASIC language cartridge. Assembler allows sophisticated program creation. A special cartridge is used to activate the educational system. All of these cartridges come with extensive instructions, many in full color.

The Atari 800 is one of the few computers that perform all tasks in full color. (My word-processing screen has a light-blue background with white letters—much easier to view than Apple's and Radio Shack's white-on-black, or PET's green-on-black text modes.) As a programmer (or just a noodler), you can draw color pictures, create graphs or diagrams, or generally doodle by using a full keyboard of graphic symbols and commands with about an hour's instruction or study. Atari's keyboard is particularly good for text and graphics. Most keys have three uses: upper-case letters, lower-case letters, and graphics, each mode engaged by its own shift-type key.

Atari's 800 connects easily to other Atari components: the disk drive, an interface module, which is used to operate the telephone modem, and several printers.

The Atari 400 is a junior version of the 800. It has an inferior keyboard (touch-sensitive, not real keys), less internal memory capacity (the Atari 800 can go up to 48K, the 400 to only 16K), and a stripped-down number of features. It's a bit stronger than the Commodore VIC 20 described above and sells for about the same price.

BUYING SOFTWARE

Plan to spend about $800 for the 16K Atari 800 component, a few hundred dollars more for the

Atari's starter computer, the 400, can be used with a wide variety of sophisticated accessories, including printers, disc drives, and other items most often associated with the sophisticated Atari 800 computer. (Photo courtesy Atari, Inc.)

full-blown 48K machine. This is competitive with the Apple II Plus or Apple II. In comparing these two systems, you will find that many more programs are available for the Apple than for any competitive system, but Atari is encouraging the creation of new programs in hopes of eventually competing with Apple and with Commodore, also a system rich in software. When buying a computer, strong software support (in other words, the actual quality and number of programs available) is a vital concern.

Software is sold by large computer companies (Apple, Radio Shack, Atari, Commodore, and Mattel, etc.), by independent software publishers, and by clever hobbyists with a knack for marketing. The size of a software supplier has no relationship to quality: some of the finest programs have been created in basements and garages. There is no rule of thumb for the quality standard of software; one must have faith in the store or the mail-order operation where the program is purchased. Computer magazines (page 131) are good sources of information about available programs.

You will find that most available software is written for the Atari, Radio Shack, and PET systems. Under no circumstances should you attempt to use a program written for one machine on another—it will not work properly.

One of the best-selling programs in the personal computer business, VISICALC, is made by the software publisher VisiCorp. Its concept is straightforward and uniquely adapted to computers. VISICALC turns your computer screen into a calculator and worksheet—in effect, a very, very large sheet of accounting paper that appears only in small sections on your TV screen. You can position the TV "window" anywhere on the worksheet, and even split the screen to see two areas at once. In each VISICALC application, you plot rows against columns of numbers (heading each row and column with a word or date, of course). A sales manager can plot the names of salespeople in

Some of the more popular computer software, from manufacturers like Epyx, Adventure International, Creative Computing, SSI, Edu-Ware, and Data Soft. (Photo by H. Blumenthal)

one direction and their weekly earnings in the other. A teacher can plot children's names in one direction and their spelling test scores in the other. And so on. Column and row totals are always calculated automatically, and are changed automatically when you change an entry. Additionally, there is a "what if?" game that can be played on some or all of the numbers. If a teacher sees that the test scores were all too low, he or she might increase everyone's grade by 10 points, and then check the increase's effect on the year's averages, for each individual student and for the class as a whole.

VISICALC's program is sold on diskette by VisiCorp for Atari 800, Apple II, IBM Personal Computer, Commodore PET, Radio Shack TRS-80, and other systems. Remember that the diskette contains the program for a blank worksheet and all of its calculation capabilities. Once you've entered your entries (or "data") onto this worksheet, you must record what you've done on another diskette. *This must be done before you turn the computer off*, or else you will lose the program (and all the work you've done).

WORD PROCESSING

Word processing is probably the most practical reason to own a personal computer. A word processor will allow you to type onto the screen (actually into the computer's memory) and to manipulate what you've written. Once you've written and rewritten the text to your satisfaction, you may decide to print it, or to store the text for future use (and for future rewrites and edits) on a diskette. On-screen editing, where words and letters, even paragraphs and pages, can be moved, deleted, or even duplicated with the touch of a few buttons is one reason why word processing is such a convenience.

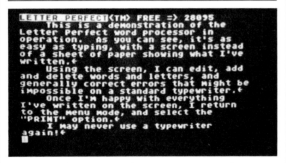

Typing on the screen is just like typing on the typewriter, except that correcting mistakes requires nothing but an electronic backspacer. The "cursor," the small white rectangle just below the text, shows where the next letter will appear.
(Photo by H. Blumenthal)

A few examples will show you just how terrific a word processor can be. I offer these examples from direct personal experience, as I'm using a Letter Perfect word processor on my Atari 800 to write and edit the entire manuscript for this book. (I will never use a typewriter again.)

The program is loaded from a diskette to my Atari 800's internal memory, and a menu appears on the screen. I select the EDIT mode, so that I can start to compose my text. I usually code each chapter with instructions, telling the printer to double-space, to number each page in succession, and to stop printing at the end of every page so that I can change sheets of typewriter paper by hand. Then I start to type. If I make a mistake, I can just back-space to the letter or word and retype (no correction ribbons, no Liquid Paper, only an electronic backspacer). If I don't like what I've written, I can go to the beginning of the line, the beginning of the page, or any place in the text and start over again. If I don't like a specific copy block at a certain point in the text, a few keystrokes will lift that block and drop it into a secondary memory (a "buffer") for later editing, or later elimination. Chronically misspelled words are no problem—a "search" mode will find each misspelling of a particular word and replace it with a correctly spelled word. (It does not contain a dictionary—I must tell it which problem words to go after, and how they are correctly spelled. It only does the replacing automatically.) All of these commands are accomplished by pressing the CTRL (short for CONTROL) key while depressing individual letters. Mnemonic devices can help you remember the codes. (I call my "eliminate everything after this point" routine "Control Yucch," because its command is CTRL/Y.)

Once it is typed, I usually SAVE the entire chapter on a disc. (To SAVE, one simply returns to the menu and selects the SAVE option.) I usually make a second copy of the chapter on another disc (for protection) and then PRINT it (another menu selection). I then edit my PRINTed copy, LOAD (another menu option) the previously recorded disc version of my masterpiece, and go back into the EDIT mode to enter my changes. Then I repeat the SAVE procedure, generally using the DELETE option to erase old versions from the diskettes.

You will find that Letter Perfect is typical of most word-processing systems; if anything, others offer even more options (e.g., being able to split the screen and look at two sections of text at once).

As with other programs, a word processor must be written for one specific computer. I used the Letter Perfect initially because there was no other word processor available for my computer, the Atari 800. Since that time, Atari has started selling its own word processor, and a company called DataSoft has introduced a program called Text Wizard. Since I started on the Letter Perfect, and all my diskettes were programmed according to that program's specifications, I could not change processing systems (even if I wanted to) in midstream.

You will find many word processors available for the Apple II, the Commodore PET, and the Radio Shack TRS-80. With trade names like SuperText and WordStar, you will find word processors and text editors (lower-level word processors) priced as low as $100 or so, and up to about $500 for personal computers (some higher). Before you buy, compare programs in a computer specialty store (see page 132); type an identical page of text into each, make a few corrections, line insertions, and deletions, and see how quickly, clearly, and efficiently the word-processing program performs. Be sure to test each program on a machine identical to your own.

One further point in favor of word processors: You can merge a good word processor with a mailing-list program, thereby generating freshly typed, personalized letters to a mailing list of thousands. Spelling and grammar checkers are available as well.

GAMES AND EDUCATIONAL PROGRAMS

Although computers have become routine in many school curriculums, there has been no single outstanding software that far surpasses all others. Scholastic (the magazine publisher) now sells educational software, as does a computer-user group called Santa Cruz Educational Software. Many textbook manufacturers and suppliers of educational materials are also entering the software market. For the latest in educational software, visit your local Computerland or other computer retail store. If you're an educator, look into Scholastic's *Electronic Learning* magazine.

Closely allied to the field of education is the computer game. Computers play great games, either as opponents (they can be taught to compete at whatever level you like) or as dazzling animated gameboards for play between human opponents.

The Atari is the best game computer, with many game cartridges available at reasonable prices. The best of these games is Star Raider, a game that uses both joystick action and keyboard control.

Star Raider seats you in the cockpit of a spaceship, requiring that you constantly adjust your velocity and energy requirements and placement in space via keyboard control while using the joystick to steer the ship, firing at enemies. The screen becomes a cockpit window, which can be adjusted for either fore or aft view or, with a keyboard command, a chart of the galaxy. One's imagination easily escapes into the adventure when playing Star Raider, particularly on a giant screen. Computer versions of arcade favorites like Missile Command and Asteroids are also available for play on the Atari system.

Although less a game than an instructional tool, Flight Simulator is an equally fascinating simulation, using diagrams of real airports to make the adventure more engaging.

Other fantasy simulations, some along the lines of Dungeons & Dragons, others based on their own witty concepts, are available from a wide range of software houses. Try Temple of Apshai (EPYX) or any of the Scott Adams Adventure programs.

ABOUT THE SOURCE AND COMPUSERVE

Anyone with a personal computer and a telephone can use the resources of the nation's most popular data bases, The Source and CompuServe. Please note that the rates and schedules listed below were correct as of early 1982; all information is subject to change.

THE SOURCE

For information, contact:

Consumer Relations
Source Telecomputing Corporation
1616 Anderson Road
McLean, Virginia 22102
800-336-3330 (except Virginia)
703-821-6660 (only in Virginia)

Sign-up Fee: $100 subscription charge, one time only.

Rates: Midnight–7 a.m., every day: $2.75/hour; 7 a.m.–6 p.m., Monday–Friday: $15.00/hour. All other times, including weekends and holidays: $4.25/hour. (All times listed are for *your* local time.)

Free Demonstration: In computer stores throughout the country.

Billing: Visa, MasterCard, American Express, or direct billing to your business.

COMPUSERVE

For information, contact your local Radio Shack store, where applications are available. An application is also included in every Atari TeleLink cartridge.

Sign-up Fee: None.

Rates: 6 p.m.–5 a.m. weekdays, all times on weekends and holidays: $5/hour. All other times: $22.50/hour, with a 2-hour minimum.

Demonstration: At many Radio Shack stores and at some computer stores. The first hour is free if you become a subscriber (provided the hour is at night).

Billing: MasterCard, Visa, direct billing to home or business.

SAMPLE OFFERINGS

Thousands of programs and stories are available from The Source and CompuServe. Below you will find a sample grouping culled from each service's index. The codes at the right of each entry are used to access each entry—e.g., type the letters "Go CIS-49" to see a computer adventure game on CompuServe.

COMPUSERVE

Editorials:
 Columbus Dispatch ....GO CDP-16
 Los Angeles Times ....GO LAT-80
 The New York Times ....GO NYT-11
 San Francisco Chronicle ....GO SFC-10
 San Francisco Examiner ....GO SFE-50
 The Washington Post ....GO TWP-60
Fashions ....GO NYT-13
Federal agency reports ....GO TWP-38
Federal diary ....GO TWP-55
Federal government schedule ....GO TWP-53
Federal publications ....GO CIS-144
Feedback program ....GO CIS-7
Financial advice:
 Raylux ....GO CIS-34
 The Washington Post ....GO TWP-37
Financial commentary ....GO RFC-1
Financial services ....GO CIS-21

Fireplaces, firewood ....GO GPO-9
Food and food preparation:
   Articles ....GO LAT-93
                                         GO TWP-94
   Food and diet ....GO NYT-13
   Food storage ....GO GPO-7
   Food-borne illnesses ....GO GPO-7
   For fitness...GO GPO-5
   Freezing...GO GPO-7
   Menus, meal planning ....GO BHG-1
   Recipes ....GO BHG-1
Football (AP wire)............................GO APN-16
Football computer game...................GO CIS-43
For sale ads ....GO CIS-24
Future prices ....GO CNS-1
Games, computer:
   Adventure ....GO CIS-49
   Blackjack ....GO CIS-48
   Football ....GO CIS-43
   Spacewar ....GO CIS-44
   Star Trek ....GO CIS-46
Gardening ....GO TWP-82
Gasoline, how to save........................GO GPO-6
Gold prices..GO CNS-1

If you read the list carefully, you will start to notice a pattern of cross-referencing and the frequent use of acronyms (NYT for *The New York Times*), even when the source of the information is not so identified in the left column.

THE SOURCE

Using The Source is not quite as simple, because of the arrangement of its information. You'll find that the codes for each item make more sense than those used above, but you will also find that CompuServe's system of branching from a general category to one that's more specific is far better arranged than the orchestration of The Source programs, most of which are simply listed individually by name.

Here's a sample list from roughly the same spot in the alphabet as the CompuServe list (certainly out-of-date by the time you're reading this, but you'll get some sense of arrangement):

Editorial ....DATA EDITORIAL
Education ....DATA EDUCAT
Electrical engineering ....DATA ELECEN
Electric vehicles ....NYTCDB (P0046)
Emergency numbers ......DATA EMER
Employee-owned com-
   panies ....NYTCDB (P0048)
Energy (savings) ....ENERGY
English lesson ....R INWORD
Equal Rights Amend-
   ment ....NYTCDB (P0049)
Equipment lease vs.
   purchase ....R LORB
Equity capital cost ....R EQUITY
ESP ....DATA ESP
Esperanto lesson ....R ESPERO
Etiquette ....DATA LORE
Exchange rates ....UNISTOX (040)
                             AUTO FRANC
Executives ....NYTCDB (P0050)
Executive selection
   (astrological) ....EMPLOYQUEST
                             CHOICEQUEST
Exobiology ....NYTCDB (0051)
Expenses ....DATA TAXTIP
Factorial stats ....INFO FACT
Fair trial vs. free
   press ....NYTCDB (P0052)
Fairs and festivals ....POST READ FAIRS-
                             AND-FESTIVALS
Fall distance stats ....INFO FALL
Family life ....NYTCDB (P0053)
                             UPI F 1485
Family shopper ....UPI F 1167
                             DATA BUCKS
Farmer (game) ....PLAY FARMER
Fashion ....UPI F 1129, 1473
Fast-food industry ....NYTCDB (P0054)
Faults (wine) ....WINE (P037)
Features index ....UPI F
Federal land bonds ....UNISTOX (061)

 The organization of these two services is dramatically different. Under GAMES, for example, The Source requires you to go to a subindex for a list of commands that will start games like Adventure, Chess, and other standards. CompuServe allows you to find the first page more directly, with a code number straight from the index. In either case, you can gain proficiency in finding most of what you're looking for within a few hours of practice.

 Both services review their libraries regularly, so it's wise to request a current index when you first decide that you would like to subscribe. A complete index is available from each service's library as well.

Every computer user should be familiar with games like HMRABI. Atari sells a version of HMRABI (it's a made-up name) called Kingdom, requiring the user to control the resources of a small country in hopes of feeding its people and increasing its borders and its productivity. A failure will cost you your head.

These and other simple computer games are available in written form (you simply type what you see in print to make your own program) in books like David Ahl's *101 Computer Games.* All such games are written in BASIC, but you must be sure to buy a book written with your specific machine in mind—otherwise you will spend hours changing commands and rewriting the programs, or, more likely, you will give it up in disgust. These games are usually text only, with no graphics or sound effects.

COMPUTERIZED DATA NETWORKS

If you're not so ambitious, or do not care to buy a program each time you want to try something new, you might consider a subscription to a data network. There are two general-interest networks available to personal computerists: The Source and CompuServe (a third network, the Dow Jones News/Retrieval Service, specializes in business information). All are used by connecting your computer to a modem, which is in turn connected to the network via a Touch-Tone phone. You will also need some inexpensive software ($20 or so) to teach your computer how to communicate with the network (Atari's TeleLink is an example).

Both services charge by the portion of hour. Each requires preregistration, mainly for the assignment of a secret entry code to be used only by you. A membership fee may be required as well.

"About The Source and CompuServe" on page 129 will show you how to contact each of these networks. Connection is easy, but some patience is required because incomplete connections do occasionally occur.

The Source and CompuServe are general-interest networks, offering not only programs—biorhythms, astrological forecasts, loan analysis, educational exercises, lots of games, and a solid selection of workaday applications—but also banks of information (the UPI wire arranged by topic, many newspapers and financial services similarly arranged). The chart on pages 130–31 lists some of the best offerings from each of these networks, as well as pricing information.

Comp-U-Card is another futuristic service which, for instance, makes it possible to use a personal computer and modem to shop for discounted merchandise.

All the services described above are quite new, but this by no means exhausts the available personal computing services. Keep in touch with these companies, and check in at your local computer store for more information about data networks.

COMPUTER MAGAZINES AND BOOKS

For more about personal computing in general, several popular magazines are your best sources of up-to-date specifics. *Popular Computing* is the best for beginners. Articles about everything in this chapter, and many topics not discussed for lack of space, cover what can be done and how to do it yourself without technical training. For an even more technical overview, try *Byte.* For more about Atari, Apple, and Commodore software, including many programs you can write yourself (with a little practice), try *Compute!* Other, smaller magazines deal with specific computer systems—they're available at your local computer retail store. Stores not only stock the latest in hardware and in software, as well as books and magazines, but will share all they know about personal computers with prospective buyers and with regular customers. At many stores you can even set up an appointment for a private demonstration. Some stores also organize informal groups of users for occasional meetings to trade information. Generally, the computer store is the single best place to learn more. Take your time and try a personal computer on for size. You will be pleasantly surprised at all you can do without any training at all.

PUTTING IT ALL TOGETHER

There are two prime aspects to putting your media room together—first, the various video accessories needed physically to connect, switch, and maintain all the equipment discussed so far, and second, the adjustments in room design necessary to create your very own media room, custom-tailored to your present and future needs.

As you begin to buy video equipment, you will acquire an impossible group of ugly black cables as well. As soon as you own two or more devices, you will have to unplug and rewire every time you want to change the input to watch television, or you will need to buy a switcher that automates the process. If you decide that production is your bent, you can find accessories that will dramatically improve your home-brewed video programs. Hundreds of other video-related accessories are available, from magic electronic boxes that improve picture quality (called "image enhancers") to plastic lids that protect your equipment from dust. If you wanted the most versatile media room, you could spend almost as much money on accessories as on the equipment itself. It is wise to know about the wide range of available accessories before you

buy; you may find that the perfect tool has been invented to meet your special needs.

The best source of information about the latest accessories are the video magazines (*Video Review*, *Video*, etc.), reviewed on pages 86–87.

For most people, the single biggest problem in creating a home media environment is the connection process. A tabletop VCR comes with two cables and one AC cord. Your cable box comes with two cables and one AC cord. A LaserVision videodisc player comes with three cables and one AC cord. It's very confusing—a tangled mess, unless you know what you're doing.

The best way to cope with the connection process is to be alone in the house, and to spend the afternoon alone. Put on some music. Then attack.

Start by planning connections on paper. Draw everything in a box diagram (see pages 134–36). Think of each signal as a train that must make stops along a continuous track. If you want to record from cable, the signal must first come from the cable into some kind of tuner (so that you can change the channel); then it must go into the VCR (so that it can be record-

SAMPLE CONNECTION DIAGRAM

It's always best to plan the connections between machines *on paper* before you start wiring up. Your diagrams need not be fancy (boxes with names of equipment are fine). But you must think about the connections in a step-by-step process.

In Figure 1 below, the signal passes from the cable station through a tuner to the TV set. Note that the lines have little arrows that show the way in which the signal is flowing.

Figure 2 isn't much more complicated in theory. There are two signals here (the cable and the cassette), but both of them pass through the VCR on the way to the TV set. A TV/VCR switch on the VCR itself allows you to choose between the two signals. The newer cable-ready VCRs allow you to eliminate the cable-TV tuner box entirely and simply use the tuner inside the VCR. The theory, however, remains the same— the signal comes from the cable system through a tuner, and then becomes one of two available signals from the VCR feeding into the one TV set. This business gets very complicated in practice if you spend too much time trying to follow the instructions that come with your VCR. Just try to think logically about the way the signal must flow, and make sure that the connectors you're using are the right ones for your TV set.

FIGURE 1

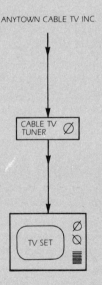

FIGURE 2

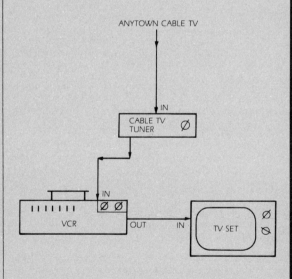

If your system becomes as complicated as the one in Figure 3, you cannot escape drawing a connection diagram before you start. The cable TV signal here is an RF signal, but the video-game signal is not. Ultimately, only one signal can be fed to the TV set, and the small aluminum game/TV switcher that comes with your videogame (or personal computer) is the only way to accomplish the connection.

Once you've invested in anything more than a VCR and cable, you should probably consider buying a switcher. Reconnecting wires every time you want to change the program source will be a bother, and probably quite a mess because of the sheer number of wires involved. On

electronic schematic diagram, it is really just an expansion of the RF switcher idea. Pick any input device and trace its signal—you will see that most can be seen on either one of two TV sets or can be recorded on the main VCR. There are several appendages to the main connection pattern, like the second VCR and Detailer in the lower left, which allow the main VCR to make fine duplicate copies of tapes, and the computer and videogame in the lower right, which can

FIGURE 3

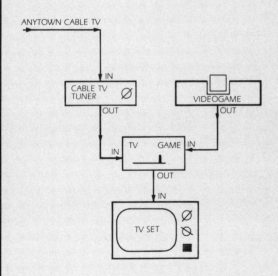

FIGURE 4

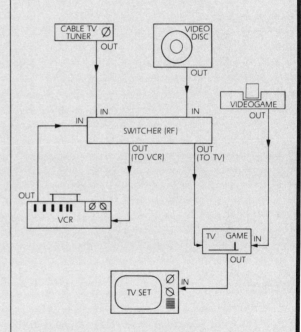

Figure 4, all the RF devices (the videodisc, VCR, and cable-TV tuner) are fed through an RF switcher, which will subsequently allow signals to pass not only to the TV set but to a second device, like the VCR, as well. Notice the game/TV box used to connect the videogame, and the RF switcher's "to TV" signal passing through it in the lower right corner.

Although Figure 5 begins to look more like an

only be seen on the second TV set. Note also that a small switcher is used to choose either the game or the computer unit before the proper signal reaches the game/TV box.

You can also connect this mass of machinery to your stereo system. The videodiscs connect just like a turntable, with a stereo audio cable. Your TV set's earphone jack can also be connected to one of the two channels on your stereo system (so that sound will come out of both speakers, you will have to switch the stereo into "mono" operation).

Since every media room is different, it is best for you to draw your own connection diagrams. The ones pictured in these diagrams represent actual connections used by the author in the development of his own media room.

FIGURE 5

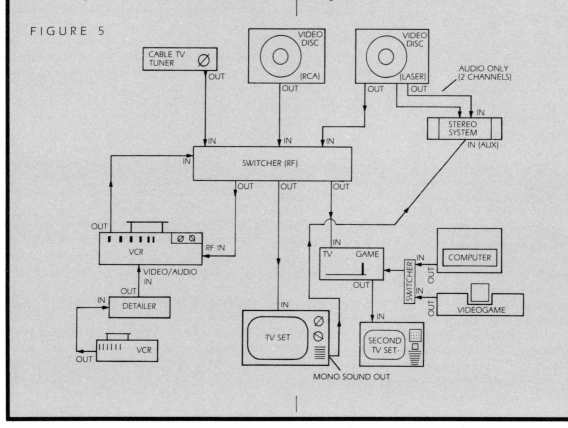

ed); and then back out of the VCR and into the TV set (so that it can be seen). Every signal path is logical. Every signal moves in a step-by-step pattern. And, contrary to the ridiculously complicated diagrams in most of the instruction manuals, the process really does make sense. If you've ever hooked up a stereo system, where the signal must flow from the turntable to the amplifier to the speakers, you should have almost no trouble hooking up video equipment. The key to connection is thinking about what you're doing (or finding a good friend who can do the job for you).

SWITCHING

If you own more devices than just a VCR or disc player, and you want to avoid rewiring every time you play a videogame, there are switchers available that will do the job with the touch of a button. Distrivid makes several switchers (known as RF switchers because they switch RF signals—see page 39 for more about RF). The Distrivid IV can accommodate three output devices—mine is hooked up to the living room television, the bedroom television, and the VCR. It can handle four different inputs (cable, VCR

Distrivid is one of several RF switchers that can help organize the mass of wires and connections that are endemic to media rooms. Everything plugs into the back, so wires are hidden away. Using the box is easy—just select the source for your main TV, your recorder, and, if you have one, a second TV set. (Photo by H. Blumenthal)

The "RCA plug" or "phone plug" is most often used when passing direct audio or video signals from machines that are near one another. It is commonly used in home stereo systems, and will also be found in videogame, personal computer, and VCR-to-monitor connections. Again, the RCA plug is used to pass direct video and audio signals (not RF signals). (Photo by H. Blumenthal)

The "coax connector" is most often used when passing RF signals. You'll find it in your cable TV system, and in connections between your home TV set and your VCR and videodisc machines. (Photo by H. Blumenthal)

playback, and, in my case, the RCA and the Pioneer disc machines). I can watch any of the four inputs on either TV set, and can even watch one signal in the living room and a different one in the bedroom. At the same time, I can record any of the signals on the VCR. Aside from relabeling the buttons on the Distrivid IV for my own clarification, hook-up was pretty easy once I sat down and took the time to make a diagram of what was coming into the switcher and what was coming out.

The only problem with RF switchers like Distrivid (there are several varieties available from a number of different manufacturers) is that they can be used only with RF signals. Distrivid cannot handle video/audio signals, so it cannot be used without modification with stereo playback devices. Video games are also a problem, because they use RCA connectors for their RF signals. Other switchers work with video signals, but they're not as easy to use as the Distrivid unit.

Note also that an RF switcher is actually a "splitter," that is, it splits a single signal among as many as three different outputs. Splitting a signal may cause weaker signals, of particular concern if you are recording for a permanent library. Clever use of the switcher will eliminate splitting problems; you can record a non-split signal and then feed the VCR's playback, which will be identical, to the TV sets in the house. RF switchers may also attract stray off-air signals in some areas.

VCR MAINTENANCE

After you've owned a VCR for some time, you will probably notice a slight disintegration of picture clarity. This deterioration is most often due to a build-up of dirt and stray oxide particles on the VCR's sensitive record and playback heads. (A few years after you buy the VCR, you will almost certainly replace the heads, at a cost of not less than $100, and perhaps as much as $300.) You can improve the pictures provided by aging heads *slightly* by cleaning them with one of several systems on the market, but the abrasion of the cleaner may cause damage beyond slightly dirty heads. It's best to leave the job of VCR cleaning to the repair shops.

Most of the videotape manufacturers make head-cleaning cassettes, among them Scotch, Fuji, and TDK. These are not nearly as effective as the Allsop cassette or the swab-and-alcohol method. Use these occasionally, every few months or so, between visits to the service shop.

If you want to keep your VCR reasonably dust-free, buy a plastic cover. There are several custom-made plastic covers available for most popular machines. Covers are available on a limited basis for other equipment as well. It's generally wise to keep all your equipment in some sort of cabinet, a semipermanent location if possible. Moving equipment around is never a good idea. A cabinet is also a good way to hide the wires (more about that later in the chapter).

VCR ACCESSORIES

If you're recording a program from television, you may want a recording free of commercials. There are several boxes that will electronically eliminate commercials, albeit not flawlessly. Shelton's Editor is the most widely advertised. This device is wired between the TV tuner and the recorder. It kicks in the VCR's PAUSE mode whenever it detects a high percentage of video black—most often the dip to black between a program and a commercial, but sometimes the black of a night scene during the body of the

These boxes are called the "editor" because they can edit the commercials out of an off-the-air recording automatically. There are three different models, each to be used for a designated VCR. One word of caution, however: The editor sometimes edits out portions of shows as well as the commercials. (Photo courtesy Shelton Video)

show, since it cannot distinguish between the two. The machine remains in pause for about 30 seconds, then restarts the recorder. It's an imperfect system, because commercials are sometimes played in a 30-second cluster, sometimes in a 60-second cluster; at times up to 3 minutes of commercials appear in sequence during a late movie. Add some 10-second station identifications, news breaks, and promotional announcements, and the entire detection procedure can occasionally result in a very confused recording. As of this writing, there was no better commercial detector than the Shelton unit (actually, there are several Shelton units, each for a select group of VCRs). There have been rumors of systems with higher accuracy (Shelton claims 95 percent), but none has appeared on the retail market.

Less reliable commercial systems will sound an alarm when black appears, but will not stop the machine—you must do that yourself. There is also a system that will flag color commercials during black-and-white movies, terrific for old-movie buffs.

Under normal circumstances, if you are duplicating a videocassette, you will lose some picture quality. In order to guard against major picture deterioration, you can pass the signal through an image enhancer. Vidicraft makes several fine enhancers under the brand name Vidicraft Detailer. Three controls are available: detail, sharpness, and core (which minimizes the "snow" caused by high detail and sharpness settings). The detail and sharpness controls are most useful; there is a real increase in clarity when these are properly adjusted. The unit is easy to operate; anyone can adjust the knobs to make the picture look right according to personal preference. The unit can be used in three modes: for black-and-white, for color, and in a "bypass" mode. If you want to see just how much the picture is being improved as a result of the Detailer, switch in and out of the bypass mode. In most cases, the difference will be significant. Image enhancers can also be used between the playback VCR and the TV set.

The Detailer mentioned above is the Vidicraft

Model II. It can accommodate three input machines and four output machines, but only one signal at a time. Vidicraft is one of several companies in the business of enhancing home video signals.

Note that image enhancers work with *video* signals as opposed to RF signals. Audio signals are unaffected.

If you're having a tough time playing prerecorded tapes, there is an electronic box known as a "stabilizer" or a "copyguard stabilizer." The stabilizer was originally designed to ensure perfect playback of prerecorded tapes on all VCRs. Most people seem to buy these boxes to dub illegally prerecorded videotapes.

This video accessory will not only stabilize pictures from finicky prerecorded tapes, but will convert an audio/video signal to an RF signal (see page 39) as well. It's made by Vidicraft.
(Photo courtesy Vidicraft)

This Vidicraft image enhancer is used to improve the clarity and color of recorded video images. The MODE knob on the left is used to tell the Detailer II whether color or black-and-white images are being shown or simply to allow the signal to pass without enhancement. The DETAIL, SHARPNESS, and CORE are used together to adjust the signal to your own preference. The final INPUT knob is used to select any one of three incoming VCR signals.
(Photo courtesy Vidicraft)

Many VCRs can duplicate prerecorded tapes without the use of any accessories. (A technical statement—your own morality will have to guide whether you take advantage of this feature or not. If you are planning to duplicate prerecorded tapes for your own use, you are probably outside the law. If you are planning to duplicate tapes for sale or paid screening, you are inviting a visit from the FBI and are risking a prison sentence and a fine.)

You probably won't need an image enhancer or a copyguard stabilizer unless you take your video very seriously.

DESIGNING YOUR MEDIA ROOM

Once you've made all your buying decisions and connected the various video devices to one another, you must decide how this pile of hardware should fit into an otherwise attractive living room or den. Even without a giant-screen television set, you really should consider the design of a media area to maximize function and viewing pleasure.

The first factor in the design of a media room is function. You must decide precisely what you need the room for, the number of people who will be using it, the practicality and convenience of individual pieces of hardware. If you're going to play a lot of videogames, you will need the videogame unit *near you*, although the screen can be anywhere in the room. If you're going to play tapes or discs, there's no need for any equipment near the seating area. You won't have any interaction with the playback machine except for loading and unloading tapes. If you're computing or doing word processing, you'll need the keyboard and the screen near you, in a convenient work (or play) area.

There are five key questions that must be answered before you start work on your media room. If you are to avoid an endless stream of bills and a pile of partially connected hardware, it is best to answer these questions honestly, before you spend any money:

1. How much money are you willing to spend on the entire project, including video equipment, installation, delivery, new furniture, and accessories, and, if it's your style, the work of a professional designer?
2. Where are you going to set up the media room? The living room, den, bedroom, large kitchen, home office, playroom are popular choices.
3. How often will you actually use your media room? How many different functions will it serve at once?
4. What kind of design do you want? How functional or flashy do you want your design to be?
5. Will your equipment be central to your room's design? Do you want the equipment hidden, or will you allow the equipment to share a design statement with other furniture and accessories?

Designers agree that good planning is the key to a successful media room. The process is not as simple as arranging furniture—the wires and connections will be a cumbersome, perhaps even dangerous impediment to arranging a media showplace on a whim.

The proper way to plan a media room is on paper. Take the time to measure the room, lay it all out on a sheet of graph paper, and don't buy anything until you feel very secure with the whole plan. Then make a shopping list, and try to make a budget, not forgetting the cost of new woodwork and possibly a paint job to conceal wires. You will be investing no less than $5000 if your room has a big screen, and probably as much as $10,000 to $20,000 if you're at all serious about creating an environment. If you're satisfied with the workmanlike and homely, you can spend less, but you will still need some cabinetry, however simple. Take your time, consult local furniture stores and video stores, and do the job right. Measure all major pieces of furniture, and most important, think about the way that you like to watch television.

The TV screen (or screens) may or may not be the design center of the room but should be visible from the room's most popular and comfortable seating area. If seats are less than 6 or 7 feet from the screen, you might pass on a projection set in favor of a good standard (e.g., glass-enclosed, old-fashioned) color TV or one of the new high-quality monitors. Any kind of screen is perfectly acceptable for your media room, but projection sets are much flashier (and much more expensive). A seating arrangement some 8 feet or more from the screen is perfect for most projection systems.

When designing around a projection system, you must be very aware of light. A projected image will always look best in semidarkness. Common sense tells you to avoid the sunniest corner of the room, but window shades, discreet placement of lighting instruments, and dimmer controls will help to correct for lighting in difficult room locations.

One further note about seating: Projection systems are usually designed for an eye level of about 4 feet from the ground. If you intend to raise a seating platform or to arrange tiers of theater-style seats, not all screens will deliver optimum images to all viewers. Choose carefully—and measure!

You can see a reasonably bright, colorful image from a projection set at about 60 degrees to the left and right of screen center (sometimes even 70 degrees, depending on the set). The best images, however, are seen head-on, or 30 degrees on each side of center. This goes only for projection sets. The clarity and color saturation of a standard glass-enclosed set is totally unaffected by viewing angle.

It's usually a good idea to sketch out exactly where the screen and seating area will be as you design your media room. Use these two elements as "anchors," and then arrange other furniture and equipment to complete the room. No special furniture is essential in the design of your media room—the creative use of ordinary furniture will usually do the job. Several manufacturers do sell customized video cabinets, to help place the video gear in an organized environment and to hide some of the wires.

Most modern furniture stores now stock audio/video cabinets. Some of these are called "music benches," designed mainly for audio gear (try Workbench, or any store which stocks Scandinavian designs). Some are sold as deep bookshelf-style cabinets, with smoked-glass doors to hide the equipment and removable back pan-

els to make connections easy. Others have roll-out shelves. Most furniture store models are sold in simulated wood designs for less than $500. Real wood or aluminum or glass or plexiglass cabinets are available, but almost always for a premium price. You may also build these cabinets yourself, or have them built for you.

Remember, however, that all this equipment is fragile and sensitive to extremes of temperature and humidity. Leave plenty of space for ventilation (2–3 inches on back, top, and sides).

If you are considering custom work, it might be wise to talk through your ideas with a professional designer. There are a great many tricks that lead to more efficient design, particularly if you want the equipment to be inconspicuous. One designer broke through a living room wall into an infrequently used bedroom closet. He created an enclosed alcove for the equipment. When in use, the equipment was visible. When not in use, the equipment was hidden by a large flat piece of modern art. Another designer eliminated the boxy coffee-table look of a video projector by building it into a much larger kidney-shaped coffee table.

You can design your own media room, but you will do your best work if you visit a few other media rooms first (or at least look at a few pictures in *Video* magazine and publications like it). See "Suggested Designs: Your Own Media Room" at the end of this chapter.

A quality video retail store (not a discount house, unless you've come upon a very caring discounter) should be able to tell you about media rooms they've designed or supplied in your area. In the New York City area, where this book was written, both New York Video and Liberty Music/Video are involved in the design of two or three media rooms every month. Both stores encourage prospective clients to plan carefully, and to discuss plans in detail with their in-house experts before any purchase or construction begins. It is vital that the store work with you in the planning stages, even if

LAYING OUT THE MEDIA ROOM ON GRAPH PAPER

If you plan to use your media equipment as an important part of a room's overall function, it is best first to construct your room on graph paper. This is easy to accomplish in a step-by-step manner.

1. Use standard 8½" by 11" sheets of four-squares-to-the-inch graph paper. Establish the scale as 1 inch equals 2 feet. (If your room is larger than 20 feet long or 15 feet wide, you will need bigger paper.)

2. Measure the room by starting in one corner and working around in either a clockwise or a counterclockwise direction. It's best to measure each wall twice, first as one entire unit and then as the sum of each smaller portion (wall + window + wall + doorway + wall). Draw first a long line that equals the entire length of the room, and then draw darker line segments that accurately show where the windows and other openings are in the wall. Complete all four walls of the room.

3. Measure the main pieces of furniture in the room, accurate to about 6 inches. Draw each as a box or a circle on a separate sheet of graph paper, and write the name of each piece as you go. Now cut out each piece.

4. Start arranging the furniture by placing each cutout in its place on the graph paper you designed in step 2. Be particularly aware of space between furniture—be sure to leave enough room for human traffic. Also, be conscious of angles, not only in relation to the TV screen but between pieces of furniture (if you're going to use part of the room as a conversation pit, for example, be sure all chairs can comfortably face one another).

Here are four sample graph-paper media rooms. One is a small family room/bedroom (including a convertible sofa), one is a full-size bedroom, the third is a full-scale living room, and the fourth is a workroom/playroom. Each one was drawn in less than one hour.

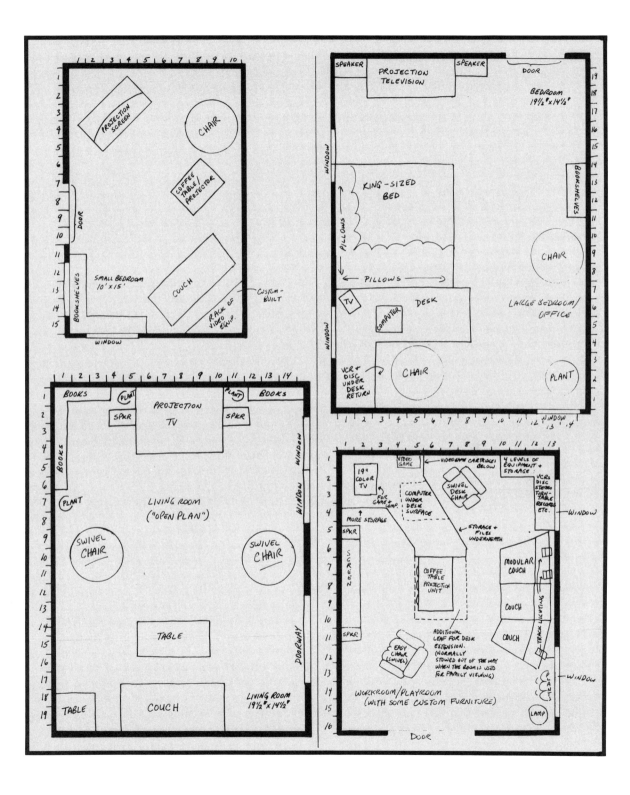

your plans seem conventional. This becomes very important when, after following all the rules, the screen just *looks* enormous and you want to trade it in for a smaller model. If you've been working with a store from the start, this should not be a problem. If you're out to save a few dollars, your discounted giant screen may turn out to be a bad purchase decision indeed.

Also consider versatility. This year you may adore your Japanese motif, but next year you may opt for a more traditional design scheme. What happens to your media room when the futons and rice-paper panels become recreation room junk? And what happens if you simply decide to move? Twenty percent of Americans move every year, so if you're average, you'll be moving within the next five years or so, according to the book *American Averages* by Barry Tarshis. If you planned well, you may have to buy a new cabinet and some extension cords, but the key features of your media room should be adaptable to your new environment.

Consider also the possibility of modular building, so that each piece of furniture can be easily moved without disturbing the entire environment. You can buy modular couches that can be rearranged in minutes at most furniture stores, and modular video cabinets from your RCA dealer. As your needs change, as new equipment comes out, as your tape and disc libraries grow, your furniture should grow with them. Smaller cabinets, which can be placed either side by side or on top of one another, do the job well. If you build a series of 24-inch-wide by 10-inch-high by 10-inch-deep box modules yourself, you will be able to house almost any VCR or videodisc, or even a tape library. If you're doing the building, leave the backs open and build the bottoms flat, so the modules can be placed on top of one another. A 5-inch-high platform is fine for informal living situations. If you're more formal, build your platforms as storage cabinets 13 inches high, so that you can keep books and record albums behind the cabinet doors.

The media room is usually a place to entertain, to show movies and videogames as big pictures. The effect of big pictures is even more awesome when big sound is added. If you are considering a full-scale media room, you probably already own a stereo system. You can use your amplifier and stereo speakers with all your video equipment. All the disc systems play back in stereo, and some VCRs do so as well. Some cable channels are delivered with stereo sound, and many PBS concerts are simulcast on area FM radio stations. Even a mono signal sounds better if it's pumped through an amplifier—connect the earphone or AUDIO OUT of your TV set to the AUX IN of your amplifier, and turn the amplifier's MONO/STEREO switch to MONO to get sound from both speakers. For best results, place the speakers on either side of the screen, at least four feet apart.

You'll get the best sound in your media room if it is about three quarters hard surfaces (bare walls and ceilings, windows), and one quarter soft surfaces (carpeted floor, drapes, large fluffy couches, soft furniture). Most normal room arrangements will provide adequate ambience. Rooms that are entirely without soft surfaces will sound a little too lively; rooms with carpeted walls and ceilings, or completely filled with furniture, will sound dead. Common sense should prevail. Consult an audio store for more specifics—and bring pictures if you like. (An equalizer, available in most quality audio stores, can solve the ambience problem for a price.)

Media rooms are most often built in living rooms and dens, but any room will do. Many large corporations are redoing their conference rooms as media rooms for group training, display of computer data, and teleconferencing. A writer's media room and study might include a small screen on the desk by the word processor and a giant screen in the distance, for viewing old movies while writing screenplays for new ones. A bedroom can be a media room, too—there's nothing more luxuriously decadent than remaining in bed for an entire day of life-size soap operas.

In all cases, try to keep the lighting soft, controlled by dimmers. The ideal lighting for a media room is situated *behind* the viewer, either glowing from the ceiling or from the floor. Track lights are fine, if they are aimed to bounce off a wall behind the viewer. For best results, keep your field of vision free of all lights. (Or turn off all other lights in the room when you're watching, but keep a light on behind you to reduce eye strain.)

As you're designing, you might also consider an extended media room, with more than one screen. One family in my neighborhood has two screens in the living room alone—a giant screen, and a small portable, which uses a headset so two soundtracks won't be heard at once. Both sets are hooked up to a switching system, along with sets in the master bedroom, in the kitchen, and, believe it or not, in the bathroom. Any set can show disc, tape, cable, or regular TV. They keep promising to install a camera in the bathroom as well, but have yet to fulfill the promise.

If you are a family that tends to center around kitchen activities, there's no reason why the media room can't be set up in the kitchen, in whole or in part. There's nothing to prevent you from having equipment in more than one room—so long as you're willing to take the trouble to interconnect everything properly.

There are no hard-and-fast rules in creating your own personal media room, just good advice and the benefit of experience. Think about function first, before you start contemplating the flash of an expensive hardware showplace. Think seriously about how all this new equipment can be integrated into your style of life. Careful planning will allow you to create precisely the kind of viewing room, electronic study, workroom, family room, recreation room, or neighborhood gathering place that will serve you for years. Or at least as long as your equipment stays current for, ever looming in the distance, there is the be-

wildering series of choices that will be posed by the incredible future of consumer electronics.

SUGGESTED DESIGNS: YOUR OWN MEDIA ROOM

The notion of a media room usually conjures up thoughts of horribly expensive showplaces, but this need not be the case. A media room is essentially a place to watch television, and it is important to keep sight of that function as you start planning and designing.

You really can build a handsomely equipped media room for under $5000, including furniture. (See photo above.) Here's a budget, based on a real shopping trip through New York City's discount stores in 1982:

–Sony 19-inch color TV (wood cabinet)—$499
–Panasonic PV-1770 full-featured VCR—$859
–10 blank TDK T-120 VHS tapes—$125
–Panasonic PV-4100 portable VCR with power supply (no tuner)—$750
–Pioneer VP-1000 videodisc player with optional remote controller—$600

–10 Laserdiscs—$250
–RCA SelectaVision Videodisc Player—$400
–10 CED discs—$250
–Atari VCS videogame—$130
–10 Atari cartridges—$250
–Vidicraft Detailer II—$219
–Distrivid IV RF switcher—$75
–"Music bench"—$350
–Additional cables, extension cords, adapters—
  $100
–Cable TV installation—$50

Total price: $4907
(If you live outside a large metropolitan area, add
at least 10 percent to the price.)

It would be difficult to argue that the media
room described is incomplete. Still, the owner
was in need of even more media equipment. In
his home office, he added some computer gear
and an additional television set, which is wired
to the main media room.

The price of the additional equipment was
$2591, which might be budgeted as follows:

–Atari 800 Computer (48K)—$750
–Atari 810 Disc Drive—$444
–Atari 825 Printer—$629
–Atari 850 Interface—$159
–Atari 830 Modem—$159
–Panasonic CX-7711 7-inch color TV—$350
–Additional cables, connectors, storage—$100

The equipment you see cost the owner roughly
$7500. The owner has been toying with the idea

of a projection screen for just over $2000
("rounding out the investment to an even
$10,000 . . . and change"). Unfortunately, he has
a one-bedroom apartment (the office area is a
corner of the kitchen), and the living room/
media room would be completely dominated by
even the smallest of the projection screen units.

In terms of design, the basic concept is "one-
wall." The Scandinavian-style music bench/wall
unit allows all equipment (including some videodiscs and audio records) to be conveniently
displayed. The bookshelves even double as videocassette storage. The drawer on the right side is
deep enough to hold videogame cartridges.

The 19-inch color TV can be seen from any
place in the room, but it is most often watched
from a couch that is situated parallel to the wall
unit, at a distance of about ten feet. The videogame unit is placed on the coffee table when in
play; it is stored in a cranny just above the white
box on the lower right. It is the only piece of
equipment that must be moved in any way prior
to use (the AC cord and the cable that connects
the game unit to the TV must be unraveled, and
a GAME/TV switch must be shifted).

All other switching is accomplished through
the Distrivid IV RF switcher.

The office Toshiba color set also receives its
signals from the Distrivid IV (four REMOTE TV
switches allow viewing of VCR, Laserdisc, RCA
disc, or cable).

Although the room design is quite different, the same basic equipment was used to create this custom media room below. With the addition of a projection screen, a Kloss Model One coffee-table projector, and some custom cabinetry, the price of converting this living room to a fully equipped media room was estimated at "just over $10,000." Note the speakers placed just below the screen surface—the best possible layout for lifelike TV sound.

The seating arrangement in this oblong room is fine for viewing, but potentially conversation limiting. The owner has solved this problem by using easy chairs that *swivel*, so that they can face either the screen or the couch. The track lighting could have been placed more strategically—it would have been more functional if it was as far back as possible in the couch's nook.

The only problem with this room is one that is easily solved. Notice the wide expanse of space in front of the projector. Nobody can stand or walk in that space without disrupting the picture. If the very same projector were hung from the ceiling (easily done by a professional), it would be more convenient. (*Photos courtesy* Video *magazine*)

If you have the space, you can integrate the projection screen into an overall sleek design. The New York City apartment below is blessed with an extremely large living room. On the far left there is a conversation pit that is totally removed from the media environment. Built-ins all on the same wall eliminate clutter and lend a futuristic touch. The far right corner is an entranceway. In the foreground is a couch, which is shaped to allow the best possible viewing angles to the projection screen.

At the center of the room, two comfortable leather chairs swivel either to the screen or to the couch for conversation. Between them, there is a custom-built coffee table that houses a Kloss Model One projector.

The coffee table itself is designed to accommodate the media room functions and to serve as a storage area. The top of the table is divided into two parts. The right side is built to slide out from under the left side, revealing controls for the projection set, a pair of cable-TV tuners (one for each of the TV sets on the wall), remote controllers for the videotape recorders, and a telephone.

The straight-on shot of the viewing wall shows

(under the speaker at the upper left) a custom switching center (mainly for stereo speakers in several bedrooms—the video switching here is really not very complicated at all). A stereo amplifier and stereo audiocassette recorder sit above the Sony color TV set (the owner prefers to watch only certain kinds of programs on the giant screen, and does a "healthy amount of viewing" on the regular-size screen). The audio turntable is safely inside the nook below the TV set (it rolls out to allow the owner to change records).

The giant screen speaks for itself. It is angled perfectly, and because of the size of the room and its brushed-aluminum paneling, the screen seems to fit right into the overall room decor. Two videocassette recorders are nested beneath the screen (note that there is sufficient open space on all sides for ventilation). The owner has been contemplating a videodisc player, but says that he is confused by the different formats and is waiting for the competition to work itself out. And just where would he put the disc player? Two possible places: either in place of one of the VCRs ("I don't really use the second one anyway") or in one of several nooks that are hiding behind the empty panels. (The designer considered possible expansion, albeit on a limited basis, when the room was first built.)

Also note the pair of speakers built into the wall above all the other equipment. All the wiring and cables are located behind the viewing wall (the backside of this wall is a closet).

Clearly this room is the work of a professional designer, the result of a great deal of planning and money. With a little imagination, however, you could use the best elements of this design in a much smaller, far less lavish media room in your own home.

If you ever have the opportunity to tour somebody else's media room before you build your own (this can sometimes be arranged through a retailer), make a list of the clever design features.

Here are some of the best ideas in the media room pictured on page 148:

1. Hiding all the cables behind the viewing wall. Using a closet to store the cabling is a good idea, but only if the closet is large enough to accommodate the wiring.
2. Nesting the coffee-table projector into a larger, more functional coffee table. The sliding top helps to hide the equipment when not in use. The front doors, which slide out of place when the projector is used, both hide and protect the lenses.
3. Adding a telephone to the coffee table.
4. It's a good idea to plot the best possible viewing area before buying a couch and then to try to buy accordingly. The couch used in this room was custom-made, but a standard modular couch and some imagination could do the job as well.
5. Swivel chairs.

Built-ins are also the key to the clean look of the next media room—built into an 86-foot yacht! A Sony coffee-table projector is the room's centerpiece, with the screen recessed into the far wall as further guard against reflected light (this recessing was necessary because of the number of windows in the room—it is not necessary in most rooms). Two stereo speakers are built into the viewing wall, just below the screen. (It doesn't matter whether the speakers are above the screen or below it, or even on the sides. Just keep them reasonably close to the screen to ensure realistic sound.)

The video equipment is racked with the audio equipment in a high-tech display in one corner of the room, to the left of the screen near the door. In fact, most of the equipment is audio gear. The owner of this yacht has only one VCR in his rack—but he also happens to own 2000 movies. Unfortunately, these are not always accessible on the boat; most are stored in his *other* media room, in his home.

The design of this room is remarkably straightforward for all its wonderfully elegant appearance. Notice the curved couch, designed to maximize viewing angles, and the large comfortable swivel chairs in the room's center. It's a very pleasant place to watch a movie, to observe activity around the boat (there are several video cameras mounted on board), or just to relax.

This media showplace was designed by Howard Holtzman & Associates, Kildeer, Illinois. (*Photos provided by Howard Holtzman*)

All these successful media rooms have several key concepts in common:

First, they were all planned very carefully before the purchases were made.

Second, they were designed to be used both as living spaces and as media rooms. You can't have one without the other and still be happy with the place you have created in your home.

Third, and most important, each was designed with *function* as the most important element in the design. It is important to set priorities relating to equipment and possible expansion according to function before you start working out the physical design.

Try your best to borrow ideas from other media rooms before you begin your own. Keep a clipping file as an increasing number of media rooms are described in the home-decorating and video magazines. Visit any media room you can

in person. Talk to your retailer about your plans, and try to buy from one store if you can. Keep them apprised of your progress—they will almost certainly be interested.

So long as you plan carefully, there is no reason why you must construct the entire showplace at one time. Try starting with a music bench, like the one at the start of this section, and fill the open spaces with books or bric-a-brac until you've completed your media room.

THE PORTABLE MEDIA ROOM

You're going to be away from home: traveling on the road, on vacation, or at the beach for an afternoon. And there's a movie you've been watching or a TV show you can't miss. There's no reason why you can't take it with you. All the equipment pictured on pages 151–53 will fit in a tote bag, under an airline seat if you like. Most of it can be packed in an attaché case. And all of it will run on batteries.

Portability has been the greatest advance in consumer electronics in the 1980s. In the 1970s, city streets were invaded by "boom boxes" blasting disco music from giant, yet portable, speakers. City dwellers lacking a taste for loud street music cursed the electronics industry for the plague of this relentless beat.

Then suddenly the streets grew silent. The musical exhibitionism afforded by boom boxes was no longer stylish. It was replaced by an ostentatious privacy. City dwellers of all ages and cultural persuasions now opted to block out street noise with personal stereos. Boom boxes were replaced by lightweight headphones and paperback-size cassette players of remarkable fidelity.

Roller skaters and joggers were among the first to buy the trendy Walkman in 1980. A year later, Walkman was only one of more than a

Sony's Walkman revolutionized portable entertainment. (Photo courtesy Sony Corporation)

dozen portable stereos available. More important, personal audio systems became socially acceptable for everyone. Accountants take lunch-hour breaks in the park, listening to jazz; young mothers block out shopping-mall noise with Chopin and Chicago; busy executives on airplanes and commuter trains withdraw to private worlds of beautiful music.

With miniaturization, all media equipment will eventually have pocket-size kid brothers. That process has clearly begun in a big way with Walkman and its knockoffs. It has also taken shape, albeit to a lesser degree, in many other electronic media.

Panasonic's Travelvision is aptly named; it is one of several truly lightweight TV sets, smaller and lighter than most radios. You wouldn't think such a small box could be a TV, but it will deliver good clear black-and-white pictures (see the photo taken from a Travelvision screen on this page) even under marginal conditions. Travelvision is a little over 1 inch high, about 3

inches wide, and 5 inches deep. It will fit into a large purse or the pocket of a man's sport jacket. The latest Travelvision sets contain Walkman-style radios as well.

The technology of color TV has not yet developed to a point where inexpensive pocket sets can be mass-produced. By the late 1980s, though, pocket color television sets should be available at popular prices. For the next few years, a color TV set will be the bulkiest element in the portable media room. Still, the 5-inch Toshiba is sufficiently small and lightweight to be carried in a tote bag with other equipment. This set has a built-in handle as well.

The Toshiba is well suited for almost any portable use. No special boxes or connectors are needed to use it with a videocassette recorder or as a TV. And, like all the devices in the portable media room, the Toshiba CA-045 can be operated on batteries for at least an hour; the battery pack is an extra piece, purchased separately. Panasonic, JVC, and Hitachi make portable color sets of comparable quality. Panasonic makes a set with a smaller color screen as well.

Panasonic's Travelvision is smaller than most portable radios, yet it contains a very clear $1\frac{1}{2}$-inch television screen (as well as an AM/FM radio on some models). Photo is actual size. It's battery- or AC-operated. (Photo by H. Blumenthal)

Toshiba's CA-045 is a portable color TV that can be operated either as a monitor or as a TV set. Battery, car, or AC operation available.
(Photo by H. Blumenthal)

Portable video recording and playback are really just beginning; portable VHS and Beta recorders were not introduced until the late 1970s. A Japanese company called Funai started marketing one of the first minivideocassette formats a short time later, sold by Technicolor in the United States. Although there are several other minisystems available, the Technicolor is currently the only portable VCR that weighs less than 8 pounds. In a truly portable media environment, this VCR would be used as a playback-only device. It can record off the air, but only with a special tuner or from a camera, and each of these pieces is too large to fit into our mythical tote bag with all the other equipment. The cassettes used in this VCR are smaller than other videocassettes, and there are no prerecorded movies or other programs available in this format. If you intend to watch tapes, you must either make copies from your library of VHS or Beta masters or watch your own productions originally recorded on this machine. The only way to solve this problem is to buy the lightest Beta VCR, which weighs in at about 9 pounds, plays commercially recorded tapes, and, to be honest, requires a slightly bigger tote bag—it's a

few inches larger in two dimensions than the Technicolor unit.

Prerecorded audio affords many more choices. When the Walkman was introduced, it was a small box that played audiocassettes, with sensational fidelity, through a featherweight headset. From there it was a short step to the transistor radio's logical successor, the FM Walkman. AM and recording capability were soon to follow.

Toshiba's AM/FM/recorder/player is an extremely clever system. It looks like most portable stereos, with a clear panel for insertion of the cassette and the usual control buttons (play, rewind, fast forward, stop/eject, as well as high tone/low tone and related functions). Playing tapes is easy enough—just place a cassette in the slot, close the door, and press PLAY. But where's the radio? It's on another cassette. Actually, two other cassettes. The FM stereo tuner is built into a cassette-size cartridge, which makes contact with the KT-R2's amplifier when locked into place. There is an AM cassette tuner available as well.

The KT-R2 will also record, in stereo. Two built-in microphones in one corner of the unit can be used for interviews and the like. The unit

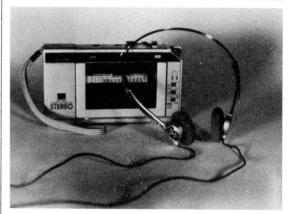

Toshiba's KT-R2 is one of the most versatile Walkman-style machines.
(Photo courtesy Toshiba America, Inc.)

can also be connected to external microphones or to a stereo system for recording of other material such as record albums.

Several playback-only cassette players are available, in stereo, from the better manufacturers. There are players available from companies you've never heard of as well—generally Oriental imports without much promise in the service area should the machine break down. There are radio-only portable stereos available from most name manufacturers as well. The same lightweight stereo headset can be used with all such systems and, with an adapter, with your home stereo system as well.

A quality audiocassette recorder can store more than words and music on tape. It can also store information and computer data when connected to *any* small computer, including an Apple, Atari, TRS-80, or any of the popular desk-top systems.

There are several personal computers that will fit neatly into a briefcase or tote bag with all the portable media gear we've already discussed. Some even offer printers.

Radio Shack's TRS-80 Pocket Computer may look like a calculator, but it is, in fact, a full-scale small computer. It can be programmed in BASIC language to solve many mathematical problems, store business records, prepare travel expense reports, and (most important to many of us) play games. Input is accomplished with the use of a small keyboard, similar to a typewriter keyboard, except that tiny keys do not allow for smooth, rapid typing. You can see what you've typed on a readout and on the optional printer. You can save what you've programmed on a cassette recorder.

The Sinclair ZX series (sold by Timex as well) looks, and behaves, much more like a professional desk-top computer. The keyboard is touch-sensitive and, although a bit cramped, works very much like a typewriter. The ZX is always used with a TV set, and will display calculations, BASIC programs, and games on any screen,

Radio Shack is one of several companies that sell pocket-size computers. Although this TRS-80 looks like a calculator, it will handle most simple computing functions. The system is even more powerful when attached to a cassette player/recorder like the KT-R2 described elsewhere in this chapter. (Photo by Radio Shack, a Division of Tandy Corporation)

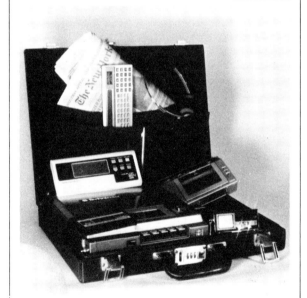

This full-scale media room fits into a standard business-size briefcase. Besides today's New York Times (an item no media room should be without), the kit includes Radio Shack's Pocket Computer, Technicolor's portable color VCR, Toshiba's KT-R2 stereo cassette recorder/player/AM/FM radio (with headset), Panasonic's Travelvision, and even a pocket-size electronic game (Computer Gin by Mattel Electronics). (Photo by H. Blumenthal)

ABOUT FOREIGN TV SYSTEMS

The technical systems of television and video vary slightly in different areas of the world, so American and Canadian equipment for the most part cannot be used elsewhere.

The United States, Canada, some South American nations, and Japan use a television system called NTSC. In this system, 525 horizontal lines create a full screen picture. These lines are scanned at a rate of 60 fields per second, so that we actually see 60 individual TV frames per second. (For how individual frames create the illusion of motion, see page 52.)

In NTSC, picture information is sent at one frequency and sound information at another. These frequencies are expressed as a ratio to one another, and this ratio is used for all broadcast, cable, and home video signals.

American/Canadian NTSC uses the television channels 2–13 and 14–83 for broadcast transmission. Other countries on the NTSC system do not transmit over the same channels, and so American NTSC TV sets cannot be used, for example, in Japan.

The television system used in most European countries, indeed in most of the world, is called PAL. PAL produces better pictures than NTSC, because a PAL screen uses 625 scanning lines to create a single screen image. That's 20 percent more detail in the same-size area. PAL scans the screen with new images only 50 times per second, as opposed to our 60 times. The way in which the color is processed within the video system is also slightly different from our own. For these three reasons, and several more subtle ones, NTSC and PAL equipment cannot be interchanged.

Beyond the video system itself, countries using PAL transmit their broadcasts at frequencies completely different from our own. Another tuning system, therefore, is required as well.

The incompatibility of PAL and NTSC equipment is a definite concern for anyone interested in, for example, European video devices not yet available in the States.

Neither TV sets nor monitors in these two systems are compatible, but you can buy an *expensive* TV/monitor from Sony's professional product line, for example, that will show NTSC, PAL, and SECAM signals.

PAL VCRs are not only incompatible with NTSC VCRs for the same video differences but also because their speeds are slightly faster. The T-180 videocassette for VHS available in Europe, for example, will play for only a few minutes longer than the tape we call T-120. This can be a real annoyance for an American abroad who sees the familiar T-120s (PAL T-120s also run for less time than their American cousins) and buys the T-180 length believing that there's one third more tape on the cassette. The speed and the video differences between PAL and NTSC will permit the use of only PAL prerecorded tapes in PAL machines, and NTSC tapes in NTSC machines. Only a dual-standard VCR (again, very expensive, designed for specialized professional use) will play tapes recorded in either format. And even then, you must have a dual-standard TV or monitor, so that when the dual-standard VCR is set for PAL, the dual-standard TV is in the same position. Also you cannot make a copy of a tape on one system for play on another (the video differences require a large-scale machine called a "standards converter," whose hourly rental charges generally start at a few hundred dollars).

The actual VHS or Beta recording tape, the blank stock itself, in PAL is basically the same as its American and Japanese equivalents. Lengths may vary, as in the T-120 (PAL) versus T-120 (NTSC) example above, but "tape is tape" and it's the same in most countries.

Videodiscs and cameras are also incompatible, as are videogames and personal computers, with a notable exception. Bearing in mind that the incompatibility between systems exists in the way that the picture is actually displayed on the screen, some of the *programs* written for game and computer units may well be interchangeable between systems. Others may be incompatible. It's still best not to buy any PAL hardware or software for NTSC equipment, or vice versa. This is an important rule of thumb when shopping in Europe (particularly in Germany, where lots of futuristic video devices are available), because returns are virtually impossible even with the best of stores.

To make this foreign standards business even more complicated, there is a third system in use in France, Russia, and many of the Middle Eastern countries. It's called SECAM, and it is totally incompatible with both PAL and NTSC. SECAM pictures are as good as PAL pictures, because of the high number of scanning lines, but its colors reach the screen in a dramatically different fashion from the manner used in the other two systems. As with PAL, it is best not to buy any SECAM hardware or software for your NTSC media room.

even the 1½-inch Travelvision with some special attachments, although the 5-inch Toshiba is much easier to read.

Both the Radio Shack and the Timex computers are designed to be part of a system. Matsushita, through both Quasar and Panasonic, has a full-scale computer that fits into a briefcase. Accessories for their Hand-Held Computer include accessory memory, a telephone modem (for communications by phone with other systems), printers, and tape data storage. It's a miracle that such a small arrangement can be so powerful—more powerful, in fact, than some desk-top systems.

Only the most fanatic media buff will actually attempt to schlepp all this electronic hardware everywhere he or she goes. As with the living-room-size media room, the portable media room should be judiciously designed as an expression of function. If you take lots of business trips and you're accustomed to working with a computer, consider an HHC for business and a personal stereo for pleasure. If you're a movie fanatic with no hope of seeing Tracy and Hepburn while on a Peace Corps mission a thousand miles from Malaysia, the Technicolor VCR and Toshiba color TV are for you—but you'll have to bring *lots* of extra batteries.

Buy slowly and carefully, always being on the lookout for something that's a few ounces lighter, a few inches smaller, a bit more versatile. Finding something that's cheaper isn't so easy—the future looks great for portability, but you'll pay dearly for the privilege of taking *Star Trek* reruns with you wherever you go.

WHAT'S NEXT?

In 1970 there was no such thing as VHS tape, Home Box Office, a videogame, or a personal computer. Nearly every device described in this book is new, the result of fantastic progress both in technological development and in marketing. Getting to this point wasn't easy. Several home tape (and film) formats preceded VHS and Beta with no success, and the number of cable networks that died in the planning stages by far exceeds the number actually on the air today. False starts are very much a reality of the video world, as promises of new developments evaporate with changed market trends or a plain inability to deliver the product as planned.

The products described in this book are here to stay, for the next five years at least. You can feel secure that VHS machines will not suddenly become antiques and that the newest videodisc machines will be serviced with software until at least the middle of this decade. The products now in development, for introduction through the mid-1980s, are generally enhancements of, rather than replacements for, current equipment configurations. However, there is reason to believe that by the end of the decade we will be watching significantly better (and wholly redesigned) TV sets, playing a new kind of videocassette or videodisc, and hearing just about everything in stereo.

The first development on the horizon is a conceptual change: component video. Each component, each operating element of the overall system, will be offered as a distinct piece of equipment. You'll soon have the chance to buy a screen, a tuner, and a speaker system, instead of a single TV set. This is already necessary because cable, discs, and tapes offer stereo sound, but standard television sets do not. Manufacturers are already showing high-quality screens for connoisseurs, first using the current technical standards for American television; and eventually using a wholly new standard, which will give TV pictures the clarity and texture once associated only with film. Japan's Matsushita has already demonstrated a new kind of television picture, whose presence hardly seems like television at all. "High resolution" pictures will use a new kind of TV screen, with pictures created not by 525 scanning lines but by 1125 lines instead. The increased number of lines will create an image with greater resolution, and greater picture

Two cameras are used to record three-dimensional images. Special glasses are needed to see them. (Photo courtesy Matsushita Electric)

quality. It will be used first in the business marketplace, but a strong consumer economy in the late 1980s could bring this new TV system home. It will be expensive, however, because new screens, VCRs, disc players, videogames, and computers will need to be designed for the new screen dimensions (a 3 × 5 instead of 3 × 4 ratio).

Matsushita is also showing a 3-D television system for future use. It is similar to a stereo photography system, where a pair of cameras are mounted at slightly off-center angles, and a pair of special glasses are worn to merge the two images, simulating depth. This particular 3-D (there are several others in development by Japanese manufacturers) requires that the viewer wear stereo glasses not unlike those used to view Vincent Price in *House of Wax* back in the 1950s. The final consumer version of a 3-D system, should one ever arrive, is unlikely to require glasses of any kind.

A "Stylesetter" TV system, representative of just how flexible video has become, is also in Matsushita's plans for the future. This one is a bit arcane, but apparently of great value to the beauty industry. A subject sits in a chair before a color TV camera. The camera creates a still image on a TV screen, and then a beautician/ operator asks the subject about preferred hairstyle, and responds by placing a plastic transparency over a special area in a housing above the TV set. Printed on this plastic overlay is the subject's choice of hairstyle. When a few buttons are pressed, the subject's image appears *wearing the selected hairstyle*. In whatever color you please.

The Stylesetter allows people to preview variations on hairstyles, beards, mustaches, and even eyeglasses. (Photo courtesy Matsushita Electric)

Of more impact for everyday life: pocket-size color TV sets will be in general distribution by the end of the decade. The change here will be to a *flat* screen, which should allow the pocket portable to be no larger than a pack of cigarettes or an overstuffed wallet. Sony's Watchman, the

Pocket-size television sets are likely to become commonplace within the next few years.
(Photo courtesy Toshiba America)

flat-screen black-and-white TV, is the shape of things to come. Their screens will use liquid crystals, the very same silver-and-black crystals that display the time on your digital watch.

Touch-sensitive screens have been used in the computer industry for years. They're filled with a chemically reactive plasma, treated to respond to the heat of a human fingertip. The educational PLATO interactive computer network uses touch sensitivity to allow users, usually children, to point to the answers to a question or problem. Example: Which of these animals is a horse? Touch any of the five drawings. The creative possibilities of this idea, now available by using a "light pen" on some personal computers to draw on the screen or to point at choices, are just beginning to surface.

Matsushita is already demonstrating an ultimate picture manipulator, which uses both a personal computer and a television camera. The camera takes a still video picture of an image— let's say a full-color drawing of a farm—and the computer stores the picture, digitally, in its memory. The computer then redisplays the very same picture in a split second, with a box graph superimposed. When you touch a light pen to one particular box, you can either change that

box's color, transpose its picture with another box's picture, or change the content of the box entirely. To go back to our example of the farm, let's say that your first box was just a patch of brown dirt, and that a few boxes over was a pig. You could duplicate the pig in your box, steal the pig from its original spot and replace it with the dirt, or paint your initials on the side of the pig.

All of this pig-painting is fun, but it is through just this sort of nonsensical playing around that a creative person begins to understand just how valuable this kind of manipulative system can be. Educators will find it a means to engage TV-trained youngsters in classroom activities, art directors will be able to create advertisements (and change those ads to meet client specifications) quickly, and engineers will be able to use the system in the design process. It is a remarkable system, certainly representative of the kinds of computer/video crossovers we will see throughout the rest of this century.

Somewhat less exotic, but infinitely more practical for the masses, will be the certain growth of

Information and amusement programs can be prepared and stored on the CompuCassette home computer system. It's particularly good for educational uses as well.
(Photo courtesy Matsushita Electric)

cable television, pay TV, subscription TV, and direct broadcast satellite TV. Some of these new technologies will become routine in our daily lives, while others will find their proper place in industry or education, or may disappear altogether.

Cable is already well on its way to becoming a dominant force in American television. One in four United States households had cable at the start of the 1980s. By the end of the decade, more than half of us will subscribe, and that number may be as high as three in four homes according to some estimates. Most of us will pay no less than $20 per month, probably over $50 per month or even more for the extended versions of cable. We will be willing to pay more because, presumably, we will be getting more—about 100 channels, according to the franchise proposals now being written. Well into the planning stages by early 1982 were these services and more, all to be operated twenty-four hours each day: a retail shopping channel, using a toll-free phone number to purchase items on the screen; a game channel, where all viewers can become contestants in the greatest continuing game show of all time; a travel channel; a self-improvement network, which would offer nothing but adult education courses on every possible topic. Satellites will remain the principal carrier of these new networks, and cable will deliver these channels to area homes and businesses. But that's only half the picture, for there is more to cable television than the one-way distribution of television signals.

Using an electronic keypad, many subscribers will regularly use cable for banking transactions; this is already available in many areas via telephone, where you actually speak with a teller who does the computer entries for you. This same keypad will be used for local shopping, for voting in local elections, for answering research questionnaires, for interacting with local on-screen educators. Qube viewers already consider some of these conveniences routine, and you will

too, once your cable operator offers all that was promised in his or her new cable franchise.

There are a few hitches in cable's growth, some of which may affect the services available to you as a viewer in certain cities. Most large cities are already served (or will soon be served) by Subscription TV (STV, known locally by names like SelecTV and ON-TV), which offers many of the same programs as those seen on Home Box Office and Showtime. Just how the STV and cable operators will coexist in America's cities remains to be seen.

Add to this mix a concept called DBS (Direct Broadcast Satellite), which will allow a satellite operator like COMSAT to beam a few of its own channels directly to your home via satellite, and the complexity of the necessary policy decisions to be made becomes clear. DBS is a concern not only for the cable and STV operator but for the local TV station, whose future is already unclear. With a truly national network now made possible, the very idea of localized television may become a memory.

In response to the industry proverb "Information will be the pay TV of the '80s," data networks like The Source and CompuServe are the leading edge of an enormous new industry. These networks, available via cheap home terminals, will be at least as important as any television programming.

One of the forms that video information has already taken is called, informally, "videotext." This is a whole new kind of television, employing still pictures, printed words and numbers, and even photographs to create a hybrid of television, an encyclopedia, almanac, daily newspaper, and a whole lot of services, like airline reservations, once reserved for proprietary operations.

The ways you'll eventually see videotext on television fall into two distinct categories: teletext and viewdata. Teletext is a one-way transmission, which usually broadcasts "piggyback" on regular TV channels and can be received by anyone with a specially adapted TV set. When you watch teletext, you are essentially watching slides, newspaper pages, inanimate graphics, each code-numbered so that, for example, #010101 would fill your screen with the day's baseball scores.

Viewdata looks like teletext, but it is a two-way system that allows you to add new information to what you see and to interact with that information for purposes of personal and business services. The viewdata system in use in Britain since 1979, called Prestel, uses telephone lines to transmit both pictures and data to and from the homes and businesses that subscribe to the system. Viewdata will also work via cable, which provides one reason for a cable versus telephone rivalry in the coming information revolution.

Perhaps the best way to distinguish between the systems is through example. Both systems will theoretically allow you to access a page of scheduled air flights between Columbus, Ohio, and Rochester, New York. On teletext, all you can do is look at the schedules. On viewdata, using a keypad, you can select a flight, charge it to a credit card, and even make arrangements for special needs.

As you might well expect, teletext is a good deal cheaper than viewdata, a situation that the folks of London, England, have experienced for years. (The British are blessed with not one but *three* videotext systems, including the Prestel viewdata and the Ceefax and Oracle teletext systems. None of these had become standard household utilities as of this writing.) An American introduction will occur upon the resolution of numerous tests now being conducted around the country.

Here is a plausible scenario for videotext use. Let's say you've got a horrible toothache and are quite sure that your upper left wisdom tooth will finally need to come out. It is New Year's Eve, and you need an appointment tomorrow, or you will consider doing the deed yourself. You go to a master alphabetical index, look up *Toothache*, and find nothing. You try *Oral Surgeon*, but find nothing here either, so you settle for *Dentist*.

Page D-D0000 appears on the screen. (If you knew the codes, you could have found the page quickly, by first typing a D for *Doctors*, then another for *Dentists*, followed by the string of zeroes common to a menu page.) D-D0000 should look something like this:

D-D0000

Make your selection by number:

1. Neighborhood listings
2. Emergencies
3. Special services
4. Supplies
5. Instruction
6. Children's dentists

You go directly to Emergencies, hoping to find a listing for a dentist or an oral surgeon who'll do the job on a holiday. (You might also try for a dentist with an advertisement in the neighborhood sections, but that could be tedious.)

Here's the next page, D-D2000.

D-D2000 *Dentists*, EMERGENCY

Make your selection by number:

1. Children's specialists
2. Prosthetics
3. Hospitals, associated with
4. Minor emergencies

You try the lists in 4, but don't find anyone available, so you take the plunge and go for the hospitals. A teletext system would probably supply you with a phone number and an address; a viewdata system might contact the dentist for you, or even leave word on an answering machine.

Visitors to RCA Space Mountain at Disney World in Florida get a glimpse of the future. Note the shape of the screen—we'll be seeing more of these movie-screen shapes on TV sets in years to come. (Photo courtesy RCA)

This index system is, of course, an amalgam of possible programs—some of which are currently testing. The key to any videotext system will not be only the number of pages of information it contains but just how easily those pages can be accessed by the common user. It's unlikely that we will see a national videotext system in this decade, however, except perhaps in the business marketplace.

Beyond videotext, reasonable predictions are hard to make. There is some serious talk of new videotape formats (incompatible, of course), including several that combine both tape recorder and camera into one portable unit.

The invention, refinement, and reinvention of such devices will continue for years. Updating your media room will be a constant process; it is likely to require major improvements due to obsolescence about every five years or so, from now on. Buying carefully and following current trends will help minimize the cost of obsolescence. Stores which *rent* video gear are already popular in some areas—but nobody's sure how rental fits into our purchasing society. Buying carefully, however, is only one way to build a showplace. For many, the media room will provide a happy excuse to spend too much money on electronic toys. And since the ultimate media room will always be out of date, keeping it new—nosing around electronic stores to catch a glimpse of the latest miracle—will provide much of the fun of consumer electronics. You can depend on the introduction of a new razzle-dazzle dream machine for each and every Christmas—the latest fix in a pleasant addiction that's spreading across the Western world.

"All of those bells and whistles will cost ya," an old TV engineering friend used to say. "Yup. You can do anything you like. But it'll cost ya."

GLOSSARY

AC. Alternating current, or the kind of electrical power available when you plug into a wall outlet in the United States or Canada, where AC is rated at 110–120 volts.

AFT. Automatic fine tuning, which saves some dial twisting when you tune to a TV or radio channel.

AHD. Audio High Density, the audiodisc equivalent of VHD videodiscs. AHD discs are playable on VHD machines.

ATC. American Television and Communications Corporation, an operator of many cable systems.

BASIC. Beginner's All-Purpose Symbolic Instruction Code. It's a language in common use in most personal computers.

BETA. Formerly Betamax, a home videocassette format whose name comes from the Beta (Greek letter)-like way in which the recording tape is threaded through the machine mechanism (as illustrated on page 64).

BNC. A type of video connector that uses a half twist to lock into place.

CATV. Community Antenna Television, now commonly called cable TV.

CED. Capacitance Electronic Disc system, also known as the RCA-type disc, sold by manufacturers listed on page 48.

CEEFAX. Britain's teletext system.

CNN. The Cable News Network. See chart on page 96 for a more complete description.

COAX. Short for "coaxial cable," the various sizes of thick cable used to connect video devices to one another, and to connect homes to a cable-television system.

DBS. Satellite broadcasts made directly to subscribers' homes. The letters stand for Direct Broadcast Satellite.

DC. Direct current, or the kind of electrical power generally available from batteries or car cigarette lighters (actually an outlet for the car's battery), or from AC adapters (which allow battery-operated devices to use a converted version of AC).

DIN. European video connector.

ENG. Electronic news gathering. Also refers to the popular use of lightweight, professional-quality TV cameras and recorders.

EP. Extended play. Sometimes used in place of SLP to represent the slowest speed on a VHS machine.

ESPN. Officially, the Entertainment and Sports Program Network. More accurately, a 24-hour sports channel for cable television. See chart on page 96 for a more complete description.

FCC. Federal Communications Commission, regulatory agency for many of the products and services mentioned in this book.

FREQUENCY SYNTHESIS. A high-quality TV tuning system which compares the frequency received with the actual spectrum position of a given channel, and locks to the correct frequency.

HARDWARE. All video and computer equipment is called hardware (see "software").

HBO. Home Box Office. A large pay-television entertainment and movie network, mainly seen on cable systems.

IC. Integrated circuit, the subminiature electronic part that houses the "chip" that is the "brain" of most machines in this book.

IP. Information provider (to a videotext system).

JVC. Short for Japan Victor Company, owned by Matsushita. JVC has developed many video innovations, notably the VHS home video recorder.

LP. VHS "long-play" speed, which allows a 60-minute tape to play for 120 minutes.

LPTV. Low-power television, used to service a specific audience segment in a small broadcast area.

MDS. Multipoint distribution service, or television channels or programs distributed via microwave to hard-to-reach or specialized locations.

MONITOR. In broadcast TV, a screen which shows video pictures but does not contain an audio system or tuner. In home video, high-quality or component TV sets, with or without tuners and audio systems.

MONO. Short for "monophonic," the one-channel ancestor to stereophonic (or "stereo"). Regardless of the number of speakers in, for example, a TV set, if they're all playing the same exact sound, you're listening to mono.

MSO. Multiple-system owner (of cable-TV systems).

NCTA. National Cable Television Association.

NTSC. Color TV system used in America, Canada, and Japan, requiring NTSC VCRs, TV sets, videogames, computers, and camera.

OEM. Original equipment maker, a manufacturer who makes standardized products for sale by other manufacturers (e.g., the first RCA VCRs were made by an OEM—Matsushita, mother corporation to Panasonic and Quasar).

ON-TV. Subscription television service in Los Angeles, Cincinnati, Phoenix, and other major cities. A brand name of STVs operated by Oak Communications.

ORACLE. British version of teletext.

PAL. European equivalent of NTSC, which will not allow U.S. equipment to be used abroad (and vice versa).

PRESTEL. British version of viewdata.

PROM. Programmable Read-Only Memory. A videogame cartridge is sometimes called a PROM, because it contains computer programming that can only be read and not "written on" by a computer, and also because its information is fed directly to the ROM portion of computer memory.

QUBE. Warner-Amex's name for interactive, multichannel cable systems involving their proprietary hardware. (The "Qube console" pictured on page 100 is only part of the system.)

RAM. Computer memory space generally available to the user (random-access memory).

RCA PLUG. Also called a "phono plug," the connector commonly used in stereo (and some video) hook-ups.

RF. Radio frequency. The combined audio and video signal superimposed on another "carrier" signal.

ROM. Computer memory space reserved for internal instructions (read-only memory).

SATCOM. RCA communications satellite series (SATCOM I, etc.).

SECAM. A third video color system, used in Russia, France, and the Middle East, incompatible with PAL and NTSC.

SLP. VHS "super-long-play" speed, which allows a 60-minute tape to play for 180 minutes.

SOFTWARE. Programs recorded or created for playback on videodisc, videocassette, home videogame, or home computer.

SP. VHS "standard play" speed, which allows a 60-minute tape to play for 60 minutes.

STV. Subscription television, or over-the-air pay television, usually on a UHF channel. SelecTV, ON-TV, and WHT are brand names of STV services.

TVRO. TV receive-only. A satellite receiver system incapable of sending signals.

UHF. Ultra-high frequency; better known as the range of TV channels from 14 to 83.

U-MATIC. Sony's name for $\frac{3}{4}$-inch VCRs and cassettes.

VCR. Abbreviated form of videocassette recorder—whether the cassettes use $\frac{3}{4}$-inch, $\frac{1}{2}$-inch, or $\frac{1}{4}$-inch tape. All VCRs both play and record (although there are some that are only video players on the market in the $\frac{3}{4}$-inch format).

VCS. Atari's videogame system, actually "Video Computer System," not to be confused with its Personal Computer System, which is a full-scale desk-top computer.

VHD. Video high density, the videodisc system sold by Panasonic, GE, and JVC. See page 48 for a complete chart of manufacturers.

VHF. Very high frequency, better known as TV channels 2–13.

VHS. Short for Video Home System, the most popular 1/2-inch videocassette format in the world.

VIC. Commodore's low-priced Video Interface Computer, also known as the VIC 20.

VIR. Vertical Integral Reference, the signal sent by broadcasters that can be interpreted by some TV tuners to lock into prescribed colors.

VTR. Videotape recorder. Includes all VCRs, but usually refers to the open-reel models used by professionals. (Pictured on page 61.)

WESTAR. Western Union's satellite series.

APPENDIX: SOFTWARE LIBRARY

While you are building your media room, you will probably also be building a software library containing tapes, discs, videogame cartridges, and computer programs. New software is released daily, so it is wise to use the following lists of "ten bests" as guidelines for starting your own collection. Nearly all these titles are available on VHS and Beta cassette; many are also available on CED, Laser, and/or VHD disc formats.

NOTE: Just prior to this book's publication, VHD went out of business. Product that was to be available from VHD may or may not be available from your local store under other labels.

VIDEOCASSETTES AND VIDEODISCS

Musicals

1. *Cabaret.* (Tape: CBS/20th Century-Fox; CED: same)
2. *Easter Parade.* (CED: RCA)
3. *Fame.* (Tape: MGM/UA; CED: same)
4. *42nd Street.* (Tape: 20th Century-Fox; LV: same)
5. *Gigi.* (Tape: MGM/UA; CED: same)
6. *Grease.* (Tape: Paramount; CED: same; LV: same; VHD: VHD Programs)
7. *Singin' in the Rain.* (CED: RCA)
8. *That's Entertainment.* (Tape: MGM/UA; CED: same)
9. *West Side Story.* (Tape: 20th Century-Fox; LV: same; VHD: VHD Programs)

10. *Yankee Doodle Dandy* (Tape: 20th Century-Fox; LV: same)

Classic Films (prior to 1960)

1. *Adam's Rib.* (Tape: MGM/UA; CED: RCA)
2. *The African Queen.* (Tape: 20th Century-Fox; LV: same)
3. *Bus Stop.* (Tape: 20th Century-Fox)
4. *Casablanca.* (Tape: 20th Century-Fox; CED: RCA; LV: 20th Century-Fox)
5. *Citizen Kane.* (Tape: VidAmerica and The Nostalgia Merchant; CED: RCA)
6. *Gunga Din.* (Tape: VidAmerica)
7. *King Kong.* (Tape: VidAmerica and The Nostalgia Merchant)
8. *A Night at the Opera.* (Tape: MGM/CBS; CED: same)

9. *The Philadelphia Story.* (Tape: MGM/UA; CED: RCA)
10. *A Streetcar Named Desire.* (Tape: 20th Century-Fox)

7. *The Odd Couple.* (Tape: Paramount; CED: RCA)
8. *The Pink Panther.* (Tape: 20th Century-Fox; LV: same; CED: RCA; VHD: VHD Programs)
9. *The Producers.* (Tape: Magnetic Video)
10. *The Sunshine Boys.* (Tape: MGM/UA; CED: same)

Contemporary Classics (1960-present)

1. *All the President's Men.* (Tape: Warner Home Video)
2. *American Graffiti.* (Tape: MCA; LV: same; VHD: VHD Programs)
3. *Butch Cassidy and the Sundance Kid.* (Tape: 20th Century-Fox; CED: RCA; LV: 20th Century-Fox)
4. *Doctor Zhivago.* (Tape: MGM/UA)
5. *The Godfather* Part I and Part II. (Tape: Paramount—*The Complete Epic,* a new version of both films presented as a single feature, or individually; LV: same; VHD: VHD Programs—individual films only)
6. *The Graduate.* (CED: RCA)
7. *Kramer vs. Kramer.* (Tape: Columbia Pictures; LV: same)
8. *On Golden Pond.* (Tape: 20th Century-Fox; CED: RCA)
9. *Ragtime.* (Tape: Paramount; VHD: VHD Programs)
10. *Rocky.* (CED: RCA; VHD: VHD Programs)

Comedy

1. *Airplane.* (Tape: Paramount; CED and LV: same; VHD: VHD Programs)
2. *Animal House.* (Tape: MCA; LV: same; VHD: VHD Programs)
3. *Annie Hall.* (Tape: 20th Century-Fox; LV: same; VHD: VHD Programs)
4. *Arthur.* (Tape: Warner Home Video—for rental only)
5. *Blazing Saddles.* (Tape: Warner Home Video)
6. *M*A*S*H.* (Tape: 20th Century-Fox; LV: same; CED: RCA)

Action/Adventure

1. *The Bridge on the River Kwai.* (Tape: Columbia Pictures; LV: same)
2. *Bullitt.* (Tape: Warner Home Video)
3. *Deliverance.* (Tape: Warner Home Video)
4. *Enter the Dragon.* (Tape: Warner Home Video)
5. *The French Connection.* (Tape: 20th Century-Fox; LV: same)
6. *Jaws.* (Tape: MCA; LV: same; VHD: VHD Programs)
7. *Magnum Force.* (Tape: Warner Home Video)
8. *Patton.* (Tape: 20th Century-Fox; LV: same; CED: RCA)
9. *Smokey and the Bandit.* (Tape: MCA; LV: same)
10. *Star Wars.* (Tape: 20th Century-Fox; CED: RCA)

Science Fiction and Horror

1. *Alien.* (Tape: 20th Century-Fox; LV: same)
2. *Carrie.* (Tape: 20th Century-Fox; LV: same)
3. *A Clockwork Orange.* (Tape: Warner Home Video)
4. *Close Encounters of the Third Kind.* Special Edition (Tape: Columbia Pictures)
5. *The Exorcist.* (Tape: Warner Home Video)
6. *Forbidden Planet.* (Tape: MGM/UA; CED: same)
7. *Halloween.* (Tape: Media Home Entertainment)
8. *Psycho.* (Tape: MCA; LV: same)
9. *2001: A Space Odyssey.* (Tape: MGM/UA; CED: same)
10. *War of the Worlds.* (Tape: Paramount; CED: RCA; LV: Paramount)

Recommended for Children

1. *The Black Stallion.* (Tape: 20th Century-Fox; CED: RCA; LV: 20th Century-Fox; VHD: VHD Programs)
2. *Davy Crockett, King of the Wild Frontier.* (Tape: Walt Disney Home Video)
3. *The First National Kidisc.* Children will adore this game-filled LaserVision activity disc, which is both fun to play and instructional as to that system's capabilities.
4. *The Adventures of Huckleberry Finn.* There are several film versions of this Mark Twain classic, but the 1939 Mickey Rooney version is by far the best. (Tape: MGM/CBS)
5. *Mary Poppins.* (Tape: Walt Disney Home Video)
6. *Unicorn Tales* (I and II). In the late 1970s, NBC's local TV stations hired a talented troupe of performers to update fairy tales. The resulting series, *Unicorn Tales,* is up-to-date, full of color and life, and extraordinarily entertaining for children. Each story is based on a theme drawn from fairy tales but told in a contemporary situation in which a real child copes with a problem or conflict. (Tape: 20th Century-Fox)
7. *The Wizard of Oz.* (Tape: MGM/UA; CED: same)
8. *Benji.* (Tape: Fotomat)
9. *The Pinwheel Songbook. Pinwheel* is a wonderful program for pre-schoolers that appears daily on the Nickelodeon cable channel, and this cassette presents some of the best original songs and stories from that series. Brad Williams's puppets are clever and imaginative, and George James's songs are bright, funny, and sensitive to the world of children. With Jim Jinkins, Dale Engle, Arline Miyazdki, and Betty Rozek. If you have young children in the house, and you're not yet familiar with the *Pinwheel* characters, you and the children are in for a treat. (Tape: Warner Home Video)

Foreign Films

1. *Black Orpheus.* (French-Portuguese) (Tape: CBS/20th Century-Fox)

2. *Breaker Morant.* (Australian) (Tape: Columbia Pictures)
3. *Bye Bye Brazil.* (Brazilian) (Tape: Warner Home Video)
4. *La Cage aux Folles.* (French) (Tape: 20th Century-Fox)
5. *Cousin, Cousine.* (French) (Tape: CBS/20th Century-Fox)
6. *The Harder They Come.* (Jamaican) (CED: RCA)
7. *My Brilliant Career.* (Australian) (Tape: Vestron Video)
8. *Small Change.* (French) (Tape: Warner Home Video)
9. *The Sorrow and the Pity.* (French, Swiss, and West German) (Tape: Columbia Pictures)
10. *Z.* (French-Algerian) (Tape: Columbia Pictures)

Theater/Performing Arts

We will see a tremendous increase in the number of Broadway and Off Broadway plays produced for video in the immediate future. Both Showtime and The Entertainment Channel offer one new production each month, while Bravo, HBO, and ARTS service also feature plays. Many of these productions will be made available in home video formats.

1. *The Boys in the Band.* Starring Cliff Gorman, Leonard Frey, and Laurence Luckinbill. (Tape: MGM/CBS)
2. *Camelot.* Starring Richard Harris as King Arthur and Meg Bussert as Guinevere. Recorded on Broadway as an HBO special, at the Winter Garden Theatre. (No distributor assigned as of this date)
3. *Candida.* A television version of George Bernard Shaw's play. With Blythe Danner, Edward Herrmann, and Austin Pendleton, who also directed. (Tape: VTN)
4. *Eubie!* One of the more engaging black musicals of the late 1970s/early 1980s, this Eubie Blake revue is full of hummable tunes. (CED: RCA stereo; VHD: VHD Programs)
5. *H.M.S. Pinafore.* The D'Oyly Carte Opera Company. (Tape: 20th Century-Fox)
6. *The Life and Adventures of Nicholas Nickleby.* The distinguished stage version of the Charles Dickens novel, produced in Britain expressly for TV. (Tape: CBS/20th Century-Fox—in stereo, an 8-hour, 4-cassette presentation)
7. *The Nutcracker.* (Tape: CBS/20th Century-Fox; CED: RCA)
8. *Piaf.* Starring Jane Lapotaire singing a dozen of Edith Piaf's songs. (Tape: CBS/20th Century-Fox)
9. *Pippin.* Bob Fosse's production, starring Ben Vereen, William Katt, Chita Rivera, and Martha Raye. (Tape: Family Home Entertainment; CED: RCA stereo; LV: Pioneer Artists; VHD: VHD Programs)
10. *A Spectacular Evening in Paris.* American actress Lauren Hutton and French journalist/impresario Yves Mirousi take viewers on a tour of Paris's best-known nightspots. (Tape: VidAmerica)

Above, a partial list. Consult your retailer to find out about release dates on *Sweeney Todd, Tintypes, Canterbury Tales, The Country Girl* (with Faye Dunaway), *Othello* (with James Earl Jones), *Broadway Follies, The Me Nobody Knows,* and *Lena Horne: The Lady and Her Music.*

You should also know about a series Magnetic Video sells under the banner of Video Playhouse. These were originally shown, on a subscription basis in movie theaters, as the American Film Theatre. Katharine Hepburn stars in Edward Albee's *A Delicate Balance,* Topol stars as *Galileo* in the Bertolt Brecht play, and Lee Marvin and Fredric March star in Eugene O'Neill's *The Iceman Cometh.* Pinter's *The Homecoming,* Ionesco's *Rhinoceros* (with Zero Mostel and Gene Wilder), John Osborne's *Luther,* and Simon Gray's *Butley* (with Alan Bates) are also in the series. All are good, though none extraordinary.

Music/Concert

1. *Blondie: Eat to the Beat.* With the energy of New Wave rock 'n' roll, Blondie created a visual approach that is as aggressive as their music. Every song is presented as an individual work, with costumes, abstract settings, and a strong style. The first real video record album—a new form. Songs include: "Dreaming," "Accidents Never Happen," and "The Hardest Part." (Tape: Warner Home Video; CED: RCA)
2. *The Last Waltz.* Quite simply, a rock 'n' roll masterpiece. The farewell concert by The Band, staged in San Francisco's Winterland, was captured on film by director Martin Scorsese (*Raging Bull, Taxi Driver*) and cinematographers Laszlo Kovacs and Vilmos Zsigmond. Special guests include Dr. John, Neil Young, the Staple Singers, Neil Diamond, Joni Mitchell, Paul Butterfield, Eric Clapton, Muddy Waters, Emmylou Harris, Bob Dylan, Van Morrison, Ringo Starr, Ron Wood, and Ronnie Hawkins, and San Francisco poets Lawrence Ferlinghetti and Michael McClure.
3. *An Evening with Liza Minnelli.* In this 1980 concert (originally done for HBO), Liza Minnelli gives a terrific performance, and every minute on this stereo disc is winning (Tape: 20th Century-Fox; LV: Pioneer Artists, under the title *Liza*)
4. *One Night Stand: A Keyboard Event.* Keyboard artists Herbie Hancock, Stanley Clarke, Ron Carter, Bob James, Hubert Laws, Sir Roland Hanna, Bobby Hutcherson, Charles Earland, George Duke, and Eubie Blake appeared individually and collectively in 1980 at Carnegie Hall to put on an incredible show. (Tape: CBS/20th Century-Fox)

5. *Richard Pryor: Live in Concert.* This is uncensored comedy, a terrific performance based almost entirely on taboo themes; recorded at the Long Beach Civic Auditorium. (Tape: Vestron; CED: RCA)

6. *Paul Simon.* A live concert recording, handsomely produced, showing Simon and band doing a great job on his more recent work. (Laserdisc: Pioneer Artists)

7. *Rod Stewart Live at the Los Angeles Forum.* This is one of the very few tapes that really do capture a stage performance. Songs include: "Tonight's the Night," "Don't Ya Think I'm Sexy," "Maggie Mae," and others. (Tape: Warner Home Video; CED: RCA stereo)

8. *The Charlie Daniels Band: The Saratoga Concert.* The Daniels band is one of our best concert groups, and this stereo tape shows them at their best. Songs include: "The Devil Went Down to Georgia," "The Legend of Wooley Swamp," "In America," and ten others. (Tape: 20th Century-Fox)

9. *Peter Allen and the Rockettes.* A great idea— Peter Allen and the Rockettes were made to perform together. Allen is totally at home in the cavernous Radio City Music Hall, filling the stage with his singing and dancing and carrying on. (Tape: 20th Century-Fox)

10. *Elephant Parts.* Michael Nesmith's integration of pop music and video is entertaining, effective, and original; he is one of a few artists now creating for video and music as a single medium. This first effort was impressive enough to win the 1981 Grammy Award for "Video of the Year." (Tape: Pacific Arts; LV: Pioneer Artists)

More and more musical artists are making videotapes, and this category will swell in the coming years. Look for currently available performances by Devo, Dire Straits, Grover Washington, Jr., The Tubes, Joni Mitchell, Paul McCartney and Wings, Queen, Electric Light Orchestra, Alice Cooper, The Beach Boys, James Taylor, Fleetwood Mac, The Rolling Stones, Olivia Newton-John, REO Speedwagon, and an increasing number of classical and jazz artists. Classical, opera, and jazz artists, whose audience is limited, will be releasing tapes and discs—as the sheer number of VCRs and disc players increases.

Instructional

As more and more people buy VHD and Laserdisc players, there will be instructional programs on almost every subject. For now, only a limited number of subjects are covered on video, some more competently than others. The catalog from VHD Programs, unavailable at the time this book was published, will be filled with nonfiction and instructional programs on a wide variety of topics; these can be played only on the VHD disc player, however.

Below are some of the programs already available:

1. *Caring for Your Newborn.* World-renowned pediatrician Dr. Benjamin Spock presents information about baby care. The tape and the disc are arranged by chapters, so that you can find precisely the topic you need in a few minutes. The demonstrations and explanations are very good, showing real babies and their parents. Extremely useful for new mothers and fathers. (Tape: VidAmerica; CED: RCA)

2. *Julia Child—the French Chef, Volume I.* Four programs that originally aired on WGBH, Boston, and PBS stations. All the dishes can be made in your own home, without fancy ingredients. (CED: RCA)

3. *Titus Chan's Flavors of China.* An absolutely terrific instructional tape about Chinese cooking, hosted by the ingratiating (and frequently funny) cook Titus Chan. We see a great many dishes presented clearly and simply, along with most of the techniques and tricks common to the art of Chinese cookery. Chan also takes us shopping, showing how to choose the freshest fish, the best vegetables, and so forth. The trip to a real Chinese kitchen (in a restaurant) is extremely helpful if you're at all serious about Chinese cooking in your home. The desserts are ambitious, prepared on a yacht for naval officers in Hawaii. (Tape: Warner Home Video)

4. *The Touch of Love . . . Massage.* A straightforward demonstration of sensual massage (performed by a nude couple). There are twelve chapters, including an introduction, a preparation chapter, unifying strokes, and nine specific entries on parts of the body. (Tape: MCA; Laserdisc: MCA)

5. *Steve Strandemo's Racquetball Instruction.* Teaches the fundamentals, using the unique capabilities of

the VHD system: still frames, chapter and frame access, slow motion, and so forth. Certainly the shape of things to come. (VHD: VHD Programs)

6. *The World's Greatest Photography Course.* This is a complete course in 35mm photography. The emphasis is on seeing pictures, on composition and use of color and contrast. Your television screen becomes the viewfinder for many of the lessons on *Photography*; the various special-effects modes are used in demonstrating and practicing the basics of good picture-taking. (Tape: VidAmerica; VHD: VHD Programs)

7. *Aerobicise.* Ron Harris made quite a splash hit on Showtime with his between-the-movies tapes of shapely women exercising to bouncy music. A blend of video art, erotica, and exercise instruction, it contains 113 minutes of instruction. (Tape: Paramount)

8. *The Master Cooking Course.* Craig Claiborne and Pierre Franey teach gourmet cooking in this videodisc (which is designed for use with the book of the same name, published by G. P. Putnam's Sons. (LV: Optical Program Associates)

9. *The Famous Photographers Series, Volume 1: David Chan.* David Chan is one of *Playboy* magazine's top photographers (he specializes in features like *Girls of the Southwest*). We see Chan at work, photographing Jill DeVries, Suzanne Shaheen, and Sherral Snow, and hear explanations of lighting, makeup, wardrobe, and technique. (Tape: Sherwood Video—selected stores)

10. *Jane Fonda's Workout Tape.* An exercise program. (Tape: KVC; CED: RCA)

There simply are not enough programs in this category, but that situation will change dramatically in the next two to five years. For now, browse through the NVC guides (see page 88) for information about specialty programs from smaller distributors, producers, and suppliers.

Cartoons and Animation

Sooner or later, every major cartoon series will be made available, at least in part, for home video. The list below details several full-scale animated features and then lists some of the cartoon collections available.

1. *Alice in Wonderland.* (Tape: Walt Disney Home Video)
2. *Animal Farm.* (Tape: Media Home Entertainment)
3. *The Bugs Bunny/Road Runner Movie.* Sort of a *That's Entertainment* of Warner Brothers cartoons, hosted by that great Hollywood star Bugs Bunny. If you're a fan, you can't do much better: the best of Bugs, Daffy Duck, Elmer Fudd, Porky Pig, and, of course, Road Runner. Chuck Jones produced and directed. (Tape: Warner Home Video)
4. *Dumbo.* (Tape: Walt Disney Home Video)
5. *The Hobbit.* Originally released as a TV movie in 1977, this is a delightful (albeit cursory) version of the J. R. R. Tolkien fantasy. (Tape: Thorn/EMI; CED: RCA)
6. *Race for Your Life, Charlie Brown.* A legitimate motion-picture feature (not a TV special, although these are available as well), with the expected assortment of Charles Schulz characters. (Tape: Paramount; CED: RCA)

Keep your eyes open for more Disney films (as rental tapes), and for the release of Ralph Bakshi's catalog (*American Pop, Fritz the Cat*). There have been a surprising number of animated TV specials over the years that will find their way to market as well.

If you are a cartoon lover, you might complete the list of ten from the following selections:

A. *A Charlie Brown Festival.* (CED: RCA)
B. *Terrytoons, Volume I: Featuring Mighty Mouse.* (CED: RCA; Tape: Magnetic Video, in different versions)
C. *Mr. Magoo, Volumes I and II.* (Tape: Columbia Pictures)
D. *Disney Cartoon Parade, Volume I.* (Tape: Walt Disney Home Video; CED: RCA)
E. *Tom and Jerry Cartoons.* (Tape: MGM/CBS; CED: MGM/CBS)
F. *Mickey Mouse and Donald Duck Cartoon Collection, Volumes I, II, and III.* (Tape: Walt Disney Home Video)

You might also consult the NVC guides for information about Chip 'n' Dale, Betty Boop, Dinky Duck, Gerald McBoing-Boing, Little Lulu, and lots of others.

Sports

1. *Baseball Fun and Games.* This is a great gift for a baseball fan, produced by Major League Baseball. Joe Garagiola hosts a program chock-full of baseball bloopers, players' goofs, questionable calls by the umps, and (most fun of all) baseball trivia quizzes. (Tape: VidAmerica)

2. *Baseball's Hall of Fame: The Game and Its Glory.* Baseball fan Donald Sutherland conducts a fact-packed tour of the Baseball Hall of Fame in Cooperstown, New York—a particularly realistic survey of the game's past, thanks to the clever use of stock footage from years past. Again, produced by Major League Baseball. (Tape: VidAmerica)

3. *Boxing's Greatest Champions.* This is a fine compilation of the greatest fighters of all time: Sugar Ray Robinson, Rocky Marciano, Muhammad Ali, and Joe Louis in their best fights. (Tape: VidAmerica)

4. *The Boys of Summer.* The television version of Roger Kahn's classic tale of the Brooklyn Dodgers. This is a documentary, with a strong story line as told by Duke Snider, Pee Wee Reese, Preacher Roe, Carl Furillo, Clem Labine, Carl Erskine, Roy Campanella, Joe Black, and host Sid Caesar. (Tape: VidAmerica)

5. *Greatest Sports Legends, Volumes I, II, and III.* The best from the syndicated TV series, repackaged for home videocassettes. Each legend is treated in a 15-minute film biography. Volume I: Joe Frazier, Jesse Owens, Eddie Arcaro, Sam Snead. Volume II: Gordie Howe, Willie Shoemaker, Don Budge, Roy Campanella. Volume III: Mark Spitz, Secretariat, Gayle Sayers, and Roger Ward. Each volume sold separately. (Tape: 20th Century-Fox)

6. *Grudge Fights.* An action-packed hour for boxing fans. These "grudge fights" are thirty-four of the most exciting rematches in boxing history. Ali–Frazier, Louis–Schmeling, and Dempsey–Tunney are among the best. (Tape: VidAmerica)

7. *How to Watch Pro Football.* An interactive disc that you can stop, slow down, and otherwise manipulate as you learn the fine points of watching football on television. The people at Optical Programming Associates originally created this program to show off the Laserdisc machines, but the

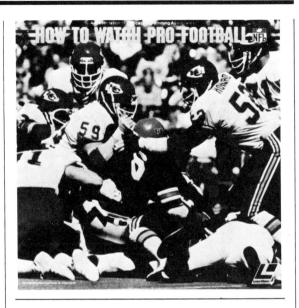

idea proved to be so practical that MCA released a slightly revised version on videocassette. (Tape: MCA; Laserdisc: MCA)

8. *The Super Bowls.* Like many sporting events, the Super Bowl series has been recorded for posterity. Each of the tapes is a 30-minute highlights program narrated by John Facenda. Each Super Bowl (I–XV) sold separately. (Tape: NFL Films Video)

9. *Miracle of Lake Placid: Highlights of the 1980 Winter Olympics.* Ninety minutes of highlights, taken from ABC's network coverage of the games. The best footage: Eric Heiden's speed races, Linda Fratianne's figure skating, and the sensational U.S. Hockey Team. (Tape: Magnetic Video; CED: RCA)

10. *The Two Best World Series Ever.* Highlights of the 1975 World Series (Cincinnati Reds versus Boston Red Sox) and the 1978 Dodgers versus Yankees series. The tape is 60 minutes long, 30 minutes for each series. (Tape: VidAmerica)

If you are interested in more specialized programming, it is best to browse not only in the video stores (which tend to keep only the major labels' inventory) but through the NVC books and any mail-order catalogs you can find. There are a vast number of tapes available, on subjects from gardening to religion, with blooper reels, old TV shows (lots, from *Amos 'n' Andy* to *Watch Mr. Wizard*), medical instruction, and some unusual topics if you take the time to look.

The video magazines mentioned earlier in this chapter are also good sources for additional information about software.

All the entries listed above were available in early 1982, but not every supplier will have every tape.

Each month, several dozen new cassettes hit the market. If your favorite films are not available yet, just keep asking.

Keep your eyes open for cassettes that are available only on a rental basis, through CBS's First Run for example. Rental-only films tend to be the newest movies on the market—some will still be in theatrical release when you first borrow them from your local video retailer.

ATARI/ACTIVISION: TEN BEST VIDEOGAMES

Here's a list of the ten best videogames for the Atari VCS videogame unit.

1. *Space Invaders.* The arcade classic. Shoot at the alien force while dodging their fire. This game is an institution, complete with national competitions (Atari).
2. *Asteroids.* Another arcade classic. A single player controls a ship, floating in space, shooting at threatening asteroids flying toward the ship from every direction (Atari).
3. *Missile Command.* A space-target game where your guns are used to stop oncoming waves of alien missiles. This is a very fast, high-tension game—one of the best around (Atari).
4. *Super Breakout.* Each time your paddle hits the ball, it is deflected into a wall of bricks, and eliminates each brick it hits. The idea here is to eliminate all the bricks on the screen. With several variations on the original Breakout. It's simple to play and thoroughly addictive (Atari).
5. *Skiing.* Choose either a slalom or a downhill course. The action is remarkably like skiing,

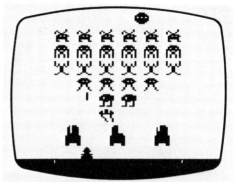

SPACE INVADERS* Game Program™
* Trademark of Taito America Corp.
Trademark of ATARI, INC.

ASTEROIDS™ Game Program™

MISSILE COMMAND™ Game Program™

SUPER BREAKOUT™ Game Program™

where gradual movements of the skis are used to maximize time scores. One of the best single-player games around (Activision).

6. *Boxing.* You control a boxer, jabbing and ducking punches, prancing around the ring. It feels a lot like a real match and is great fun (Activision).

7. *Night Driver.* In the dark of night, you see only the guardrails. You must keep your car on the road and race the clock for either best time or greatest distance covered (Atari).

8. *Donkey Kong.* The crazy arcade favorite, with multiple screens (Coleco).

9. *Warlords.* A Breakout variation, where defense and offense must be combined to first break through enemy castle walls and then hurl fireballs at enemy kings (Atari).

SKIING   AG-005

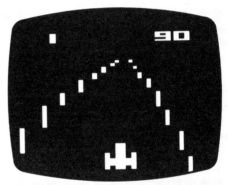

NIGHT DRIVER® Game Program™

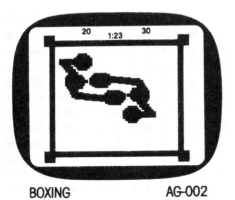

BOXING   AG-002

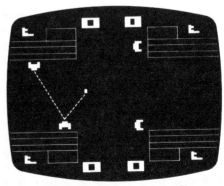

WARLORDS™ Game Program™

10. *Pac-Man.* Maneuver your Pac-Man character through the maze, avoiding the ghosts. Based on the fantastically successful coin-op game (Atari).

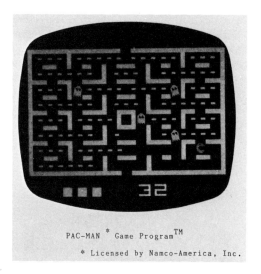

PAC-MAN * Game Program ™

* Licensed by Namco-America, Inc.

MATTEL INTELLIVISION: TEN BEST VIDEOGAMES

Here are ten of the best videogames for the Mattel system, all manufactured by Mattel.

1. *Major League Baseball.* Choose the pitch (fast, slow, curve, inside, outside), bat, bunt, field, run bases, even steal. One of the best, most realistic sports adaptations ever made.
2. *NFL Football.* Select your plays from a play book; then act and react as you would in a real game. This is also an astonishingly good sports adaptation.
3. *Electric Company Word Fun.* Three wonderful games with an educational slant, for kids: a Scrabble variation, a monkey hunt for letters to form words, and a target game that teaches vowels.
4. *U.S. Ski Team Skiing.* Fully thirty different courses, fifteen slalom and fifteen downhill. The key factor is accuracy—good control will result in good speed scores.
5. *NASL Soccer.* You control the man with the ball, and the computer builds a realistic match around your player. Very exciting and quite realistic. Also try NHL Hockey.

Major League Baseball

Electric Company Word Fun

U.S. Ski Team Skiing

NASL Soccer

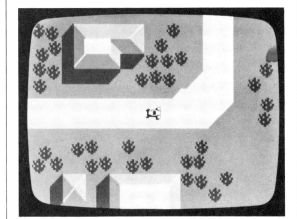

Auto Racing

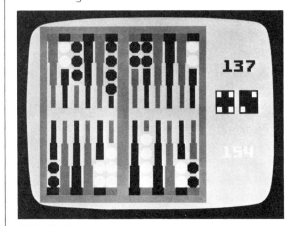

ABPA Backgammon

6. *Auto Racing.* Five very long courses full of hairpin turns. You see only the current portion of each course as you race. This is a tough one, which requires practice; good reflexes are also essential.

7. *ABPA Backgammon.* A clear rendition of the board game, with the computer as an adept opponent. There is no doubling, however.

8. *PGA Golf.* A 9-hole course with all possible obstacles, played by first choosing a club and then selecting power and direction of swing. Very realistic.

9. *Tennis.* For two players, a reasonably accurate re-

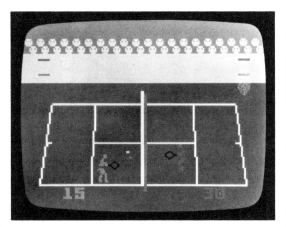

Tennis

Electric Company Math Fun

production of the game, including many strategy features you wouldn't expect to see in a video-game.

10. *Electric Company Math Fun.* For grade-school children, a flashcard drill involving a jungle environment—every time you get an example wrong, your gorilla falls into the river. Silly fun, but effective with children.

INDEX